The American Lawrence

UNIVERSITY PRESS OF FLORIDA

Florida A&M University, Tallahassee
Florida Atlantic University, Boca Raton
Florida Gulf Coast University, Ft. Myers
Florida International University, Miami
Florida State University, Tallahassee
New College of Florida, Sarasota
University of Central Florida, Orlando
University of Florida, Gainesville
University of North Florida, Jacksonville
University of South Florida, Tampa
University of West Florida, Pensacola

THE
American Lawrence

Lee M. Jenkins

UNIVERSITY PRESS OF FLORIDA
Gainesville/Tallahassee/Tampa/Boca Raton
Pensacola/Orlando/Miami/Jacksonville/Ft. Myers/Sarasota

Copyright 2015 by Lee M. Jenkins
All rights reserved
Published in the United States of America

First cloth printing, 2015
First paperback printing, 2021

26 25 24 23 22 21   6 5 4 3 2 1

Library of Congress Cataloging-in-Publication Data
Jenkins, Lee M. (Lee Margaret), author.
The American Lawrence / Lee M. Jenkins.
pages cm
Includes bibliographical references and index.
Summary: Although contemporary scholarship views D. H. Lawrence as a distinctly English author, Lee M. Jenkins argues for a reassessment of his relationship to American modernism and his American literary contemporaries, including "Studies in Classic American Literature" and "The Plumed Serpent."
ISBN 978-0-8130-6050-7 (cloth) | ISBN 978-0-8130-6837-4 (pbk.)
1. Lawrence, D. H. (David Herbert), 1885–1930—Criticism and interpretation.
2. Authors, English—20th century—Biography. 3. American literature—20th century—History and criticism. 4. Modernism (Literature)—United States. I. Title.
PR6023.A93Z634 2015
823'.912—dc23   2014033286

The University Press of Florida is the scholarly publishing agency for the State University System of Florida, comprising Florida A&M University, Florida Atlantic University, Florida Gulf Coast University, Florida International University, Florida State University, New College of Florida, University of Central Florida, University of Florida, University of North Florida, University of South Florida, and University of West Florida.

University Press of Florida
2046 NE Waldo Road
Suite 2100
Gainesville, FL 32609
http://upress.ufl.edu

Contents

List of Figures vi
Acknowledgments vii
List of Abbreviations ix

Introduction: D. H. Lawrence, *Americano* 1

1. Hands-up, America!: *Studies in Classic American Literature* 26
2. Under Our Home Eye: Lawrence and American Modernism 47
3. Tales of Out Here: "St. Mawr," "The Princess," and "The Woman Who Rode Away" 81

Conclusion. Wilful Women: Lawrence's Three Fates and Georgia O'Keeffe 102

Notes 111
Bibliography 127
Index 145

Figures

1. Dorothy Brett, *Lawrence's Three Fates*, 1958   107
2. Georgia O'Keeffe, *The Lawrence Tree*, 1929   108

Acknowledgments

I am grateful to the following friends, colleagues, and Lawrentians for help and advice of various kinds: Donna Alexander, Graham Allen, Jerold Auerbach, Nancy Brown, Christopher Castiglia, Dick Collins, Tonio Colonna, Claire Connolly, Lisa Costello, Patricia Coughlan, Fiona Cox, Alex Davis, Mark Faulkner, Felicia Fergusson, Nuala Finnegan, Shelley Fisher Fishkin, Anne FitzGerald, Alan Gibbs, Jane Goldman, Eleanor Green, Margaret Mills Harper, Sarah Hayden, Sean Hignett, Charles K. Hyde, Cate Huguelet, Earl Ingersoll, Bethan Jones, Padraig Kirwan, Catherine La Farge, John (Pen) La Farge, Holly Laird, Kate Marshall, Julianne Newmark, Maureen O'Connor, Martin Padget, Lesley Pollinger, Paul Poplawski, Jahan Ramazani, Beth Silbergleit, Tim Youngs, and Eric White.

I owe special thanks to Neil Roberts, for encouraging me both in person and by his own fine example to write about Lawrence, and to the late Keith Sagar, who kindly sourced the image of Dorothy Brett's *Lawrence's Three Fates* reproduced here. At the University Press of Florida, I am indebted to my editor, Shannon McCarthy, for her unfailing patience, enthusiasm, and support for my book; to Amy Gorelick, who commissioned it; to my project editor, Eleanor Deumens; and to my copy editor, Elizabeth Detwiler. My sincere thanks to the two readers for the University Press of Florida, whose astute reports helped me shape the book in its final form. As always, my thanks to Alex Davis, who has traveled twice to New Mexico with me and to other Lawrence locations in Italy, France, and England.

I gratefully acknowledge financial assistance in the production of this book from the School of English and the College of Arts, Celtic Studies, and Social Sciences at University College Cork, and the National University of Ireland.

An earlier version of parts of the first chapter of this book appeared as "*Studies in Classic American Literature* and American Studies" in *D. H. Lawrence Review* 37.2 (2013): 44–59.

Extracts from the *Cambridge Edition of the Letters and Works of D. H. Lawrence*, published by Cambridge University Press, are reproduced by permission of Pollinger Limited on behalf of the Estate of Frieda Lawrence Ravagli.

Final thanks to the parties below for permission to reproduce the two images in this book.

Brett, Dorothy (1883–1977): *Lawrence's Three Fates*. 1958. Reproduced courtesy of Keith Sagar.

O'Keeffe, Georgia. *The Lawrence Tree*. 1929. Hartford (Conn.), Wadsworth Atheneum Museum of Art. Oil on canvas. 31 × 40 in. The Ella Gallup Sumner and Mary Catlin Sumner Collection Fund. 1981.23 © Georgia O'Keeffe Museum / DACS, 2014. Wadsworth Atheneum Museum of Art / Art Resource, N.Y. / Scala, Florence.

Abbreviations

Works of D. H. Lawrence

A	*Apocalypse and the Writings on Revelation*. Edited by Mara Kalnins. Cambridge: Cambridge University Press, 1980.
FSLC	*The First and Second Lady Chatterley Novels*. Edited by Dieter Mehl and Christa Jansohn. Cambridge: Cambridge University Press, 1999.
IR	*Introductions and Reviews*. Edited by N. H. Reeve and John Worthen. Cambridge: Cambridge University Press, 2005.
K	*Kangaroo*. Edited by Bruce Steele. Cambridge: Cambridge University Press, 1994.
LEA	*Late Essays and Articles*. Edited by James T. Boulton. Cambridge: Cambridge University Press, 2004.
MM	*Mornings in Mexico and Other Essays*. Edited by Virginia Crosswhite Hyde. Cambridge: Cambridge University Press, 2009.
P	*The Poems*. Edited by Christopher Pollnitz. Cambridge: Cambridge University Press, 2013.
PH	*Phoenix: The Posthumous Papers of D. H. Lawrence*. Edited by Edward D. McDonald. London: Heinemann, 1936.
PH II	*Phoenix II: Uncollected, Unpublished, and Other Prose Works by D. H. Lawrence*. Edited by Warren Roberts and Harry T. Moore. New York: Viking Press, 1970.
PL	*The Plays*. Edited by Hans-Wilhelm Schwarze and John Worthen. Cambridge: Cambridge University Press, 1999.

PS   *The Plumed Serpent*. Edited by L. D. Clark. Cambridge: Cambridge University Press, 1987.
PU   *Psychoanalysis and the Unconscious and Fantasia of the Unconscious*. Edited by Bruce Steele. Cambridge: Cambridge University Press, 2004.
Q   *Quetzalcoatl*. Edited by N. H. Reeve. Cambridge: Cambridge University Press, 2011.
RDP   *Reflections on the Death of a Porcupine and Other Essays*. Edited by Michael Herbert. Cambridge: Cambridge University Press, 1988.
SCAL   *Studies in Classic American Literature*. Edited by Ezra Greenspan, Lindeth Vasey, and John Worthen. Cambridge: Cambridge University Press, 2003.
SEP   *Sketches of Etruscan Places and Other Italian Essays*. Edited by Simonetta de Filippis. Cambridge: Cambridge University Press, 1992.
SM   *St. Mawr and Other Stories*. Edited by Brian Finney. Cambridge: Cambridge University Press, 1983.
STH   *Study of Thomas Hardy and Other Essays*. Edited by Bruce Steele. Cambridge: Cambridge University Press, 1985.
WL   *Women in Love*. Edited by David Farmer, John Worthen, and Lindeth Vasey. Cambridge: Cambridge University Press, 1987.
WWRA   *The Woman Who Rode Away and Other Stories*. Edited by Dieter Mehl and Christa Jansohn. Cambridge: Cambridge University Press, 1995.

Letters of D. H. Lawrence

i   *Letters of D. H. Lawrence: Volume I, September 1901–May 1913*. Edited by James T. Boulton. Cambridge: Cambridge University Press, 1979.
ii   *Letters of D. H. Lawrence: Volume II, June 1913–October 1916*. Edited by George J. Zytaruk and James T. Boulton. Cambridge: Cambridge University Press, 1981.
iii   *Letters of D. H. Lawrence: Volume III, October 1916–June 1921*. Edited by James T. Boulton and Andrew Robertson. Cambridge: Cambridge University Press, 1984.
iv   *Letters of D. H. Lawrence: Volume IV, June 1921–March 1924*. Edited by Warren Roberts, James T. Boulton, and Elizabeth Mansfield. Cambridge: Cambridge University Press, 1987.

v	*Letters of D. H. Lawrence, Volume V, March 1924–March 1927.* Edited by James T. Boulton and Lindeth Vasey. Cambridge: Cambridge University Press, 1989.
vi	*Letters of D. H. Lawrence: Volume VI, March 1927–November 1928.* Edited by James T. Boulton and Margaret Boulton, with Gerald M. Lacy. Cambridge: Cambridge University Press, 1991.
vii	*Letters of D. H. Lawrence: Volume VII, November 1928–February 1930.* Edited by Keith Sagar and James T. Boulton. Cambridge: Cambridge University Press, 1993.
viii	*Letters of D. H. Lawrence: Volume VIII, Previously Uncollected Letters and General Index.* Edited by James T. Boulton. Cambridge: Cambridge University Press, 2000.

Introduction

D. H. Lawrence, *Americano*

> In direction I am more than half American.
> I always write really towards America.
>
> D. H. Lawrence, letter to Amy Lowell

"Can non-Americans write American literature?"[1] John Muthyala, who asks the question in his study titled *Reworlding America*, answers yes, they can. In *The American Lawrence*, I read D. H. Lawrence as a non-American who, in one period of his career at least, wrote American literature.

There is no American Lawrence in the sense that we speak of the American Auden. Unlike Auden, Lawrence would remain a British subject; during the three years he spent in the New World between 1922 and 1925, Lawrence stayed in the United States on six-month-long visitor's visas, moving across the border from New Mexico to Mexico as each elapsed. Literary citizenship is another matter, however, and Lawrence himself floated the idea that he was "more than half American" in a letter he sent to Amy Lowell from Sicily, the year before he traveled to the United States for the first time.[2] Taking him at his word has far-reaching implications, for our understanding of Lawrence and of American literature alike: it means calling in question the still-dominant domestic definition of the English Lawrence and the integrity of nation-based traditions, British and American. Read as "more than half American," Lawrence sets national canons out of kilter, on both sides of the Atlantic.

Under a globalizing rubric like Muthyala's, Lawrence's American oeuvre, the core of which consists of the poems, essays, and fictions he wrote in and about New Mexico in the early to mid-1920s, may be classified as American literature. Yet Lawrence is left out of the loop, his American writing bypassed in the transnational circuits of contemporary scholarship. His absence is explained not only by the "presentism" with which the transnational paradigm has been charged but also by Lawrence's own imbrication with American literary criticism in its formative, nation-building phase. The Lawrence who wrote American literature has been occluded by the Lawrence who wrote *about* it, in the set of essays begun in England in 1917 and published in book form in New York in 1923 as *Studies in Classic American Literature*. The case I want to make in what follows for Lawrence's pertinence to new paradigms in American studies is thus contingent on a reappraisal of his contribution to the old American studies.

Certain Americanists and an Englishman

In an early review of *Studies in Classic American Literature* for the *New York Evening Post Literary Review*, the American critic Stuart Sherman informs his readers that Lawrence "has been visiting us, sojourning physically, I believe, in New Mexico." With suitably dry humour, Sherman pictures Lawrence there, at the edge of Taos desert, "wearing a sombrero, driving a Ford, drinking iced water qualified perhaps with white mule, reading the Albuquerque *American*, and smoking Camel cigarettes." Lawrence, Sherman says, is a "good guest," who observes the customs of the host culture; adopting the peccadilloes of the locals, he even gives a passable imitation of a "genuine *Americano*."[3] What a genuine Americano might be is a moot point, and one to which I will return. "Out there in New Mexico under sombrero," Sherman's Americano Lawrence is, in any case, a straw man: the real target of his review is the English author of *Studies in Classic American Literature*, who imitates American "habits and manners" by phrasing his book about American literature in the American vernacular.

Sherman deciphers the ersatz Americanisms of *Studies in Classic American Literature* as the signature, not of a wannabe American who talks the talk in the belief that imitation is the sincerest form of flattery, but of a "gifted alien," a mimic man who flatters to deceive. In Sherman's judgment, the English Lawrence "has borrowed our language and discussed our classics in order to deliver, in a style intelligible to us and with illustrations suited to our comprehensions, his own message." *Studies in Classic American Literature*, that is, "has a thesis," which, Sherman finds, is the same thesis propounded in Lawrence's novels and in his philosophical writing—the colonization of the passional instincts of the body and of the "blood" by the idealizing and intellectualizing forces of the mind.[4] Sherman's point is that the book says more about Lawrence himself than it does about the American classics that it purports to study.

Writing more than seventy years later, however, and with the benefit of the longer view, Lawrence Buell points out that *Studies in Classic American Literature* is "the first thesis book *about American literature* to endure" [my emphasis].[5] But if *Studies in Classic American Literature* still endures in American studies, it is as a black book. Lawrence's *Studies*, which tests its thesis on a select group of "classic"—male, white, antebellum—authors, is deemed complicit with the now superannuated and ideologically suspect processes of national canon-formation that defined American literary studies in the post–World War I decade of its inception.

As Paul Giles remarks, Lawrence's *Studies* also "anticipates the epistemology of American studies in its 'mythic' phase." The "widely influential nature" of Lawrence's book in the period of the Cold War is in inverse ratio to its reception by Americanists today, who reject, often in polemical terms, the method and mind-set of their myth and symbol precursors: R.W.B. Lewis, Richard Chase, Charles Feidelson, Henry Nash Smith, and Leslie Fiedler.[6] According to Donald E. Pease, the myth and symbolists were "soldier-critics" who "produced the patriotic fictions in whose name they could retroactively claim to have fought the war." In Pease's critique, the myth and symbol school promulgated "the state fantasy of American exceptionalism" by identifying in classic or canonical American literature the "foundational signifiers" of the U.S. national metanarrative—the myth of Virgin Land, for example, and of the American Adam. Thus, during myth and symbol's tenure in the academy, "the field of American Studies collaborated with . . . the cultural apparatus" of the nation state.[7]

In the 1990s, American studies took the transnational turn, and, rebranded as the New American studies, turned its back on the insular notion of a national narrative the legitimacy of which had been contested since the cultural turn of the 1960s and the opening up of the American canon in the following decade. Philip Rahv's argument in *The Myth and the Powerhouse* (1965) that the recourse to myth belies a fear of history (the powerhouse) would now be taken up by a cohort of critics who rejected the "'consensus' history which ignores fundamental conflicts and tensions in American culture."[8] The myths of uniqueness and of American Exceptionalism encoded in the "classic" canon by the myth and symbolists have duly been exploded, and today American literature is understood, not as a world apart, but as part of a wider world. American literary studies now navigates a "world of fluid borders" as scholars embark on the cartographic enterprise defined in Giles's recent study of that title as *The Global Remapping of American Literature*.[9]

As the spatial coordinates of American criticism shift, and the national scene recedes into the transnational distance, the English Lawrence is caught somewhere between the devil and the deep blue sea. Identified by Sherman as a gifted alien who, in mimicking the native tongue mocks the "national spirit," Lawrence, in Giles's more recent assessment, is an essentialist who intuits in the American classics "an alien quality, which belongs to the American continent and to nowhere else" (*SCAL* 13).[10] There is a curious reversal here: New Americanists consign *Studies in Classic American Literature* to the reactionary rearguard of their discipline, whereas Sherman, who was old-school even by the critical standards of the 1920s, places Lawrence's book closer to what is now the leading edge of American literary theory. In his review, Sherman locates the English Lawrence in the borderland state of New Mexico in order to position the pro tem "Americano" author of *Studies in Classic American Literature* at a tangent, in a more than geographical sense, to the national narrative his book nominally underwrites.

Clearly, Lawrence did regard "classic" American literature, in its manifest, if not in its latent or symbolic meaning, as a national literature, and *Studies in Classic American Literature* would subsequently be co-opted in institutionalizing it as such. But Lawrence's book itself is concerned less with the incarnation than with the "post mortem" decomposition of a national narrative in the American classics (*SCAL* 148). For Lawrence, antebellum American literature augurs what Pease would call a *post*-national imaginary, albeit that Lawrence's vision of the American future is hardly identical with Pease's. Lawrence's spirit of place may be an essentialist notion, but that does not mean that it is a national, still less a nationalist, one: as Jon Thompson argues, "Lawrence uses a fair part of 'The Spirit of Place' to clear the field of familiar American myths."[11] The spirit of place as Lawrence defines it in *Studies in Classic American Literature* is a continental quality, anathema to the national spirit so stalwartly defended by Sherman in his review of Lawrence's book. Far from being "conditioned to an alien nationalism" in America, or in his American writing, Lawrence was himself the alien, even if he was, as Sherman concedes, a gifted one.[12]

Placing Lawrence

During the war years, in the latter stages of which the first version of *Studies in Classic American Literature* was begun, England had become an alien nation for Lawrence. In "Democracy," an essay directly related to his work-in-progress on the "Whitman" chapter for *Studies*, Lawrence would assert that "*Nation* is a dead ideal"—"England, France, Germany, America—these great Nations, they have no vital meaning any more" (*RDP* 66). Written after the signing of the Treaty of Versailles in June 1919 and before Lawrence's departure from England for Italy in November of that year, "Democracy" rejects the empty promise of League of Nations internationalism even as it picks over the post mortem remains of the war-torn national ideal. A noncombatant with a German wife, Lawrence was harried in an England caught up in the patriotic frenzy of the war.

The posttraumatic shock of his wartime experience is registered in "The Nightmare" chapter of Lawrence's Australian novel, *Kangaroo* (1923), where, in a searing anatomy of nationality and its discontents, Richard Lovatt Somers, the protagonist and a close fictional surrogate for the author, is described as "[o]ne of the most intensely English little men England ever produced, with a passion for his country, even if it were often a passion of hatred" (223). In Somers, we can discern F. R. Leavis's obdurately English Lawrence (a figure of the author that has proved somewhat more durable than the Leavisite Great Tradition itself): Leavis would use Lawrence's testament that "I am English, and my Englishness is my very vision" as the epigraph to his *D. H. Lawrence: Novelist*.[13]

Kangaroo gives equal sanction, however, to the countervailing view of Lawrence, in which the English novelist championed by Leavis and by Raymond Williams as the wayward heir of George Eliot and Thomas Hardy is displaced by the unaffiliated and footloose exile. "The ties were gone," Lawrence writes of Somers, and of himself: "He was loose like a single timber of some wrecked ship, drifting the face of the sea. Without a people, without a land" (*K* 259). Roots or routes—these competing discourses, which claim Lawrence for an English tradition or define him as deterritorialized nomad—replicate what, in "Democracy," Lawrence perceives as the false binary between the bounded national subject and world citizenship *sans frontiers*. His own postwar credo, expressed in the introduction to *Fantasia of the Unconscious* (1922), was that "[t]he promised land, if it be anywhere, lies away beneath our feet" (*PU* 68). For extended periods between September

1922 and September 1925, the promised land, in Lawrence's characteristically down-to-earth definition of it, was an American place.

Michael North may well be right to opine that Lawrence's quest for "an organic community to which he might belong" proved fruitless, because "the only place he finally belonged was in transit."[14] But if he was a rootless déraciné, Lawrence was also a topophile; in more than the strict sense of the term Lawrence was a travel writer, for whom the poetics of space and of place was as generative a principle as the dynamics of transit he admired in Whitman's verse of the open road. L. D. Clark argues in his study of Lawrence and the symbolism of travel that the writing Lawrence produced in and about New Mexico "constitutes one of the most outstanding achievements in response to place" in modern literature.[15] Moreover, together with the final version of *Studies in Classic American Literature*, which was completed in northern New Mexico, the poems, essays, and fiction he composed in Taos and its environs comprise a record of Lawrence's acculturation to the human and physical environment of the U.S. Southwest.

In Sherman's skit on the Englishman abroad, the southwestern state of New Mexico is the stamping ground of the Americano Lawrence. The epithet may be more apt than Sherman's amusing use of it supposes, I want to suggest, insofar as the moniker Americano puts what it means to be American under semantic pressure. Now that the word has entered the esperanto of a multinational like the Starbucks corporation, of course, an Americano means a cup of coffee (named after the first mate of the *Pequod* in *Moby-Dick*, the U.S.-owned coffee chain is a global flagship for the American empire portended in Melville's novel). Nonetheless, to ask what is an Americano? is still to put a hemispheric spin on the famous question "What is an American?" posed in Crèvecoeur's American classic, *Letters from an American Farmer*. The term Americano filters through the Hispanophone Americas as a measure both of identity and of difference, shifting its signification according to geographical context.

In October 1923, when Sherman's review of *Studies in Classic American Literature* appeared, his Americano Lawrence was in fact sojourning, not in New Mexico, but across the border in Guadalajara. In Mexico, the term Americano connotes any inhabitant of the American continent (with the compound noun, *norteamericano*, designating the U.S. national in particular). By contrast, in New Mexico, Americano carries the Hispanic inflection of a state that is both on the physical periphery of the nation and on the outer edge of U.S.-American identity as well. This is the New Mexico advertized at the turn of the century by Charles F. Lummis as "the United States which is *not* the United States" due to its "quaint" ethnological demographic, the greater quotient of its population consisting of Native Americans and those Lummis refers to as "Mexicans."[16] When Lummis's *The Land of Poco Tiempo*, a book Lawrence would read en route there, was published in 1893, New Mexico was *not* the United States in a constitutional sense; annexed by the United States at the end of the Mexican-American War in 1848, New Mexico would not be admitted to the Union until 1912.

In the late nineteenth century, in the Upper Rio Grande region of northern New Mexico where Lawrence would later live, Americano had acquired a meaning specific to that struggle for statehood: the word (the abbreviated form of *hispanoamericano*) was adopted in this period by the Spanish-American settler population, anxious to differentiate itself from the *mexicanos*, mixed-race Mexican immigrants and migrants. The Hispano-Americans disdained by Lummis as the "inbred and isolation-shrunken descendants of the Castilian world-finders" were in fact proud of the roots in the region that they could trace back to the Spanish Conquest and, by extension, to European blood.[17] In this context, Americano signifies both an evolving Hispanic consciousness among Nuevo Mexicanos, and, so crucial to their demand for statehood, political allegiance to the American nation.[18]

Although he was no Americano in the local sense, the Lawrence who lived and worked in northern New Mexico as an amateur ranchero as well as a professional writer was more than merely a sojourner there. In the 1920s, his writing was appropriated to local traditions of New Mexico modernism promoted by Mary Austin and Alice Corbin Henderson, among others, who discerned in the indigenous cultures and in the verbal and visual art of Anglo emigrés to the state alike a desert aesthetic different in kind from the standardized culture of the U.S. mainstream. The cosmopolitan localism of the sort sponsored by Austin and Henderson in the 1920s anticipates Tom Lutz's concept of countercosmopolitanisms and related theories like the "regional transnationalism" posited by Laura Doyle in her contribution to the 2009 inaugural issue of the *Journal of Transnational American Studies*. Doyle is arguing along the same lines as Austin and Henderson when she suggests that regional cultures tilt national axes.[19]

For the reason Doyle suggests, regions—and in particular borderland regions like New Mexico—have occupied a strategic position in theories of literary transnationalism since the 1990s. For instance, in his 1998 position piece, "The Myth of 'America' and the Politics of Location," Paul Jay recommends that "our criticism can best be revitalized by paying more attention to locations that are *between* or which *transgress* conventional national borders—liminal margins or border zones in which individual and national identities migrate, merge, and hybridize."[20] Jay is drawing here both on Mary Louise Pratt's influential concept of the "contact zone" as a "space of colonial encounters" and on Carolyn Porter's observation that national borders form pressure points at which the received geopolitical and historical definitions of "America" are "at once internally fissured and externally relativized."[21]

Like Porter and Jay, Lawrence understood America, and indeed experienced it at first hand, as something more, and other, than the United States. Indeed, his own American writing proves the transnational point, that American literature is not a field-imaginary the boundaries of which are coextensive with national borders, but a hemispheric phenomenon, a literature of the Americas as well as a planetary geo-literature. Instead of being read within the expansive contours of the transnational paradigm, however, Lawrence, like other writers of the modernist generation, whether American-born or non-nationals, tests its temporal and ideological limits and limitations.

American literary studies "became consolidated and institutionalized in the modernist era," as Giles notes.[22] In part at least as a consequence of Fredric Jameson's ascription of a temporal paradigm to modernism and spatial culture to postmodernism, modernist writing, both critical and creative, is treated as a toxic zone by New Americanists who, after the spatial and transnational turns, define their praxis in contradistinction to that of their predecessors in the 1910s and 1920s.[23] The Progressive intellectual Randolph Bourne, author of the 1916 essay "Trans-National America," has been singled out from his cohorts as a lonely prophet of the new transnationalism (this notwithstanding Bourne's close involvement with *Seven Arts*, a New York-based little magazine that, in the 1910s, was an organ of the indigenous modernism nurtured by Alfred Stieglitz, and included Lawrence on its list of non-national contributors).[24] In the judgment of revisionist Americanists like Giles and Walter Benn Michaels, who stipulate that their criticism should be "read against the grain of the American polis," a Stieglitz-school modernist manifesto like William Carlos Williams's *In the American Grain* (1925), tainted with blood-and-soil nativism, is tantamount to fascism. Bertrand Russell famously levied the same charge against Lawrence's writing, of course, and the fact that *In the American Grain* is profoundly indebted to *Studies in Classic American Literature* only compounds the suspicion with which Williams's book, like Lawrence's, is regarded in American studies today.[25]

Wai Chee Dimock's *Through Other Continents: American Literature across Deep Time* (2009) calls a long-overdue truce between New Americanists and the modernists. Dimock makes the modest claim that her book merely reflects a broader transnational "sea change" in American studies. Yet, in using Ezra Pound as a major point of reference, Dimock is, in effect, redrawing the map to encompass modernists who more often remain off the chart, or lurk in the margins marked "Here be dragons."[26] By steering a tricky course between modernist aesthetics and ideology, Dimock rediscovers Pound for transnational American literary studies. Pound's "epic spiral, prenational in its genesis and subnational in its babel of tongues" represents a "challenge to the national," Dimock argues. She can thereby find in *The Cantos* a working model of her own theory of American literature across deep time: threading the "long durations" of other cultures "into the short chronology of the United States," her work, like Pound's, effects "a scale enlargement along the temporal axis" of American literature that "also enlarges its spatial compass."[27]

According to Mexican writer Heriberto Yépez's ex-centric and provocatively eccentric study of the psychopoetics of American empire, "*spatialization is the fundamental element not just of Whitman's and Pound's poetry, but, also, in general, of U.S. culture from its very origins. (The States-United is the dystopia of the Co-Here)*."[28] In her use of Pound, Dimock is arguably recuperating an anterior transnationalism or "*Co-Here*" in modernism, translating the obsolescent critical vocabulary of "international" modernism into the idiom of the new transnationalism. The international is the new transnational: so William J. Maxwell concludes, in his response to Jahan Ramazani's analogous theory of a transnational poetics.[29] In the context of American studies, however, Dimock's work, like that of Ramazani in the postcolonial field, is exemplary: rowing against the contemporary current to recover modernism as a usable past for American studies, Dimock's book perhaps predicts a turn in the transnational tide itself.

In *Through Other Continents*, "classic" American literature, like that of the Pound era, is conceived as a global meshwork, a transhistorical skein of intertextual strands. Dimock pulls the thread that connects the writing of the American Transcendentalists and world religions, an implication of which is that a transnational philosophy might also be salvaged from the modernist myth-kitty. Is the Emerson who, as Dimock puts it, "lumps . . . together" all "the Bibles of the world" that different from the modernists, Pound among them, for whom the comparative mythology of Sir James George Frazer's *The*

Golden Bough proved so fruitful a source, or from the Lawrence who, in a move that is wholly characteristic of modernism's primitivist syncreticism, likened the belief-system of the ancient Etruscans to that of present-day Pueblo Indians in New Mexico? By default, deep time is nothing new; Lawrence, like Pound, was a "deep time" traveler, and J. W. Dunne's "An Experiment with Time" (1927) reminds us that theories of timespace are not the property of postmodernity alone, but are closely imbricated with the metaphysics of the modernist era.

If it is the case, as Dimock proposes, that we may, and indeed should, read "Thoreau on Three Continents," then surely we can read the Lawrence who wanted to "write a novel of each continent" on two continents, at least (iv.385).[30] To do so is to bring Lawrence into the broad transnational church of non-Americans who write American literature.

Lawrence's America

"I always write really towards America," Lawrence told Amy Lowell in 1921. America had catalyzed his writing—critical, creative, and philosophical—throughout the 1910s, and by 1916, the year he read Melville's *Moby-Dick*, Lawrence's early enthusiasm for Emerson, Whitman, and James Fenimore Cooper had developed into a profound preoccupation with the symbolic meaning of America and its literature. Begun in 1917 and eventually published, in book form, in 1923, *Studies in Classic American Literature* is the belated product of a fascination with nineteenth-century American writing that had already inflected Lawrence's attempt, in *Women in Love*, to reimagine the modern English novel. His final full-length fiction, *Lady Chatterley's Lover* (1928), marks for some readers the return of a prodigal and native son, if not to England, then to English social and literary forms.[31] But in that book English realism is filtered through the alembic of American romance, making *Lady Chatterley* a Nottinghamshire *Scarlet Letter*, Hawthorne rewritten according to lustier Lawrentian principles. Certainly, America mattered profoundly to Lawrence, both philosophically and more prosaically as a market for his work, at least in the decade between 1916, when *Women in Love* was written, and the publication of his Mexican novel, *The Plumed Serpent*, in 1926—in a writing career and life as contracted as his, this is a significant span.

America was pivotal to Lawrence's weltanschauung, or worldview. In the first version of his essays on American literature, eight of which had appeared in the *English Review* in 1918–19, the magnetic attraction of America is taken as a cosmological given. But, like its literature, America itself has a double meaning—if it is the likely birthplace of a new, postindustrial, race, this is because the United States is the nadir of a played-out, mechanical modernity, the end-product of the West rather than a redemptive rescripting of the Old World narrative of decline. Regeneration is to be effected, not according to the design of a paleface Puritan Providence, but by the resurgence of an autochthonous spirit of place. What Lawrence hears in the "sad, weird utterance" of American literature is an unconscious expression of the disintegration of the modern American psyche and democratic superstructure, and the emergence of a new age to follow—a crisis in the field-imaginary, indeed (*SCAL* 179).[32] Lawrence reads the "classic" works of American literature as prophetic books, telling of the eventual reintegration of knowing with being, and of colonizers with aboriginal continent.

Although he repudiated the material and the spiritual premises of the American Dream, Lawrence was far from immune to the allure of the New World; not only did he make a good deal of what money he had there, Lawrence also considered various American locations for Rananim, the little colony that he had begun to plan early in 1915. In the war years, America represented a sanctuary of a more expedient kind, as well, from the England in which Lawrence found himself confined, and hounded, for the duration of the conflict. Following the publication and suppression of *The Rainbow* in 1915, Lawrence had looked increasingly to an American readership and marketplace for his work. In a 1917 letter to Waldo Frank, associate editor of *Seven Arts*, he wrote of *Studies in Classic American Literature*, then in its early stages, "I hope America will publish it and read it and pay for it." To Frank, Lawrence also declared his counter-biblical covenant with the New World, assuring him that "if the rainbow hangs in the heavens, it hangs over the western continent" (iii.160, 144). Taking the long way round via Sri Lanka (then Ceylon), and Australia, Lawrence eventually made it to America in September 1922. With the exception of a single, unhappy, interlude in Europe, he remained there until September 1925, living on both sides of the U.S.-Mexico border, and competing at firsthand in the U.S.-American market as a working writer.

"The Southwest was Lawrence's America," Frederick J. Hoffman recognized.[33] The United States itself acted on him as a stimulant and an irritant in equal measure, but was nonetheless meaningful to Lawrence to a degree that marks him out from other English writers of the modernist generation, with the important exceptions of the self-styled anglo-mongrel poet Mina Loy, who had emigrated there in 1916, and of Wyndham Lewis. Lawrence himself is a prominent figure in *Paleface* (1929), Lewis's caustic analysis of the American "melting-pot," in which he appears as the transatlantic antitype of Leavis's English novelist. According to Lewis, "Mr. D. H. Lawrence, though an english writer, supplies the most important evidence of the contemporary american 'consciousness.'"[34]

D. H. Lawrence, Americano

My book is an attempt to flesh out the American, or Americano, Lawrence. The first of its three parts or extended chapters focuses on *Studies in Classic American Literature* and employs thick description in order to restore Lawrence's book to its contemporary cultural and literary-historical contexts. When it was published in New York in 1923, *Studies in Classic American Literature* made an unorthodox intervention into what was still a fledgling critical scene in the United States. That *Studies* is regarded in American studies today as a a retrograde exercise in canon-formation and national myth-making is due to a slippage in the reconstruction of the history of American literary history, a conflation of literary history with canonicity, and of Lawrence's contribution to American criticism in its early phase with his book's impact on American studies in the Cold War era. Lawrence, I suggest, has been made a whipping boy for the purported crimes and misdemeanors of the myth and symbolists. My chapter seeks to correct the literary-historical record by returning *Studies in Classic American Literature* to the horizon of its contemporary reception in the United States in the early 1920s.

Later in the American Century, Lawrence's *Studies* did indeed exert a remarkable influence on the myth and symbol critics; their fellow-traveler, Leo Marx, even suggests that Chase, Feidelson, and Lewis all "carry on where Lawrence left off."[35] So too did Leslie Fiedler: described by Arnold Goldsmith as the "most controversial of all the American myth critics, and the most important," Fiedler is also the most indebted, among his peers, to Lawrence.[36] Fiedler freely acknowledges in the prefaces to the first and revised editions of his *Love and Death in the American Novel* (1960; 1966) that the psychocritical method and the flamboyant manner of his book are modeled on Lawrence's. The homosocial thesis of *Love and Death in the American Novel* anticipates contemporary queer theory, Christopher Castiglia has suggested, and in this aspect, too, Fiedler's book looks back to Lawrence's

Studies and its analysis of the male pseudo-couple in the American classics: appropriately enough, Marcus Cunliffe saw Fiedler as Lawrence's "blood-brother," locked in a critical *blutsbrüderschaft* with his English precursor.[37] In Pease's "war of paradigms," the lines of engagement are sometimes blurred; in addition to queering the pitch of the American field-imaginary, Fiedler also contributed, with leading African American critic Houston A. Baker Jr., to the reformation of the American canon in the late 1970s and early 1980s.[38]

In a last-ditch defense of myth and symbol in the 1980s, Alan Trachtenberg drew attention to "the radical cultural criticism embodied in the formative works of the school," pointing to the "synthesis of historical scholarship and cultural criticism" in a much-maligned work like Henry Nash Smith's *Virgin Land* (1950).[39] Smith's "critical vision of Cold War America" and of American historical experience was widely shared among the myth and symbol critics, according to Trachtenberg, who analogizes their "embattled position" to that of the American critics who were excluded by the anglophile academy in the early 1920s.[40] Leo Marx, however, advises us to differentiate between these critical generations. His 1961 article "Listen to the States!" tropes on "America, Listen to Your Own," the 1920 manifesto-essay, written for but not included in *Studies in Classic American Literature*, in which Lawrence had urged Americans to hear the new voice of their own literature. Marx's survey of the scholarship of Chase, Feidelson, and Lewis leads him to conclude that "today, we all know, the world listens," and even to ask if the world is now "menaced by an international cult of American literature."[41] Pease makes the same point in more polemical terms when he argues that the myth and symbolists were the symbolic engineers of U.S. foreign policy in the Cold War era, their work a cultural corollary of the Marshall Plan and its mission "to legitimate the United States' place as the subject and telos of universal history."[42]

Whether or not the myth and symbol critics served as Cold War warriors, their affiliations with Lawrence reveal transnational and transatlantic reciprocities of the kind identified by Susan Sontag in her comments on *Studies in Classic American Literature*. On receiving the 2003 Friedenspreis des Deutschen Buchhandels (the Peace Prize of the German book trade), awarded in recognition of her role as intellectual ambassador between the United States and Europe, Sontag acknowledged Lawrence as her antecedant, and described *Studies in Classic American Literature* as "the most interesting book ever written about American culture." In her acceptance speech, delivered in Frankfurt in the year of the U.S.-led invasion of Iraq and subsequently printed in the British newspaper the *Guardian* under the title "The fragile alliance," Sontag recruits what she sees as Lawrence's prescient assessment of post–World War I America to her own critique of the "imperial program" of the United States after 9/11.

Sounding very much like a New Americanist, Sontag proposes that "literature, world literature" gives us the means "to escape the prison of national vanity." "The future of the world—the world we share," she insists, "is syncretist, impure. We are not shut off from each other. More and more, we leak into each other."[43] Sontag locates *Studies in Classic American Literature* in that "world of fluid borders" in which the New American studies finds its mobile remit. In his 2000 essay on "The Transnational Turn," Robert A. Gross had identified British cultural studies scholar and author of *The Black Atlantic* (1993), Paul Gilroy, as the forerunner of transnationalism in American studies. "Ironically, it has required . . . a view from Britain," Gross remarks, to encourage Americanists to look beyond their national borders. "For American Studies," Gross continues, "the effect is akin to looking through the reverse lens of a telescope. What once loomed large has shrunk in significance."[44] Seventy years before Gilroy's book, *Studies in Classic American Literature* had offered a view from Britain—a view which Lawrence defines in terms identical to Gross's as looking "though the wrong end of the telescope, across all the Atlantic water" (*SCAL* 55).

Sontag makes a passionate and persuasive claim for *Studies in Classic American Literature*'s contemporary relevance. But if *Studies* is to reemerge as a dissident document, it must also be understood in the very different terms of its own historical period, when the status of American literature and American criticism alike was far from assured, either at home or abroad.

A non-standard work of American criticism and literary history, *Studies* is, in addition, a remarkable and often disturbing record of Lawrence's attempt to come to terms with ethnic difference and otherness in America. In the first version of his essays on American literature, eight of which had appeared in the *English Review* in 1918–19, Lawrence insists that in approaching American culture, "we must learn to think in terms of difference and otherness" (*SCAL* 168). He was forced to practice what he had preached when he rewrote the essays on the ground in New Mexico in 1922. In *Studies*' final version, classic American literature is the vehicle by which Lawrence explores the racial and gendered tensions of the New Mexico contact zone in which he completed the work. Lawrence described the final version of *Studies* as "the first reaction on me of America itself," and that reaction, I argue, gives the text much of its new and edgy intensity, its own "American" imprimatur (iv.343).

My second chapter addresses Lawrence's relationship, both as a critic and as a poet, to the American avant-garde, to the networks of metropolitan and New Mexican modernism associated with Alfred Stieglitz and Mabel Dodge Luhan respectively. Borrowing a term from Ramazani, I explore an "affiliative connection" between Lawrence's 1923 volume, *Birds, Beasts and Flowers*, and the localized expression of key works of American poetic modernism published in the same year: William Carlos Williams's *Spring and All*, Mary Austin's *The American Rhythm*, and Wallace Stevens's *Harmonium*.[45] Transatlantic affiliations like this, I suggest, allow us to gauge the extent and nature of Lawrence's involvements with Anglo-American modernism.

Although he bears the brunt of John Carey's attack on the modernist generation in *The Intellectuals and the Masses*, Lawrence is more often conspicuous by his absence, or is a liminal presence, in narratives of anglophone modernism. Holly Laird's *Self and Sequence* opens with the statement that "Lawrence's poetry is barely acknowledged by the scholarship of modernism," a state of affairs that has changed little since the publication of Laird's fine study in 1988.[46] In Peter Howarth's recent *Cambridge Introduction to Modernist Poetry*, for example, Lawrence has "one foot in modernism and one foot outside it," as he rather awkwardly straddles the divide between modernism proper and the broader modern movement associated with the Georgian revolt against Victorian conventions.

Lawrence had the unique distinction of publishing poems in the rival Georgian and Imagist anthologies of the 1910s. During the poetry wars of the period, then, he did do a hokey cokey of a kind, putting a foot in, and out, of each camp (albeit that hokey pokey, the American name of the game, may be the more appropriate term, given the transatlantic tempo of Lawrence's modernism). Howarth, who is alert to Lawrence's American reception, postdates it, judging that Lawrence's "greatest impact on modernist poetry would really come as a cultural guru for the Olson generation."[47] My chapter demonstrates that Lawrence was no less of a guru for American avant-gardists in the 1910s and 1920s—like William Carlos Williams, who was himself a precursor of Olson and the Black Mountain School. There are keener affinities, I argue, between Lawrence and the poets, painters and intellectuals in Stieglitz's New York circle and in Mabel Dodge Luhan's New Mexico milieu than between Lawrence and his contemporaries in England, whether Georgians, members of the Bloomsbury set or, with the significant exception of H.D., the American-born modernists who, as Williams put it, had "run to London."[48]

As an Englishman coming to America, and doing so in 1922, the annus mirabilis of modernism in Europe, Lawrence reminds us that there was two-way traffic on the modernist Atlantic. Moreover, if, as Donald Davie argues, "[t]he case of William Carlos Williams remains the rock on which Anglo-American literary opinion splits," then the affiliative connection between Williams and Lawrence places the latter on the American side of the transatlantic divide.[49]

Although he continued to appear in their anthologies, in the course of the 1910s Lawrence moved away from the Georgian poets, whose vision of a regenerated New World was located within English borders and, to an extent, prosodic conventions.[50] With the publication of *Look! We Have Come Through!* in 1917, it was clear that Lawrence's greater allegiance was now to the New World poetics of Whitman; indeed, as Christopher Pollnitz notes in his introduction to the Cambridge edition of the *Poems*, in the course of the 1910s, Lawrence's affinity to Whitman had become "a critical truism" (*P* 695). As early as 1913, Walter de la Mare had critiqued Lawrence as a "sub-Whitmanesque" poet (*P* 692). Jeremy Hooker makes the point that *Look!* "is formally various, containing rhyming poems and ballads, reminiscences of Lawrence the Georgian, touches of Imagism, some Yeatsian symbolism, and even occasional lapses towards doggerel, as well as poems of Whitman-like utterance."[51] Nonetheless, in their thralldom to Whitman, a number of the *Look!* poems—"New Heaven and Earth," for instance—evince what Ramazani defines as "weak transnationalism." By contrast, *Birds, Beasts and Flowers*, which was begun in Tuscany in 1920 and completed in New Mexico in 1923, is an exemplary work of "strong transnationalism," a post-Whitmanian poetry of the present in which Lawrence engages his American precursor, but stands his own ground.[52] In this respect, I will suggest, *Birds, Beasts and Flowers* comports with the contemporaneous work of American poets like Williams, who were also, in several senses, writing out of Whitman.

Lawrence's feisty relationship with Whitman fits uneasily, at best, into what Russ Castronovo calls "the venerable tradition of source and influence studies"—a tradition that the new generation of Americanists has left behind: "by accepting the findings of an autopsy that declares literary history dead," Castronovo insists, "American literature receives new life."[53] Lawrence had made much the same point in *Studies*, where he dissects what he calls the post mortem corpus of classic American literature *and* reanimates it, giving the old American books, and the seemingly moribund phenomenon of literary history itself, a new lease of life. In any case, Whitman's influence on Lawrence, and Lawrence's influence, in turn, on an American poetics of space and place, cannot be understood according to the kinds of kinship in which a national literary genealogy consists. The sorts of poetic interchange with which my book is concerned are better understood according to the exogamous terms of reference adopted in world-system theories of genre like Dimock's, in which genre "has less to do with common ancestry than with a convergence of attributes" issuing from "widely dispersed environments" and comprising "a broad spectrum of affinities."[54]

Like Kim Herzinger's study of Lawrence's oeuvre between 1908 and 1915, my book approaches Lawrence "by 'placing' him inside the cultural matrix of his time" and reading him in relation to "the currents of thoughts which continually circulated around him." As Herzinger argues, establishing Lawrence's relationship to his cultural context has never been a major concern of Lawrentians. This might have surprised and disappointed Lawrence, who said of his poetry that it should not "be judged as if it existed in the absolute, in the vacuum of the absolute. Even the best poetry, when it is at all personal, needs the penumbra of of its own time and place and circumstance, to make it full and whole" (P 656).[55]

The New Mexico poems of *Birds, Beasts and Flowers* bear a striking affinity with the cosmopolitan localism of American poetic modernism in the 1920s. Lawrence was too slippery a fish to be caught in the tangled nets of transatlantic Imagism. But in the United States, he did hitch his wagon to *Laughing Horse*, a little magazine of New Mexico modernism edited by Walter Willard ("Spud") Johnson. Poems from *Birds, Beasts and Flowers* would also appear in the first anthology of New Mexico poetry, *The Turquoise Trail* (1928), edited by the former associate editor of *Poetry* magazine, Alice Corbin Henderson. Lawrence's significance as a philosopher of place, and as a theorist of "nodality" (MM 125), is confirmed by the essays collected in *Mornings in Mexico* (1927) and *Reflections on the Death of a Porcupine* (1925), as well as *Studies in Classic American Literature*'s "The Spirit of Place."[56] My chapter draws on Lawrence's own discourse of place, on ecopoetics, and on phenomenological paradigms, to read Lawrence's American and New Mexican poetry. As Jonathan Bate has argued:

> The deed of title which is constituted by a poem of dwelling is not a legal document. Poets who find their home in a specific environment have an imaginative, not a proprietorial, interest in belonging. The ecopoetic vision is inclusive, not exclusionary.[57]

Birds, Beasts and Flowers' "Autumn at Taos" and "The Blue Jay" are poems of dwelling, in Bate's and Gaston Bachelard's sense.

In my third chapter, I turn to the fiction Lawrence wrote in northern New Mexico in the summer of 1924. "St. Mawr," "The Princess," and "The Woman Who Rode Away" are read here as an American trilogy in which Lawrence engages, and profoundly unsettles, the generic conventions of American wilderness romance and related modes like that of the Indian captivity narrative. As borderlands fictions, these stories put under local pressures the national imaginary anatomized in *Studies in Classic American Literature*, published the year before.

Jay argues that "[l]iterature written in 'contact' or 'border' zones, in geographical and cultural spaces 'between' clearly demarcated lines of political and social division, almost always deals in fairly explicit—and often conflicted or unresolved—ways with issues related to the history of this contact."[58] Lawrence's borderland tales are no exception: their symbolic meaning, I will suggest, subverts rather than sanctions "the national symbolic order."[59] In classic American literature, Pease contends, "[t]he national narrative produced national identities by way of a social symbolic order that systematically separated an abstract, dismebodied subject from resistant materialities, such as race, class, and gender."[60] The reverse is the case in Lawrence's American stories, the Anglo, Indian and "Mexican" protagonists of which are caught in New Mexico's triethnic trap. Lawrence's stories demythologize the New Mexico advertized by Lummis and subsequent promoters of the place as the Land of Enchantment.

Regeneration through Violence (1973), the first book in Richard Slotkin's revisionist trilogy on the mythology of the American West, deconstructs "the myth of the essential America" by way of Lawrence's verdict, in *Studies in Classic American Literature*, that "[t]he essential American soul is hard, isolate, stoic, and a killer" (65). In *Studies*, Slotkin says, Lawrence "expresses and partially explains" the "psychological conflict implicit in European confrontation of a New World wilderness."[61] That conflict and confrontation, I argue, is also the subject of Lawrence's New Mexico fictions.

In the judgment of Simone de Beauvoir, Lawrence wrote "guidebooks for women": his New Mexico stories, "The Woman Who Rode Away" in particular, are often adduced as chauvinist cases in point, and read as cautionary tales in which wilful women get what they deserve.[62] It is worth pointing out, in Lawrence's defense, that he did write one book *with* a woman: *The Boy in the Bush* (1924), which was co-authored with the Australian Mollie Skinner, and that his three New Mexico stories were sparked by mooted collaborations with Mabel Dodge Luhan and Catherine Carswell. Elaine Feinstein has demonstrated that Lawrence's writing was consistently enabled, in creative as well as in more material ways, by women; in a wider sense, it is also the case, as Linda Karrell puts it, that authorship is "a form of production that invariably reveals the presence of others," albeit that this is "something our traditional understanding of the author persists in ignoring or displacing," a problem which is particularly acute in relation to a writer like Lawrence.[63] In my chapter, Lawrence's tales "of out here" (v.136), as he called the New Mexico stories, are read in relation to the feminized matrix in—and against—which they were written, a context that, I argue, inflects in important ways the interrelated issues of agency, gender, and genre explored in the tales.

My book is itself a collaborative effort, drawing as it does on the work of Lawrentians who have charted what James C. Cowan calls Lawrence's "American journey," among them Cowan himself, Keith Cushman, Virginia Crosswhite Hyde, Earl Ingersoll, Julianne Newmark, Neil Roberts, and Keith Sagar. I am no less indebted to the model scholarship of the editors of the *Cambridge Edition of the Letters and Works of D. H. Lawrence*. Although its chapters are roughly chronological in sequence and provide a contextual narrative of Lawrence's various transactions with America, my book is not intended as a critical biography of his American years—for that, we have David Ellis's definitive *Dying Game*, the final volume of the *Cambridge Biography of D. H. Lawrence*. My purpose, which is different in kind, is to explore the implications of Lawrence's encounters with America and American literature for our understanding of his own oeuvre, of transatlantic modernism, and of American literature in a globalized world. Nonetheless, since Lawrence's engagements with American literature, as critic and as practitioner, are bound up with his lived experience there, the remainder of this introduction provides a background for the chapters to follow.

That Lawrence did, after many prevarications and diversions, travel to America in 1922 was due in no small part to the persuasive powers of Mabel Dodge Luhan, the *salonnière* and patroness of the arts who had written to him the year before to invite him to visit her in Taos, New Mexico. In a good deal of Lawrence scholarship, when she is not deemed downright baleful, Luhan cuts a comical and even a ludicrous figure, this despite the leading part she played both in Lawrence's response to the America he believed her to personify, and in the writing he produced there.[64] Among the problems Mabel has posed for critics is the basic one of nomenclature—what should we call her? Since her names, or at least her surnames, are legion, "Mabel" has been the default but unsatisfactory option for the woman who published her autobiography and her memoir of Lawrence under the name of Mabel Dodge Luhan.

When Lawrence first met her, she was Mabel Dodge Sterne. In 1923, she married the Pueblo Indian Antonio (Tony) Lujan, but chose to use a phonetic form of his name—Luhan—because, she explained, her anglophone friends couldn't manage the Spanish *jota*. The heiress to a considerable manufacturing fortune, she was born Mabel Ganson in Buffalo in 1879. After the death in a hunting accident of her first husband, Karl Evans, Mabel moved to Europe with their young son, meeting her second husband, the architect Edwin Dodge, in Paris. During her ensuing period of Renaissance self-fashioning at the Villa Curonia, near Florence, "Mabel Dodge" emerged (with the help of Gertrude Stein) as a modern icon. Mabel returned to the United States in 1912, basing herself in Greenwich Village, and marrying her third husband, the Russian-born artist Maurice Sterne, in 1917.

With what Lincoln Steffens described as her "centralizing, magnetic, social faculty," Mabel now became "the Magna Mater of twentieth-century America's first rebel generation," presiding over what was "perhaps the most famous salon in American history." Among the movers and shakers who attended her "Wednesdays" at 23 Fifth Avenue were political radicals like her one-time lover John Reed and cultural impresarios like Alfred Stieglitz, reflecting her involvement in activism and in the arts alike.[65] In 1913, she helped to organize both the Paterson Strike Pageant and the Armory Show, the watershed exhibition of modernist painting mounted at New York's 69th Regiment Armory on Lexington Avenue. Here, she distributed copies of her own privately printed edition of Gertrude Stein's "Portrait of Mabel Dodge at the Villa Curonia" (1912), introducing Stein's post-impressionist prose to an American readership in a publicity stunt also designed to promote the avant-garde persona of "Mabel Dodge" herself. Her motives aside, the launch of Stein's word-portrait emphasizes the symbiotic relationship between the verbal and visual arts in the emergent American modernism of the 1910s—William Carlos Williams would later remark that the Armory Show represented "a break" for writers and artists alike, much as the first exhibition of post-impressionist painting had done for London modernists in 1910.[66] In New Mexico, Mabel's circle would include painters she had known in the

New York years, like Andrew Dasburg; Georgia O'Keeffe, who had moved to Manhattan a year after Mabel had left the city, came to New Mexico in the first instance at her invitation. Jean Toomer, Willa Cather, and Robinson Jeffers were among the writers connected to her in Taos.

Mabel had left Manhattan for New Mexico at the end of 1917 in reaction to the United States' entry into World War I in April: hotbeds of domestic radicalism like the Salon Dodge were now perceived as threats to homeland security. But there was another impetus for her move. Shortly after their marriage in August of that year, Mabel had sent Maurice Sterne to the Southwest on the pretext that "there are wonderful things to paint. Indians" (actually, her autobiography reveals that she wanted to put some distance between Maurice and the sexual temptations of Village bohemia). Sterne wrote from Santa Fe that he had found an "object in life" for her there, even if he had not found one for himself. Mabel's mission was to "Save the Indians, their art-culture—reveal it to the world!"[67] She duly followed Sterne to the Southwest. Finding that Alice Corbin Henderson, another Anglo emigré with a keen interest in indigenous cultures, was already in situ in Santa Fe, Mabel went north, to the more remote Taos. There, she would create a cultural hub of her own, housed in the extraordinary adobe hacienda and compound, built with the assistance of Tony Lujan, which adjoins the tribal lands of Taos Pueblo. Tony, who would become her fourth husband, was the Taos Indian whose face Mabel would claim she had already seen, superimposed upon Sterne's features, in a dream.

In November 1921, Mabel read an extract from Lawrence's *Sea and Sardinia* in the *Dial*. She wrote to him at once, urging him to come to New Mexico, convinced that he, alone, could describe "this Taos country and the Indians . . . so that it is as much alive between the covers of the book as it is in reality."[68] Lawrence had already heard reports of Taos from Gertrude Stein's brother, the art-collector Leo Stein, and feared he would encounter "a colony of rather dreadful sub-arty people" there (iv.111). In fact, Mabel had little to do with the artists' colony that had been established in Taos at the turn of the century, and Lawrence would forge a friendship with at least one of the modernist painters in her circle, Dasburg.[69] After spending less than a fortnight as her guest, however, Lawrence was chafing against "living under the wing of the 'padrona'" (iv.305). A later visitor to Taos, Georgia O'Keeffe, would move to Abiquiu "to avoid the stresses and strains of Mabeltown."[70] For his part, Lawrence briefly considered going south to Santa Fe, before deciding to decamp instead to the Sangre de Cristo Mountains to the north of Taos.

He envisaged creating a little community there, to which even Mabel might, from time to time, belong. In a letter to their mutual friend Bessie Freeman, Lawrence urged her to sell her home in Los Angeles and "take up the next 'homestead' lot to us," suggesting that "Mabel would take up another lot adjoining" (iv.333).

The preferred location for this communal homestead was a ranch purchased by Mabel in 1920 and owned by her son, John Evans. This was the Flying-Heart Ranch, later renamed Lobo and then Kiowa by Lawrence, on which he would live, with wife Frieda and the English painter Dorothy Brett, in 1924, and again with Frieda alone in 1925. But in 1922, with winter approaching and a huffy Mabel refusing to cooperate, the dilapidated property was not a viable prospect. So, in early December, the Lawrences moved to the Del Monte Ranch, a less isolated location a little further down Lobo Peak. Together with Knud Merrild and Kai Götzsche, two Danish painters they had befriended in Taos, the Lawrences rented cabins from the Hawke family, who owned the place. Now on his own terms and at a strategic distance from Mabeltown, Lawrence could attempt to establish a version of the "little colony" that he called Rananim. At first, Rananim had been an "Island idea," but Lawrence would soon propose mainland American sites for it, including a former plantation in Florida owned by the composer Frederick Delius (ii.259, 277). Wartime travel restrictions kept Lawrence in England, so he briefly considered Lady Ottoline Morrell's Oxfordshire estate, Garsington Manor (which, during the war years, served as a rural extension of the Bloomsbury enclave), as a substitute, telling Morrell in a letter that "I want you to form the nucleus of a new community which shall start a new life amongst us" (ii.271).

David Cavitch notes that, after the war, "[t]he central locations for his symbolic projections were to be the American Southwest and Mexico."[71] But living in America had made Lawrence sceptical of New World utopias like the pantisocracy on the banks of the Susquehanna proposed by Coleridge and Southey, and the Brook Farm experiment in Massachusetts that Hawthorne had fictionalized in *The Blithedale Romance*. In *Studies in Classic American Literature*, which he finished revising at Del Monte, Lawrence writes of Brook Farm, "[t]here the famous idealists and transcendentalists of America met to till the soil and hew the timber in the sweat of their own brows" in "an atmosphere of communal love," until, inevitably, "they fell out like cats and dogs" (99)—much as Lawrence and Mabel had done. In *Studies*, Lawrence writes that "it is perhaps easier to love America passionately" from a distance. "When you are actually *in* America," he admits, "America hurts" (55).

It may be the case that despite his search for what Victor Turner would term ideological *communitas*, Lawrence ultimately belonged only, as North argues, in transit. But Del Monte, and later the Kiowa Ranch, were significant way stations, at least, on what Lawrence called the savage pilgrimage of his postwar years (iv.375).[72] Keith Sagar, who insists that Rananim remained a vital ideal for Lawrence, has also suggested that the misanthropy inculcated in him during the war years prompted Lawrence to re-envisage it as "a colony without people."[73] Yet the four months in which Lawrence and Frieda, Merrild and Götzsche homesteaded together at the Del Monte Ranch made for a more harmonious experience than either Brook Farm, or the Lawrences' own earlier and disastrous attempt at a life in common with John Middleton Murry and Katherine Mansfield in Cornwall. Earlier in the 1910s, the "constitution" of Rananim had been a broadly socialist one; in his memoir of Lawrence, Merrild suggests something similar when he recalls that the gang of four "worked hard at roofing, carpentering, plastering, glazing, paperhanging, painting, whitewashing . . . One of us suggested that we form a Del Monte Local of the I.W.W." (the International Workers of the World, or "Wobblies"). The men from Del Monte, Merrild writes, forged a "unit of manly togetherness."[74]

"Men are free when they belong to a living, organic, *believing* community," Lawrence insists in *Studies*, and "[n]ot when they are escaping to some wild west" (17). He could not of course belong in any meaningful way to the local believing community of Taos Pueblo, and Lawrence dismissed European alternatives, like George Ivanovich Gurdjieff's Institute for the Harmonious Development of Man, as "a sickly stunt" (iv.555) (when she died of tuberculosis at his Fontainebleu-Avon Institute, Gurdjieff became known as "the man who killed Katherine Mansfield").[75]

The colonies established by the printer, artist, and Catholic convert Eric Gill seem to have appealed to him more.[76] The last piece of writing Lawrence completed, just days before his death in March 1930, was a review of Gill's *Art-Nonsense and Other Essays*, in which he remonstrates with the author's Christian credo but praises the ethics of "living experience" derived from Gill's Morrisite commitment to what, in one of his *Pansies* poems, Lawrence celebrates as "Things men have made with wakened hands" (*P* 388). What Gill calls "God" Lawrence defines as "a state which any man or woman achieves when busy and concentrated on a job which calls forth real skill and attention, or devotion. It is a state of absorption into the creative spirit" (*IR* 357). As a related *Pansies* poem puts it, "if, as we work, we can transmit life into our work, / life, still more life, rushes into us to compensate, to be ready / and we ripple with life through the days" (*P* 389). This is the "great truth which Mr. Gill has found in his living experience, and which he flings in the teeth of modern industrialism" (*IR* 357). Del Monte seems to have been, if not a believing community, then an extemporized cooperative of kinds: Lawrence revised or completed *Studies in Classic American Literature*, *Kangaroo*, and *Birds, Beasts and Flowers* there, while Merrild worked on illustrations for the book jackets.⁷⁷

In the spring of 1923, Lawrence and Frieda traveled to Mexico with the poet Witter Bynner, whom they had met in Santa Fe, and Bynner's then lover and amanuensis, Spud Johnson. After some weeks in Mexico City, the party moved on to Chapala, in the state of Jalisco, where Lawrence wrote *Quetzalcoatl*, the first version of *The Plumed Serpent*, using Bynner and Johnson as models for the characters of Owen Rhys and Bud Villiers. That summer, instead of visiting England with Frieda as they had planned, Lawrence went to California, where Merrild and Götzsche had found journey-work as decorators in Santa Monica. With Götzsche, he returned to Mexico, traveling in the north of the country and then staying in Guadalajara until he sailed for Europe to join Frieda, in London, in December.

Later that month, Lawrence hosted the infamous dinner at the Café Royal—the Last Supper, as Catherine Carswell, who was one of the guests, would later name it—at which he tried to persuade a number of his friends to become his disciples and follow him in what William York Tindall describes as "his second coming to New Mexico."⁷⁸ Back in England, and unhappy there, Lawrence had revived the notion of an American Rananim. Murry—with whom Frieda may have been having an affair in Lawrence's absence—is the Judas-figure in Carswell's account: he accepted Lawrence's invitation only to renege on it later. The sole recruit to his New Mexico colony was Dorothy Brett, who had herself become Murry's lover after the death of Katherine Mansfield in January 1923. Lawrence had met the Honourable Dorothy Brett—"who paints, is deaf, forty, very nice, and daughter of Viscount Esher"—in 1915 (iv.546). "Brett," as she preferred to be called, traveled with the Lawrences to New Mexico in March 1924 and would make Taos her permanent home.

The trio stayed in Taos as Mabel's guests until May, when they moved up to the Lobo Ranch, as Lawrence named it; he changed its name to Kiowa in August. Mabel had made the ranch over to Frieda soon after the Lawrences' return to New Mexico: it was the only property or real estate they would own.

Not wanting to be in her debt, Frieda sent to Europe for the manuscript of *Sons and Lovers*, which she gave to Mabel in return. Appropriately enough, Mabel would subsequently hand on the manuscript of Lawrence's oedipal masterpiece to her psychoanalyst—A. A. Brill, who was Freud's first translator in America—in lieu of fees. Soon after the move to Kiowa, Lawrence wrote the essay "Pan in America" and, over the summer there, three fictions that are closely related to it and to each other: "St. Mawr," "The Princess," and "The Woman Who Rode Away." In October, the Lawrences, and Brett, left for Mexico, this time settling in Oaxaca, where Lawrence completed *The Plumed Serpent*. In January 1925, after a falling-out, Brett returned to New Mexico. Lawrence, now very ill, followed soon afterward with Frieda: he had finally been diagnozed as tubercular and had difficulties crossing the border at El Paso. From April to early September, when they left America for the last time, the Lawrences once again lived at Kiowa, now without Brett who, after their departure, looked after the ranch as a caretaker of kinds. Georgia O'Keeffe stayed with her there in 1929, and *The Lawrence Tree* (originally titled *Pine Tree with Stars at Brett's*) is O'Keeffe's tribute in paint to Lawrence's tributes, in his New Mexico poetry and prose, to the spirit of the place.

The Kiowa Ranch is a recurring reference point in the fiction Lawrence wrote there. It is the proving ground for the philosophical essays collected in *Reflections on the Death of a Porcupine* and for the theory of environmental expression put forward in "Pan in America," an essay published in 1926, but written immediately after Lawrence had moved to the ranch. "What can a man do with his life but live it?" Lawrence asks in the essay. "And what does life consist in, save a vivid relatedness between the man and the living universe that surrounds him"? (*MM* 160). As Lawrence's biographer and sometime friend, Richard Aldington, would remark, "to realise what that mountain-side and his ownership of those American acres meant to him, read the last fifteen pages of 'St. Mawr,' the last essay of *Mornings in Mexico*, and the essays called 'New Mexico,' 'Pan in America' and 'Taos.'"[79]

1

Hands-up, America!

Studies in Classic American Literature

> I am doing a set of essays on "The Transcendental Element in American (Classic) Literature." It sounds very fine and large, but in reality is rather a thrilling blood-and-thunder, your-money-or-your-life kind of thing: hands-up, America!—No, but they are very keen essays in criticism—cut your fingers if you don't handle them carefully.—Are you going to help me to hold up the *Yale Review* or the *New Republic* or some such old fat coach, with this ten-barrelled pistol of essays of mine, held right in the eye of America? Answer me that, Donna Americana. (iii.156–57)

Writing to Amy Lowell, alias "Donna Americana," from Cornwall in 1917, D. H. Lawrence describes the work-in-progress that some six years later would be published in New York as *Studies in Classic American Literature*. In the same year, criticism in America was defined by one of its native practitioners, Van Wyck Brooks, as uncertain of "its place, its bearings, its conditions." American literature itself was a "naissant literature."[1] Little had changed by 1923, when Lawrence's book came out—at least according to the foreword to *Studies*, which is addressed to Americans and would not be reprinted in the English edition. Here, in a bravura performance of the stagey Englishness that characterizes much of the early prose that he produced in the United States, Lawrence taunts the homegrown critics in whose stead he must act as "midwife to the unborn homunculus" of their national literature. "Never was such a barren absence of creative criticism as in the U.S.A.," Lawrence complains, in a version of the foreword written in 1922 (*SCAL* 11, 389).

Studies in Classic American Literature itself is creative criticism, of course, and with a vengeance. Lawrence's reading of its literature is premised on a radical transvaluation of American values, in which national pieties are recast as antinomian, Nietzschean aphorisms: so, democracy in America is "a rattling of chains," Benjamin Franklin is "the first dummy American," and the "essential American soul" is "hard, isolate, stoic, and a killer" (*SCAL* 17, 20, 65). His "megaphonic insertions"—Anaïs Nin's memorable phrase for Lawrence's bullhorn use of uppercase type—suggest that another model for *Studies* may be the manifestos of Italian Futurism Lawrence had read in 1914.[2] Indeed, Lawrence identifies in the American classics a proto-Futurist aesthetic of the "extreme":

> The furthest frenzies of French modernism or futurism have not yet reached the pitch of extreme consciousness that Poe, Melville, Hawthorne, Whitman reached. The European moderns are all *trying* to be extreme. The great Americans I mention just were it. (*SCAL* 12)

Studies is criticism but not as we know it: creative criticism of an order matched only in a few works that owe a debt to Lawrence's own—like William Carlos Williams's *In the American Grain* (1925) for instance, and, more markedly still, Edward Dahlberg's *Can These Bones Live?* (1941), and Charles Olson's *Call Me Ishmael* (1947).

But if *Studies* is defined as sui generis, or approached solely in the terms of the countertradition that it instantiated, then it is easy to deem the book a curiosity, disconnected as such from the heated debates of its day as to the function and status of criticism in America. In fact, Lawrence was in the thick of it, playing for high stakes in what was a risky period for American criticism. Into the early 1920s American literature was still widely regarded as a subset of English literature and had little pedagogical standing in an academy committed both in principle and in its neoclassical curricular practice to the New Humanism developed by Irving Babbitt and Paul Elmer More.[3] In this context, the very title of Lawrence's book cocks a snook at the establishment.[4]

A critical movement had emerged outside of the universities in the confident years of the 1910s, a time "when dozens of novelists and poets were 'discovering' America, and a spirit of rebirth was in the air."[5] But this little renaissance was nipped in the bud when the United States entered the war in 1917, and into the 1920s "the critic in this country" was, in Brooks's words, still "so new a type" as to be "regarded as an undesirable alien."[6] Lawrence's credentials, as an English practitioner of American literary criticism, were doubly suspect; he was alien on two counts, as non-national and critic both. A *Current Opinion* notice of *Studies*, titled "D. H. Lawrence Bombs Our Literary Shrines," duly brands him an insurgent, and one whose reputation as a troublemaker has preceded him.[7] Seeking the relative safety of a niche market, Lawrence's American publisher, Thomas Seltzer, priced his edition of *Studies* accordingly: the U.S. edition sold at the steep price of $3.[8] Even those who liked his book suggested that "a foreigner" would "hardly have enough understanding of the American soul" to produce a definitive literary history of the United States (which, in Lawrence's defense, was not his intention).[9] Several of the more prominent reviews of *Studies* in the American press insist that Lawrence's right to speak on the subject is abrogated by his outsider status. Maurice Francis Egan, writing in the *Literary Digest International Book Review*, dismisses him as an English interloper, complaining that *Studies* offers "a criticism of a life of which Lawrence knows nothing." Likewise, in his *Bookman* review, Raymond Weaver charges Lawrence with an "ignorance of American literature" that is "comprehensive and profound"—this despite the fact that Lawrence had consulted Weaver's *Herman Melville: Man, Mariner and Mystic* when he was revising his own book.[10]

A copy of *Moby-Dick* that he came across by chance in 1916 seems to have sparked Lawrence's fascination with the American classics. Early in 1917, he asked Robert Mountsier, an American friend who would later act as his agent in the United States, to send him Everyman's Library editions of Melville's *Typee* and *Omoo*, together with works by Cooper, Whitman, Crèvecoeur, Hawthorne, Emerson, Franklin, and Poe (see iii.65–66). The intensive period of reading that followed yielded the first version of *Studies in Classic American Literature*—eight essays that appeared in the *English Review* between November 1918 and June 1919. Envisaging a book, Lawrence compiled a typescript for his then U.S. publisher Benjamin Huebsch; this included seven of the *English Review* articles, together with unpublished essays on Dana and Melville, and an essay on Whitman that Lawrence (rightly) feared would prove unfit to print: this is the "ten-barrelled pistol of essays" that Lawrence had at first hoped that Amy Lowell would help him place in the *New Republic* or *Yale Review*. The project then stalled until the summer of 1920, when Huebsch ceded the U.S. rights to the book to Seltzer. Lawrence emended the essays for what he expected would be their imminent publication, but two years later he was still at work, recasting them into the text that Seltzer eventually brought out on August 27, 1923. The book that Lawrence boasted would bring about the belated birth of a national literature in America had exceeded its own due date.

The 1923 *Studies in Classic American Literature* is itself the belated offspring of what Lawrence called his "metaphysic" or "philosophy" (iii.143). In their first version, his American essays contain "a whole Weltanschauung" or worldview (iii.400). Europe and America have replaced Rome and Carthage as "the great poles of negative and positive vitalism," but because the New World has not yet achieved a perfect polarity with the Old, America remains "Europe in negative reality, reflected to enormity" (*SCAL* 171, 177). In the first version of *Studies*, the Puritan settlers' "recoil" from their New World environment—their repression of the magnetic attraction of aboriginal America, or what Lawrence calls the Spirit of Place—is interpreted as a process of psychic as much as of territorial colonization, as the domination of mind over body, and of intellect over instinct (174).

Key to this early version of *Studies* is "a new science of psychology" in which Lawrence systematizes and offers "proofs" for the belief in somatic or blood-consciousness that he had begun to articulate as early as 1913 (iii.400):

> My great religion is a belief in the blood, the flesh, as being wiser than the intellect. We can go wrong in our minds. But what our blood feels and believes and says, is always true. (i.503)

Later in the 1910s, Lawrence would locate nonmental consciousness—what the *Birds, Beasts and Flowers* poem "Cypresses" calls "marrow-thought"—"in the nerve centres of the body rather than exclusively in the blood" (*P* 250; *PU* xxiv). In the 1918–19 *Studies*, expositions of the biological psyche are interlarded with readings of the American classics, producing what might be called a method of anatomy *as* criticism. In the essay on Crèvecoeur, for instance, Lawrence introduces the unsuspecting reader of the *English Review* to the then-obscure author of *Letters from an American Farmer* by way of the cardiac and the solar plexuses, the upper and lower nerve centers that, he explains, are the respective seats of spiritual and of sensual consciousness in the breast and the bowels.

This is dubious physiology, which owes more to New Age arcana than it does to anatomical science. But what Lawrence called his new science should be understood as an attempt to approximate those "ancient cosmic theories" in which "science and religion were in accord," and thereby to reconcile belief systems or kinds of knowledge that modernity judges to be antithetical (*SCAL* 260). In this regard, the first version of *Studies* is akin to W. B. Yeats's

A Vision (1925; 1937), which also purports to be a new science, albeit one in which, as Kathleen Raine observes, "not matter but mind—consciousness—is the ground of reality as we experience it."[11] Like Lawrence's, Yeats's system is a hybrid, assembled in part out of the late nineteenth- and early twentieth-century epistemologies and new sciences—anthropology, ethnography, psychoanalysis, philosophies of history, and theosophy—that were the *prima materia* for the modernist *bricoloeur*. Yeats was, for a brief period, a committed theosophist; Lawrence was not, but a good deal of the weltanschauung of his American essays in their early form is nonetheless extrapolated from esoteric myths and texts, as well as from Frazer and Frobenius.[12] Of these, the theory of "psycho-physiology" in James M. Pryse's *The Apocalypse Unsealed* (1910) is a particularly potent influence in the first version of *Studies*: the plexuses, ganglia, and chakras in the essays are harvested from Pryse, with whom Lawrence would engage again in his own *Apocalypse*, the reinterpretation of Revelation that forms the final instalment of his "philosophy."[13]

The Book of Revelation is analogized to American books in the first version of *Studies in Classic American Literature*; both offer "cypher-account[s]" of "the conquest of the lower or sensual dynamic centres by the upper or spiritual dynamic consciousness" (205). In *Studies* itself, however, Lawrence's quarrel is not with John of Patmos but with Freud, that "psychiatric quack" (*PU* 7). As Anne Fernihough notes, the basis of "Lawrence's objection to Freud is the concept of the ego as a coercive occupying force."[14] In a letter to Huebsch, Lawrence claims that his theory of pre-cerebral, somatic consciousness entails such a devastating critique of the Freudian theory of the unconscious that even the Freudians are convinced by it—"I *know* they are trying to get the theory of primal consciousness out of these essays" (iii.400). It may be that Lawrence, keenly aware of the U.S. market, is making a hard sell here, pitching *Studies* to an America in thrall to Freudian ideas. In 1922, when he rewrote his American essays for book publication, Lawrence took out most of "the esoteric stuff," the golden snakes, postulants, and other paraphernalia of the old religions (iv.405). He had already transferred what he called his "'pollyanalytics,'" the theory of the biological psyche and its jargon, into *Psychoanalysis and the Unconscious* (1921) and *Fantasia of the Unconscious* (1922), books that were also written for an American readership (*PU* 65).[15]

Lawrence wrote up the new, exoteric, version of *Studies* in situ in the United States, "Americanising" the essays as he revised them (iv.338). In the 1923 text, for instance, American literature is less often read comparatively with English literature (what is an expanded analogue between Franklin and *Frankenstein* in the 1918 essay survives only as a passing reference in the corresponding chapter of 1923). He also rewrote the book in a racy, demotic style, so that, as David Cavitch comments, "American slang explodes across nearly every page."[16] But his Yankeeisms and vulgarisms exasperated even those reviewers, like Henry Irving Brock, who admired Lawrence's critical "acumen." In his *New York Times Book Review* notice, Brock complains that Lawrence's sentences "might often be composed by a gum-chewing Main Street soda-fountain cut-up or a blear-eyed bar-room bum."[17] Stuart Pratt Sherman, writing in the *New York Evening Post*, likewise notes that Lawrence "has attempted to master the idiom and actually to write his book in the vernacular."[18] Sherman likens Lawrence, as a practitioner of the American vulgate, to H. L. Mencken, author of *The American Language*. Since Sherman's antipathy to Mencken was a matter of public record, the comparison was hardly complimentary. Sherman has a dig at "mencken-ese," and perhaps at Lawrence's working-class origins as the son of a miner, too, when he remarks that the "coal-heaver style" is now regarded as passé. While he remained unconvinced by its argot, Sherman would subsequently acknowledge *Studies'* "original critical force."[19]

John Macy's review for the *Nation* finds *Studies* to be "independent" and "eccentric" in equal measure. Macy is perplexed less by the book's Americanisms than by the traces of the physiological lexicon, left over from the *English Review* essays, which remain in the 1923 book. "I do not understand the Lawrentian physics and anatomy," he complains: "In what other physiology than Mr. Lawrence's is it written that 'the poles of the will are the great ganglia of the voluntary nerve system, located behind the spinal column in the back,' or that love is the 'prime cause of tuberculosis'?" Macy predicted, accurately enough, that Lawrence's book would "baffle the stupid" in other respects as well, that it would "offend the patriotic" and cause "quarrels."[20] Nonetheless, *Studies'* rebarbative quality matched the critical temper of the times in the United States, where the domestic critics were busy quarreling among themselves. Brooks and his generation of "Young Intellectuals" were engaged in a blood feud or "vendetta" with the "professors," while Sherman, who was one of the professors as well as a professional reviewer, exchanged salvos for over a decade with Mencken, who had found the prototype for his own "trenchant" opinions in the "critical jehads" of Edgar Allan Poe.[21]

"Against the whole corps" of the critics stood J. E. Spingarn, a "professor in rebellion" as Mencken describes him, who occupied what neutral ground there was in the critical scene, and who with good reason would define criticism in America in the early 1920s as "guerrilla warfare."[22] Spingarn would bring the warring factions together as editor of the 1924 volume, *Criticism in America: Its Function and Status*, which reprints landmark essays by Brooks, Mencken, and Sherman, among others. Spingarn notes in his preface that the collection marks "the first fundamental discussion of the nature of criticism in American literature," but his book also demonstrates the lack of consensus as to the function and the status of that criticism.²³

Lawrence liked to position himself at a cool English remove from these American culture wars, even as he entered the fray. For example, some six months before *Studies* itself came out, Lawrence claimed in a review for the *Dial* that he had "never heard" of either Mencken or Paul Elmer More (*IR* 221).²⁴ Probably he did know of More (who was the editor of the *Nation* when Lawrence's fiction was first reviewed there in 1913), and everyone knew who Mencken was. Lawrence certainly did, since he had argued with "somebody from Baltimore called Mr. Mencken" in 1921, in the foreword to his own *Fantasia of the Unconscious* (Mencken had dismissed *Fantasia*'s prequel, *Psychoanalysis and the Unconscious*, as "hollow and highfalutin nonsense") (*PU* 56–57). Lawrence's response—"Apparently *to menckenise* is to manufacture jeering little gas-bomb phrases against everything deep and earnest"—is a cheap shot, dredging up the pro-German sympathies leveled at Mencken by Sherman in the war years (*IR* 221).²⁵ Lawrence's feigned ignorance of the Sage of Baltimore is, of course, a deliberate slight, and the provenance of his remark—a review of *Americans* (1922), by Mencken's enemy, Sherman—adds insult to the injury.

Lawrence had written his review of Sherman's *Americans* as he was preparing to send the revised version of his own book on American literature to Seltzer. In the review, Lawrence tries out the coal-heaver style to which Sherman would take exception in *Studies* itself; he places himself on familiar terms with Sherman's "GREAT MEN" ("Waldo" and "Andy" [Carnegie]), and is downright rude to Hawthorne, calling the author of *The Marble Faun* a ferret (*IR* 221, 226). That Sherman himself is addressed as "Professor Sherman" is a courtesy in keeping with the conventions, although "Mr. Lawrence" may also be poking fun at the stuffy professoriate, as Brooks and his cohort routinely did. In Lawrence's mock-heroic description of him, Sherman is an Odysseus, steering his "little ship of Criticism" between the Scylla of Mencken and the Charybdis of More (Sherman's book opens with a characteristic thrust against Mencken and concludes, at the other end of the critical spectrum, with More) (*IR* 221). Sherman, who seems to have taken Lawrence's ribbing in good part, responded in kind: his lively review of *Studies*, which is titled

"America Is Discovered," represents Lawrence as a would-be Columbus, laying critical claim to the literature of the New World. True to form, Lawrence later approached Sherman in his capacity as editor of the *New York Herald Tribune Books*, offering his services as a regular reviewer.[26]

Reviewing Sherman's book allowed Lawrence to test his own very different construction of American literary culture against Sherman's celebration of "the Religion of Democracy" and his stalwart defense of Puritanism (*IR* 223). Sherman was the protégé of More and of Irving Babbitt, who called for the revival of Puritan values and claimed that the younger generation of critics misrepresented the Puritans and their legacy. Speaking on behalf of the Young Intellectuals, Waldo Frank inveighed against "the clamped dominion of Puritan and machine," dismissing Babbitt and More as "cultural sextons" whose vocation was to "guard their dead."[27] Both parties, Russell Reising suggests, confected a strategically simplified Puritanism "in order to make it serve as the source of everything right or wrong with twentieth-century America, typecasting the Puritans as heroes or villains in the drama of American history and identity."[28]

Sherman was better disposed to the American Moderns than his mentors, albeit that his greater tolerance for contemporary American writing was a facet of the fervid nationalism he espoused in the war years as a practitioner of what Ernest Boyd termed "Ku Klux Kriticism."[29] In any event, Sherman remained a staunch defender of America's Puritan heritage, which he believed was coterminous with "the national genius." In his 1917 *Smart Set* piece, "Criticism of Criticism of Criticism," Mencken pillories both the Puritan and the patriotic pieties of "Prof. Dr. Stuart P. Sherman," with his "maxim that Puritanism is the official philosophy of America, and that all who dispute it are enemy aliens and should be deported."[30] Mencken would subsequently claim that, for Sherman, "the test of an artist is whether he hated the Kaiser in 1917 . . . and prefers Coca-Cola to Scharlachberger." But for all Mencken's sniping at Sherman, it was More who was the "really tempting quarry," so much so that even Mencken, the arch iconoclast, would "sometimes join the barbarians, and help them to launch their abominable bombs against the embattled blue-noses."[31]

Lawrence's sympathies were with the barbarians at the gates, rather than with the "professors who guard the past."[32] *Studies* presents a virulent but variant strain of what Michael Kammen calls the "Puritan-bashing" that was endemic in radical circles in the American Twenties.[33] Lawrence regarded the "mechanical democracy" of the United States as a mere "marking-time," the product of the Puritan recoil against the continental spirit of place, the genius loci of the real America (*SCAL* 177)—as Sherman commented in his review of *Studies*, Lawrence is of "the Party of Nature" not "the Party of Culture."[34] If Sherman was "the darling of the old guard" of Babbitt and of More, then the defiance of Puritan prohibitions in his creative practice had already made Lawrence a poster boy for the avant-garde circles in which his critical work would receive its warmest reception.[35] Shortly after *Studies* came out, for instance, the guru of the New York avant-garde, Alfred Stieglitz, wrote approvingly of it in a letter to Lawrence. In his reply, Lawrence remarked that "the voice of America is absolutely silent nowadays": in criticism like Sherman's, he says, we hear "only echoes or catchwords" (iv.499). The implication is that *Studies* itself is to be America's new broadcast medium.

Lawrence was seemingly vindicated when, the year after its publication, *Studies* was hailed as nothing less than "the foundation for a new American critical literature."[36] This extravagant claim is made in the first monograph to appear on Lawrence, Herbert J. Seligmann's *D. H. Lawrence*. Subtitled "An American Interpretation," Seligmann's book is dedicated to Stieglitz and was brought out by Thomas Seltzer, Lawrence's own publisher in the United States at the time, so clearly some log-rolling was in motion. Seligmann himself was an ardent Lawrence fan (he would be fired by the *New York Sun* for writing a positive review of *Lady Chatterley's Lover*). However partisan Seligmann may have been, his high opinion of *Studies* was shared by Fred Lewis Pattee, whose credentials—he is regarded as the first "Professor of American Literature"—were impeccable.[37] In his "Call for a Literary Historian," which also appeared in 1924, Pattee rejects the extant literary histories as "stereotyped" and "timid," arguing, much as Lawrence himself had done in his 1922 foreword to *Studies*, that "if American literature has suffered from any single inadequateness that inadequateness has been in its criticism."[38] The "new historian," Pattee recommends, must write "not in the dry-as-dust lecture form, but in chapters thoroughly readable." Because Lawrence's "amazing volume" is "detached from class-room thinking," it is a model for the kind of "fearless" new literary histories for which Pattee calls. For Pattee, at least, the "startling" quality of *Studies in Classic American Literature* is inseparable from its formative contribution to American criticism.[39]

Red America

"Never trust the artist. Trust the tale." This is Lawrence's famous definition of the "proper function of a critic," to "save the tale from the artist who created it" (*SCAL* 14). Discarding authorial intention and privileging the intrinsic "double meaning" of the tale, Lawrence sounds more like a precursor of the New Critics than of Pattee's new historians (*SCAL* 12). He was anything but, of course, and Lawrence would elsewhere dismiss "critical twiddle-twaddle about style, and form" as "mere impertinence, and mostly dull jargon" (*STH* 209). The New Criticism privileged ambiguity as a tensional property of the well-wrought text: for Lawrence, the double meaning in the American Classics is symptomatic of a schism in the national psyche. The essays in Lawrence's *Studies* are case studies as much as studies in criticism, explorations of the psychopathology of American life as reproduced in its literature. In the early 1910s, the philosopher George Santayana had defined America as "a country with two mentalities," one "all aggressive enterprise" and the other "all genteel tradition."[40] After Santayana, Brooks's critique of the Genteel Tradition in *America's Coming-of-Age* (1915) points up the dichotomy between highbrow idealism and the lowbrow catchpenny opportunism of American commerce. Lawrence's is a more radical theory of national bipolarity, which also finds the preconditions for American doubleness in Puritan origins.

"The Spirit of Place," the first chapter of *Studies*, prepares the ground with the Pilgrim Fathers. Their emigration had a "dual motion," a positive as well as a negative impetus: as Lawrence puts it in the mystical-lyrical first version of the essay, they "went like birds down the great electric direction of the west, lifted like migrating birds on a magnetic current. They went in subtle vibration of response to the new earth" (174, 177). That duality is replicated in the double meaning of classic American literature, its writers giving their "mental allegiance to a morality which all their passion goes to destroy" (156). In the 1918–19 *Studies*, the colonization of the New World is treated ahistorically, understood as a physiological "conquest," a systemic suppression of passional by intellectual modes of understanding (404). Nonetheless, the "old American art-speech contains an alien quality, which belongs to the American continent and to nowhere else," and is an expression of the "shifting over from the old psyche to something new, a displacement" (*SCAL* 13). The 1923 *Studies* differs from the 1918–19 version in color-coding this process—the paleface cast of Puritan thought, the native hue of aboriginal America—making the relationship between the body and the body politic more explicit, but repeating the primitivist and gendered equation of European-Americans with the mind and will and indigenous peoples with the body and being and, by extension, with the continent itself. "You have got to pull the democratic and idealistic clothes off American utterance, and see what you can of the dusky body of IT underneath," Lawrence insists—if the prudish Puritan can't quite bring himself to touch America, he can at least be a Peeping Tom (19).

Lawrence's manifesto for that dusky "Red America" is a foreword he had written for *Studies* in Sicily in 1920 (*SCAL* 384). When the publication of the book stalled, the piece was published as "America, Listen to Your Own" in December of that year in the *New Republic*—so Lawrence did, eventually, manage to hold up that "old fat coach," at least. His demands, though, aren't those of the common outlaw: "The President should not look back towards Gladstone or Cromwell or Hildebrand, but towards Montezuma," Lawrence insists. Americans

> must take up life where the Red Indian, the Aztec, the Maya, the Incas left it off. They must pick up the life-thread where the mysterious Red race let it fall. They must catch the pulse of the life which Cortes and Columbus murdered. There lies the real continuity—not between Europe and the new States, but between the murdered Red America and the seething White America.

Lawrence calls on his readers to "turn to America, and to that very America which has been rejected and almost annihilated" (*SCAL* 384).

Lawrence's article was printed in the *New Republic* together with a response from Walter Lippmann, a founding editor of the journal; Lippmann dismisses Lawrence's vision of Red America as "mostly paste and paint," commenting that "Mr. Lawrence is plainly in the Noble Savage phase."[41] But if Lippmann had a point, so too did Leslie Fiedler when he argued in *The Return of the Vanishing American* in 1968 that Lawrence had some "nerve" as "an expatriate Englishman" to "talk seriously" about the "soul of the Red Man" in the early 1920s.[42] In 1919, Waldo Frank had remarked on white America's widespread "indifference" to Native America; given that indifference, it is indeed remarkable that *Studies* should be not only a key document in the modern criticism of American literature but also one that situates the Native American at the center of the national imaginary.[43] That said, however, it is the "soul," as opposed to the living reality, of the Native American with which Lawrence is primarily concerned, making *Studies* complicit with the myth of the vanishing Indian that Fiedler, who was committed to the struggle for Native American civil rights, explores and explodes in his book.

The myth of the vanishing Indian had surfaced in James Fenimore Cooper's *The Last of the Mohicans* in 1826 and it remained in circulation almost a century later. The Indian, still vanishing but stubbornly refusing to disappear altogether, reappears in Zane Grey's 1925 bestseller *The Vanishing American* and, in more complex ways, in the pivotal, New Mexico, section of Willa Cather's *The Professor's House*, published in the same year. Walter Benn Michaels has defined both of these as nativist novels in which the Indian, because he is vanishing (or, in the case of Cather's Anasazi cliff-dwellers, is long gone) may safely be assimilated to notions of an authentic Americanness without the taint of miscegenation.[44] Lawrence may have subscribed to the myth, but he understood its ideological premise well enough: indeed, Lawrence anticipates Michaels when he remarks, in his review of William Carlos Williams's *In the American Grain*, that "the only hundred per cent American is the Red Indian, and he can only be canonized when he is finally dead" (*IR* 257).

Williams's book, which is itself one of Michaels's exemplars of nativist modernism, posits an intimate relationship between the Indian and the white American that stops short of actual consanguinity: "The blood means nothing," Williams says, because "the spirit, the ghost of the land, moves in the blood, moves the blood."[45] The Indian is likewise coterminous with the land in *Studies in Classic American Literature*: as Neil Roberts notes, Lawrence's vision of a regenerated America entails "a future for the white man, not for the Indian," since it is a future premised on the "assimilation of the aboriginal people to the land."[46] The natural environment thus becomes a psychic reservation of continental proportions, the habitat of an angry aboriginal genius loci—which is something that Hawthorne understood, Lawrence says, but Cooper didn't. Neither, it seems, did Williams, who suggests that "as a natural expression of the place, the Indian himself is the flower of his world." The Indian has bequeathed his world to "us," to modern Americans, so although "[w]e are not Indians," Williams claims that "we are men of their world."[47] What Williams argues here anticipates Gary Snyder's thesis, summarized and endorsed by Wai Chee Dimock, that "[w]e become 'Native Americans' by virtue of the descendants we can imagine, the kinds of people we would like to bequeath the world to."[48] By contrast, the "continuity" Lawrence posits between "murdered Red America" and "seething White America" consists in anything but a serene narrative of inheritance: for Lawrence, the return of the native is the return of the repressed. The Indian may never "possess the broad lands of America again," but "his ghost will," and will "come back unappeased, for revenge" (*SCAL* 42). After the genocide of Native peoples, the Indian inhabits what René Bergland calls the "national uncanny," haunting the American imaginary.[49]

Criticism in the Contact Zone

In the period in which Lawrence was completing the final version of *Studies in Classic American Literature*, the land rights of the Pueblo Indian people of northern New Mexico was a live issue, and the vanishing American front page news. "I arrive in New Mexico at a moment of crisis," Lawrence remarks at the beginning of his article "Certain Americans and an Englishman," begun in October 1922, and published in December of that year in the *New York Times Magazine* (*MM* 105). In September, the month he came to the United States, Lawrence had added his name to the "Protest of Artists and Writers Against the Bursum Bill," the signatees to which included Zane Grey, Vachel Lindsay, and Carl Sandburg. Like this document, "Certain Americans and an Englishman" was produced in defense of the territorial integrity of the pueblos, threatened by legislation introduced in July 1922 by New Mexico Senator Holm O. Bursum. Although the campaign to prevent the infringement of Indian rights provided for in the Bursum Bill would prove successful, Lawrence continued to believe that the "end of the Pueblos" was inevitable, and his target in "Certain Americans and an Englishman" is as much the crusade against it as the Bursum Bill itself (*MM* 109). Lawrence mocks what he sees as misguided efforts to save the Indians on the part of "highbrow palefaces" (*MM* 107) like his hostess in Taos, Mabel Dodge Luhan, and his fellow-guest John Collier, whose 1922 article "The Red Atlantis" spearheaded opposition to the Bursum Bill's attempt to usurp Pueblo Indian land titles (in his later capacity as Commissioner of Indian Affairs, Collier would broker the "Indian New Deal" of the 1930s). Lawrence reverts to the anti-Bursumites in *Studies in Classic American Literature*, where he interprets their "desire to glorify" the Native American as the flip side of the "desire to extirpate the Indian," and inveighs against the "minority of whites [who] intellectualise the Red man and laud him to the skies," the "high-brow minority with a big grouch against its own whiteness" (*SCAL* 43).

Topical interpellations like these mark a signal difference between what David Ellis calls the "New Style *Studies*" and the earlier, 1918–19, version of Lawrence's American essays.[50] Armin Arnold, who judges that in their original form, the essays "are completely different and in many ways superior to those published in the book of 1923," blames Lawrence's "violent hate against Mabel Dodge and Toni Luhan [*sic*]" for the lack of quality control in the final version.[51] But it is Lawrence's refusal—or inability—to hive off lived experience from literary exegesis that gives the final version of *Studies* its edge, and its immediacy. Completed in New Mexico, the 1923 *Studies* is the product of what Mary Louise Pratt, in her study of travel writing and transculturation, defines as the "contact zone." The contact zone is a "space of colonial encounters"

> in which people geographically and historically separated come into contact with each other and establish ongoing relations, usually involving conditions of coercion, radical inequality, and intractable conflict.[52]

In the 1923 *Studies*, Lawrence's readings of classic American literature are spliced with despatches from the contact zone, making his book the unsettling record of his own acculturation to the reality of the Red America he could only imagine in the first version of the essays. Indeed, for Jon Thompson, who rightly notes that *Studies* "refuses easy classification," the book is "one of the greatest covert autobiographies in world literature."[53] In its final form, *Studies* is also embroiled in the racial and gendered politics of the American color line, the line that Mabel Dodge had so publicly and defiantly crossed in her relationship with the Taos Indian, Antonio Lujan. As David Ellis comments, the "life-choice" implied in Lawrence's advice to Americans to turn to their own "dark, aboriginal continent" had been "precisely Mabel's own," when she took up with Tony.[54]

Tony Lujan was the first flesh-and-blood Native American Lawrence encountered. He was not, Ellis remarks, quite the Chingachgook that Cooper's novels had led Lawrence to expect (in fact Lawrence complained to his mother-in-law in a letter that Tony was "ugly as a pancake" (v.239)).[55] Tony acted as driver and guide for Mabel's many visitors to Taos, including Willa Cather and Georgia O'Keeffe, who both liked him far better than Lawrence did; O'Keeffe had to be dissuaded from calling the first car she owned "Tonybel" after Tony, who had taught her to drive, while Cather is thought to have modeled the character of Eusabio, in *Death Comes for the Archbishop*, in part at least on Tony Lujan.[56] Lawrence found the relationship between fiction and fact harder to negotiate. In *Studies*, he complains that Cooper's Leatherstocking books, which had stimulated his interest in Native Americans in the first place, now impede his firsthand experience: "This popular wish-fulfilment stuff makes it so hard for the real thing to come through, later" (*SCAL* 44). Clearly, the real thing, the reality of the New Mexico contact zone, has taken him out of the comfort zone of Cooper's fiction: "displacements hurt," Lawrence writes. "This hurts" (*SCAL* 13). On the ground, Red America repelled as much as it attracted him. For all its Puritan-bashing, then, the final version of *Studies in Classic American Literature* exposes what Richard Aldington divined as Lawrence's own "unconscious Puritanism."[57]

Post Mortem Effects: The American Classics

The nation-building legacy of the Puritan colonists is coldly appraised in the "Benjamin Franklin" chapter of *Studies in Classic American Literature*. Here Lawrence debunks a founding father and American idol, describing Franklin as a "dummy American" who preached a mechanistic and mercantile creed that would be passed on, via Andrew Carnegie and John Wanamaker, to Henry Ford (*SCAL* 20). Evidently, Stuart Sherman's "new attempt [in *Americans*] to make us like Dr. Franklin" has failed: "I can't stand Benjamin," Lawrence admits (*IR* 223; *SCAL* 28). Franklin, for Sherman, is exemplary of the "national genius animated by an incomparably profound moral idealism" that is expressed in condensed form in the proverbs Franklin peddled as "Poor Richard." One of these—"It is hard for an empty sack to stand upright"—Sherman even parses as a "piece of imagist verse . . . a one-line poem of humor, morality, insight, and imagination all compact."[58]

Lawrence, who was himself of course a bona fide if an uncommitted Imagist, is less appreciative of the "moral tag[s]" in *Poor Richard's Almanack*. Lawrence recalls with a shudder his exposure as a child to Franklin's proverbs, which were a staple of the almanacs his father bought. "It has taken me many years and countless smarts to get out of that barbed wire moral enclosure that Poor Richard rigged up," Lawrence admits. In metaphors appropriate to the "wild and woolly" Southwest where he rewrote the essay—and perhaps thinking of the Taos Indians' name for him, red wolf (*MM* 113)—Lawrence sets about menacing "Benjamin and the American corral," reserving his severest censure for Franklin's complicity in the genocide of Native America (*SCAL* 25). According to Franklin, it is "'the design of Providence to extirpate these savages in order to make room for the cultivators of the earth'"—to which Lawrence's rejoinder is that the Indians had themselves cultivated the earth "as much as they needed. And they left off there. Who built Chicago? Who cultivated the earth until it spawned Pittsburgh, Pa.?" (25–26).

The "strange gods" that Lawrence invokes in place of Franklin's "storekeeper" god "come forth from the forest," the appropriate environment for what, in the next chapter of *Studies*, Lawrence calls "the aboriginal Indian vision carrying over" (26, 21, 35). It is that "rudimentary American vision" that is captured in those passages in Crèvecoeur's *Letters from an American*

Farmer that give us "glimpses of actual nature," the "[i]nsects, snakes and birds he glimpses in their own mystery, their own pristine being" (34–35). This is the American "IT"-factor: the expression of the American whole soul in American art-speech is palpable when Crèvecoeur speaks in "the voice of the artist in contrast to the voice of the ideal turtle" (18, 35). The trouble with Crèvecoeur, though, is that he "wanted to be an *intellectual* savage," and in this respect he differs from Franklin, for whom killing the Indian rather than pretending to be one was the more practical expedient (41). In the physiological terms of the 1919 essay, "Franklin lived in the breast . . . Crèvecoeur in the bowels" (194). Between them, Franklin and Crèvecoeur represent what Lawrence defines as white Americans' "dual feeling about the Indian" (43).

The next two chapters of *Studies* turn to James Fenimore Cooper, and nominally apply the color line that divides Cooper's fiction into "two classes," the "white novels" and the "Leatherstocking Series" (45). But the first of these chapters, on "Fenimore Cooper's White Novels," opens with an extended meditation on the "Red Man" (42), revealing the remarkable extent to which Red America—or what T. R. Wright calls Lawrence's "red mythology"—shapes the structure, as well as the thesis, of the final version of Lawrence's text.[59] Consider the difference between the essay published in the *English Review* in 1919 as "Fenimore Cooper's Anglo-American Novels" and the corresponding book chapter of 1923: both have lengthy pretexts, but where the former is prefaced by a recapitulation of Lawrence's new science of "the great nerve-centres of the sympathetic and voluntary system," the later version takes up the narrative of Indian dispossession begun in the Franklin chapter (SCAL 204). According to Lawrence,

> While the Red Indian existed in fairly large numbers the new colonials were in a great measure immune from the daimon, or demon of America. The moment the last nuclei of Red life break up in America, then the white men will have to reckon with the full force of the demon of the continent. (42)

In the meantime, Lawrence insists, there can be no "mystic conjunction between the spirit of the two races" of the kind envisaged by Cooper, nor can there be a "reconciliation in the flesh" (43, 44). "The Red Man and the White Man are not blood-brothers," Lawrence asserts (56).

Between the early and the final versions of the Cooper essays, Lawrence has recanted his belief in *blutsbrüderschaft*, in the "stark, stripped human relationship of two men, deeper than the deeps of sex" (*SCAL* 58), the limits of which he had tested in his own fiction of the period, and which surely underlies his attraction to a national literature that, after Lawrence, has been defined as homosocial, if not overtly homosexual.⁶⁰ The 1919 essay on the Leatherstocking books is a largely sympathetic account of the Cooper who

> dreamed his true marriage with the aboriginal psyche. All futurity for him lay latent, not in the white woman, but in the dark, magnificent presence of American warriors, with whom he would be at one in the ultimate atonement between races. (217)

The 1923 *Studies*, however, finds the intercultural male bonding of American bromance mere "[w]ish-fulfilment" (52), and Lawrence pillories Cooper's desire to substitute Chingachgook for the "WIFE" who is his other half in "ACTUALITY" (53).

Lawrence's evident discomfort with sex across the color line inflects his reading of "Fenimore Cooper's White Novels." Lawrence clearly has Mabel Dodge and Tony Lujan in his sights when he presents what is seemingly a purely speculative scenario: "Supposing an Indian loves a white woman, and lives with her." "He will probably be very proud," Lawrence continues of the Indian, "especially if the white mistress has money" (as Mabel did, of course), but "at the bottom of his heart he is gibing, gibing, gibing at her" (44).⁶¹ It is Lawrence, of course, who is doing the gibing—at Mabel, the wealthy white woman whom Tony must resist because he is a man (even if he is a kept one), as well as an Indian. In 1925, Mabel would publish an article defining her liaison with Tony (the couple had married in 1923) as a "Bridge between Cultures." Lawrence's 1919 essay on "Fenimore Cooper's Leatherstocking Novels" had described the (man-to-man) love between Natty Bumppo and Chingachgook in similar language, as "the bridge over the chasm" (222), but rewriting the essay in 1922, Lawrence now judges that interracial relationship to be a bridge too far: "The red life flows in a different direction from the white life" (56). Lawrence would work through and largely overcome his resistance to mixed marriage between the composition of *Quetzalcoatl* in 1923 and its subsequent rewriting as *The Plumed Serpent*, but his discomfort leaves its mark on *Studies*.

Cooper's Leatherstocking books "form a sort of American Odyssey," Lawrence says, but they make for an anodyne epic in which American literature's trademark double meaning is substituted for the "devil, Circes and swine and all" of the saltier Homeric original—so "Natty is a saint with a gun" (*SCAL* 54). The masterwork of American doubleness, though, is *The Scarlet Letter*: Lawrence remarks on the "perfect duplicity" of Hawthorne's novel (*SCAL*

95) which, in his reading of it, both dramatizes and endorses the white American repression of blood-knowledge. "The mind is 'ashamed' of the blood: as the act of coition. And the blood is destroyed by the mind," Lawrence remarks: "Hence pale-faces" (SCAL 83). Its "marvellous under-meaning" makes *The Scarlet Letter* "one of the greatest allegories in all literature," and as such it is the exemplary American text for Lawrence's psycho-critical method: "You *must* look through the surface of American art," he insists, "and see the inner diabolism of the symbolic meaning" (SCAL 95, 81).

Hawthorne's Hester Prynne, in the person of "the Female Devotee," is the epitome of the "KNOWING" woman (SCAL 87, 82) and one of several surrogates in the 1923 *Studies* for Mabel Dodge Luhan, who, Lawrence told her in a letter, embodied the "vice of 'knowing'" (iv.576). If Hawthorne's Hester reflected his ambivalence toward feminist contemporaries like Margaret Fuller, then Lawrence's Hester reveals the gendered insecurities of his own historical period, insecurities that, David Minter notes, "increased after the war." Hester thus represents the "colossal evil of the united spirit of Woman, WOMAN, German woman or American woman" that "in the last war, was something frightening" (SCAL 89). In "the diabolic trinity, or triangle, of the scarlet letter" (SCAL 94), Lawrence seems to have found an inverted reflection of his own circumstances in the period in which he was revising his essay on Hawthorne's novel, caught as he was between a German woman (Frieda) and an American one (Mabel).[62]

For the white American, "America has never been a blood-home-land. Only an ideal home-land" as well as one "of the pocket" (SCAL 105). This is the motive for the imaginative conquest of the sea in the work of Richard Henry Dana and Herman Melville. Of these, Melville is the greater "seer and poet of the sea" (SCAL 122). There is "something really overwhelming" in *Moby-Dick*, Lawrence says, which accounts, perhaps, for the uncharacteristic extent to which he quotes from Melville's "great book" in his own book (SCAL 142, 146). The quest, in *Typee* and *Omoo*, for what Melville in one of his poems describes as "Authentic Edens in a Pagan Sea," confirms Lawrence's own conviction that "[o]ne cannot go back" to "the past, savage life" (SCAL 126).[63] Those who would go back, Lawrence says, are "renegade," like those "'reformers' and 'idealists' who glorify the savages in America. They are death-birds, life-haters" (SCAL 127). Melville isn't a renegade, but he is an idealist and a democrat, and once again Lawrence inverts the terms of national self-definition when he figures democracy in America as a form of bondage: "a long thin chain was round Melville's ankle all the time, binding him to America, to civilisation, to democracy, to the ideal world" (*SCAL* 130). Like the Book of Revelation, Melville's great book *Moby-Dick* is a "cypher-account" of the mind's conquest of "blood-being" (205), the white whale the symbol of "the deepest blood-being of the white race . . . hunted, hunted, hunted by the maniacal fanaticism of our white mental consciousness." In its mission to seek out and destroy the "last phallic being of the white man," the voyage of the *Pequod* is that of a mind-bound, mechanical modernity, hell-bent on its own destruction (*SCAL* 146).

"If the Great White Whale sank the ship of the Great White Soul in 1851, what's been happening ever since?" Lawrence asks (*SCAL* 147).[64] "Post mortem effects" is the answer, and *Studies* concludes with Lawrence's assessment of Walt Whitman as America's "post mortem poet" laureate (148, 151). In the variant earlier versions of the "Whitman" chapter, Lawrence had used the American poet as a foil for his own visions of self and of society, but in the final version, under the demythologizing pressures that also shape his new reading of Cooper, Lawrence rebukes Whitman for subscribing to the notion of a "new world" built on "manly love, the love of comrades" (*SCAL* 153).

The 1919 "Whitman" essay, which had proved too controversial to publish, focused more explicitly on the homosexual nature of the Whitmanian principle of fusion, against which Lawrence had asserted his own belief in polarity, his insistence that individuals must "maintain their sheer single, separate integrity" (*SCAL* 366). In this version of "Whitman," Lawrence's physiological preoccupations overwrite his reading of Whitman's verse ("[t]he vagina, as we know, is the orifice to the hypogastric plexus, which, in the old words 'is situated amid the waters,'" while the "cocygeal centre"—the chakra point at the base of the spine—is "the dark node which relates us to the centre of the earth, the plumb-centre of substantial being" [*SCAL* 365]).

The 1921–22 "Whitman" essay, a shortened version of which was published in the *Nation and Athenaeum* and reprinted in the *New York Call* in 1921, likewise differentiates Whitman's dream of democratic camaraderie from Lawrence's vision of the "sacred relationship of comrades" on which "the making of a new world" depends (*SCAL* 415). But now, in line with the new trajectory of the first of his "leadership" novels, *Aaron's Rod* (1922), and anticipating the Don Ramón-Cipriano relationship in *The Plumed Serpent* (1926), Lawrence reformulates homosocial bonding as hero worship, "a hot belief of men in each other, a culminating belief, culminating in a final leader and hero." The "sacred tyrannus" embodies the principle of natural aristocracy that, Lawrence asserts, constitutes "true democracy" (*SCAL* 415, 416).

Harold Bloom has pointed out that his disavowal of the American democratic ideal precipitated a crisis in Lawrence's "extraordinary passion" for the Whitman "to whom he owed his own rebirth as a poet."[65] Lawrence concedes as much in the "Whitman" chapter of the 1923 *Studies*. The greater part of the chapter is given over to the antics of a cartoon-strip Walt, but midway through Lawrence stops short, and acknowledges, briefly but movingly, that "Whitman, the great poet, has meant so much to me" (155). Among the classic American writers, Lawrence concedes, Whitman was "the first to break" the "mental allegiance given to a morality which the passional self repudiates" (156). This makes him "the first white aboriginal" (157), albeit that Lawrence charges the Whitman who follows the American way in his "great fierce poetic machine" with the reckless endangerment of that aboriginal vision:

> ONE DIRECTION! toots Walt in the car, whizzing along it.
> Whereas there are myriads of ways in the dark, not to mention trackless wildernesses. As anyone will know who cares to come off the road, even the Open Road.
> ONE DIRECTION! whoops America, and sets off also in an automobile.
> ALLNESS! shrieks Walt at a cross-road, going whizz over an unwary Red Indian. (*SCAL* 152)

Vital Criticism

Like other key works of modernist criticism written during World War I and in its aftermath, *Studies in Classic American Literature* represents a radical reconfiguration of literary history and its uses in the postwar era: "Oh god, oh god, what next, when the *Pequod* has sunk?" Lawrence asks in his chapter on *Moby-Dick*. "She sank in the war, and we are all flotsam" (146).

In his landmark essay of 1918, "On Creating a Usable Past," Van Wyck Brooks had called for a "vital criticism" to remedy the "sterile" condition of contemporary American culture.[66] Brooks's dynamic understanding of tradition anticipates that of T. S. Eliot's "Tradition and the Individual Talent," published in the following year, with the difference that Brooks promotes the "uniqueness and distinction" of an American tradition that he would later accuse Eliot of making "an intellectual cause of attacking."[67] Brooks regarded Eliot as the epitome of Harvard, which was Brooks's alma mater, too; in its precincts, Brooks would recall, he had "never heard Melville mentioned" (Brooks had graduated in 1908, but he could just as well be speaking here on behalf of the class of 1918).[68] Brooks therefore calls on the critic to ask questions such as "[w]hat became of Herman Melville" and thus to break "the Talmudic seal" placed on the American tradition by "the professors who guard the past": Irving Babbitt and his protégés, among them Eliot and Stuart Sherman. Since neither the Puritan divines nor the genteel Boston Brahmins embody a "living tradition" lusty enough to "fertilize" the American Moderns, Brooks, like Eliot, figures the critic as a resurrection man, who retrieves from literary tradition not "what is dead" but "what is already living."[69] For the critic of American literature, this means venturing into a "limbo of the non-elect" in order to recover in neglected writers like Melville the "harbingers of an indigenous avant garde."[70]

Like Brooks, Lawrence discovers "the homunculus of the new era"—alive, if "thin, from neglect"—in the "old people, little thin volumes of Hawthorne, Poe, Dana, Melville, Whitman" (*SCAL* 11, 12). But for all *Studies in Classic American Literature*'s alleged complicity in the creation, out of these thin volumes, of a narrow, "classic" canon, a usable literary past for the American Century, what Lawrence hears in the "sad, weird utterance of this classic America" is anathema to the values—of nation, and of tradition—on which canonicity, as much in Brooks's construction of it as in Eliot's, subsists (*SCAL* 179). What America needs, Lawrence insists, is not a tradition, but "a new extension of life" (*SCAL* 385). Americans must therefore turn, not to the "bunch of culture monuments" of the "perfected" European past, but to its own continental and pre-Columbian spirit of place. If they are to enter the new era augured by the classic literature of the old people, Americans "must pass the bounds," temporal and spatial, of the nation-state (*SCAL* 384, 385).

The battle lines that divided the critical scene in the United States when *Studies in Classic American Literature* came out there in the early 1920s would be drawn again in the debate over Lawrence's own posthumous reputation. In a series of articles published in *Scrutiny* in the 1930s, beginning with "D. H. Lawrence and Professor Irving Babbitt," F. R. Leavis would name Lawrence as the major modern challenger to the classicism represented by Babbitt and, by extension, the Eliot who, as Williams Carlos Williams would claim, had returned modern poetry to the classroom.[71]

2

Under Our Home Eye

Lawrence and American Modernism

Between the publication of *Studies in Classic American Literature* in New York in August 1923 and the appearance of the first formal reviews in the American literary press, Alfred Stieglitz expressed his admiration for the book in a letter to its author. Stieglitz's "real generous appreciation," as Lawrence described it in his reply, marks a significant moment, not only in the intellectual reception of *Studies in Classic American Literature* itself in the United States but also in the close yet curiously neglected relationship between Lawrence and American modernism that this chapter seeks to reconstruct (iv.499).

The "nucleus" of the avant-garde in America, Stieglitz had played a key role in the cultural scene in New York since the opening, in 1905, of his Little Galleries of the Photo-Secession, later renamed 291 after its Fifth Avenue address.[1] Here and in the journal *Camera Work* (1903–17) Stieglitz had not only proselytized on behalf of photography as an artistic medium but had also introduced modern European painting to American audiences well before the International Exhibition of Modern Art, or Armory Show, of 1913, putting on the first U.S. shows of Paul Cézanne's lithographs and watercolors in 1910 and 1911 respectively. In the wake of the European art-invasion precipitated by the Armory Show and accelerated by the outbreak of war in Europe in the following year, Stieglitz promoted the work of American Moderns like John Marin, Marsden Hartley, and Arthur Dove, and mentored emergent American artists such as the photographer Paul Strand and the painter Georgia O'Keeffe, whom he would marry in 1924. In 1929, he launched a new exhibition space, An American Place, to show the work of his *Seven Americans*: Hartley, Marin, Dove, O'Keeffe, Strand, Stieglitz himself, and Charles Demuth.

In the 1930s William Carlos Williams would sum up Stieglitz's life work in terms that apply to his own, as a fusion of "local effort" with "forces from the outside."[2] Stieglitz's commitment to localized American expression clearly complemented his regard for an English outsider like Lawrence, which was shared within the Stieglitz circle: by Williams himself, and by the "official theoretician of 291," Paul Rosenfeld, whose embarrassingly effusive paean to Lawrence appeared in the *New Republic* in 1922: "Were this generation to lose the ministrations of his spirit, it would not be otherwise than if some liquid dripping planet of August nights were to be removed forever from us."[3] No less fulsome a tribute is Herbert J. Seligmann's 1924 monograph on Lawrence, which is dedicated to Stieglitz. *The Lawrence Tree*, O'Keeffe's painterly homage to the writer, was exhibited at An American Place in 1930, and in the following year her New Mexican *Cross* was reproduced in *Survey Graphic* magazine as a visual counterpart to Lawrence's posthumously published essay "New Mexico."[4]

The creative nexus between Lawrence and the Stieglitz circle had been formed during the war years, when, Bonnie Grad explains, "the often unreserved enthusiasm" of Lawrence's American admirers derived from their appreciation of him as a "kindred spirit."[5] Amy Lowell, who had subsidized the beleaguered Lawrence after the prosecution and suppression of *The Rainbow* in 1915, warned him that his reputation as an erotic writer would rule out a lecture tour in the United States: when Lawrence mooted a series of talks there on American literature, Lowell told him that this would be "an absolute impossibility. New England is far more puritanical than Old England."[6] But it was the Puritan-bashing, self-styled Priest of Love who appealed to nonconformists like Stieglitz: a subscriber to the 1928 private edition of *Lady Chatterley's Lover*, Stieglitz offered in the same year to show Lawrence's allegedly pornographic paintings at his Intimate Gallery in Manhattan.[7]

Educated in part in his father's native Germany, Stieglitz empathized with the persecution that Lawrence and Frieda, née von Richthofen, experienced during the war. Like Lawrence, Stieglitz considered the war "a political and spiritual outrage"; anti-German sentiment would curtail his own cultural activities when the United States entered the conflict in April 1917.[8] In May of that year, a bitterly disappointed Lawrence wrote to his friend S. S. Koteliansky, "America is a stink-pot in my nostrils, after having been the land of the future for me" (iii.124). Trapped in England for the duration of the conflict, Lawrence had looked to the United States as a sanctuary from the wartime repression which was now rife on both sides of the Atlantic. In October 1917, the month in which the Lawrences were served with a military exclusion order forcing them to leave their home in Cornwall (and interrupting the composition of the first version of *Studies in Classic American Literature*), the swansong issue of *Seven Arts* appeared in New York. This little magazine was, Bram Dijkstra notes, an "amplification of what Stieglitz stood for."[9] Lowell described it to Lawrence as "the most interesting and alive paper over here to-day"—its "having gone," she told him, was "a calamity to all of us of the younger school."[10]

Lawrence was a contributor to *Seven Arts* and had corresponded from Cornwall with Waldo Frank who, with James Oppenheim and Van Wyck Brooks, was a founder-editor of the magazine. Lawrence's story "The Thimble" (later rewritten as "The Ladybird") appeared in *Seven Arts* in March 1917, and "The Mortal Coil" (an early version of "The Captain's Doll") in July, in an issue that also carried Randolph Bourne's article "The War and the Intellectuals," a polemic against those, like the critic Stuart Sherman (later Lawrence's sparring partner in the U.S. literary press), who had supported American intervention. Sherman's contribution in the following year to the War Information Series of propagandist pamphlets would attack antiwar sentiment like Bourne's as a betrayal of the Puritan heritage that is the nation's "moral backbone"—a phrase which unpleasantly conflates what Sherman saw as Bourne's moral with his physical deformities (spinal tuberculosis in childhood had made Bourne a hunchback).[11] Bourne was placed under surveillance following his *Seven Arts* piece, and when its nervous patron withdrew her financial backing, the magazine was forced to merge with the more conservative *Dial*. *Seven Arts* was a casualty of the war, like Stieglitz's 291 and the Greenwich Village salon of Mabel Dodge (later Mabel Dodge Luhan), which both closed their doors in 1917. Before the year was out, Mabel had transferred her base of operations from New York to New Mexico.

Although he was an icon for the metropolitan avant-garde and, between 1922 and 1925, a major player in New Mexican modernist milieux in Taos and in Santa Fe, Lawrence makes a cameo appearance, when he appears at all, in most mainstream accounts of American modernism. As an English writer in the American scene, Lawrence cuts an anomalous figure even for scholars who place him in the vanguard of American cultural criticism in the 1920s—like Peter Halter, for instance, who judges that the anti-Puritanism that was "widespread among the avant-garde" in the United States "found its clearest and most vehement expression in the writings of D. H. Lawrence, Randolph Bourne, and the other *Seven Arts* critics, and, of course, [William Carlos] Williams," but who offers no explanation for Lawrence's presence in this otherwise all-American lineup.[12] One of the few critics who does read Lawrence in relation to the U.S. modernists who were his contemporaries, Walter Benn Michaels, attributes to the writing he produced in America traits of a nativism to which the English Lawrence could neither subscribe nor meaningfully contribute.[13] But among Michaels's nativist modernists, neither Stieglitz nor Williams were, to quote the latter, "pure products of America," although both were born there: of mixed Puerto Rican and English extraction, Williams was dubbed the "Hidalgo" by Wallace Stevens, and "a blooming foreigner" by Ezra Pound.[14]

As John Muthyala observes, "[o]n what basis something can be called American literature and at what point a text becomes American are not easy questions to answer." Rather, these questions beg the further question, "[i]s American literature produced only by Americans?"[15] Although Lawrence is not one of Muthyala's exemplars, he is nonetheless a suggestive case in point; the author of *Studies in Classic American Literature* confounds chauvinistic constructions of literary citizenship. A work on the national literature produced by a non-national temporarily resident in the United States, *Studies* was nonetheless marketed there in the Stieglitz idiom, as "a book that is less about writers than about America itself" (*SCAL* lvii). *Studies* duly became a counter-bible for those radical cultural nationalists who, like Lawrence, believed that the Puritans' fixation with America as *idea* had stunted an instinctive response to America as *place*.

Williams, for instance, takes his cue from Lawrence when he writes of the Pilgrim Fathers, in his *In the American Grain*, that "they, the seed, instead of growing, looked black at the world and damning its perfections praised a zero in themselves."[16] Williams found in Lawrence's book a sanction for his faith in the generative properties of the local American environment for a New World modernism, albeit that Lawrence did not share Williams's belief in the importance of the urban landscape to an indigenous avant-garde in the United States. In turn, reviewing *In the American Grain* in 1926, Lawrence predicates his assertion that "[a]ll creative art must rise out of a specific soil" on the distinction that Williams, like Poe before him, makes "between 'nationality in letters' and the *local* in literature" (*IR* 257).

Some commentators nonetheless detect in the localizing aesthetic of American modernism a backdoor nationalism: Paul Giles, for instance, suggests that in the work of Stieglitz and of Williams, "the value of particular places is validated not by their specific local characteristics or phenomenological qualities but from their synecdochic embodiment of a national impulse." Giles's argument may apply, perhaps, to John Dewey's coupling of localism with Americanism, but is less persuasive in relation to Williams's *Paterson*, or Stieglitz's Lake George *Equivalents*, works in which particular places are richly validated by their specific local characteristics. According to Gary Snyder, "commitment to pure place" is the marker of "a non-nationalistic idea of community."[17]

A local reading of Lawrence's own "American" writing, Julianne Newmark has proposed, creatively complicates critiques of nativist modernism like Michaels's (and Giles's). Drawing on cultural geographer Yi-Fu Tuan's theory of topophilia to differentiate between the abstraction of national space and the particularity of place, Newmark re-positions Lawrence in the local, northern New Mexico tradition that had been theorized in the first instance in the 1920s, by Lawrence's contemporaries Mary Austin and Alice Corbin Henderson.[18]

In the case of Lawrence and New Mexico, topophilia was an acquired condition, not love at first sight. In retrospect, Lawrence would claim that on his very first morning in New Mexico, "a new part of the soul woke up suddenly, and the old world gave way to a new" (*MM* 176). In fact, the rupture of the Old World rather than the rapture of New Mexico is the keynote of "Taos," an article written almost immediately after Lawrence's arrival there in the autumn of 1922, the opening of which reprises a passage from "The Nightmare" chapter of *Kangaroo*:

> Some places seem final. They have a true nodality. I never felt that so powerfully as, years ago, in London. The intense powerful nodality of that great heart of the world. And during the war that heart, for me, broke. (*MM* 125)

Taos (Lawrence means the ancient Native American settlement of Taos Pueblo) "still retains its old nodality. Not like a great city. But, in its way, like one of the monasteries of Europe" (*MM* 125). Lawrence may well be thinking here of the Benedictine abbey of Monte Cassino, north of Naples, where he had visited his friend Maurice Magnus in 1920, an episode he would recall in his *Memoir of Maurice Magnus*, written in 1922. In the Dark Ages, "life remained vivid" in such "little communities of quiet labour and courage" (*MM* 125). The new Dark Age brought about by the war has made the city synonymous with a malaised modernity for which little communities, and in particular a "*believing* community" like Taos Pueblo, may offer a remedy—

perhaps (*SCAL* 17). Much later, in the essay "New Mexico," Lawrence would affirm that Taos and its environs had indeed "liberated" him "from the present era of civilisation, the great era of material and mechanical development," and that the belief-system of the Pueblo people had given him "a sense of living religion" (*MM* 176, 178). In "Taos," however, Lawrence appears less sure, more alert to the problematics of the recourse to "the sense of place as a panacea for the disaffections of modern uprootedness."[19] "The Indians say Taos is the heart of the world," Lawrence reports. "Their world, maybe" (*MM* 125).

The subject of "Taos" is the San Geronimo Fiesta at the pueblo that Lawrence had attended with Mabel Dodge Luhan in September 1922, the month he arrived in New Mexico. In her memoir of him, Mabel avers that "Lawrence was really in it—he was able to go into it and participate with them and understand. It dissolved his painful isolation—breaking the barriers around him so that for a while he shared a communal effort and lost himself in the group."[20] Lawrence's account is quite different: painfully aware of his outsider status, he makes plain his reluctance to "crowd up and stare at anybody's spectacle" in the manner of the "white crowd of inquisitives" (*MM* 127, 128).[21] An "outsider at both ends of the game," Lawrence plays himself in first-response pieces like "Taos" as "a lone lorn Englishman, tumbled out of the known world of the British Empire" onto the "stage" of a Buffalo Bill–style Wild West show (*MM* 126, 113). Lawrence, an improbable agent of empire and an actor in what John Worthen has called the "Theater of the Southwest," ridicules himself along with the rest, the Anglo highbrows and artists, the war-whooping Indians, the Hispano Penitents staggering under their crucifixes—the ethnic mélange of a "mixed up" New Mexico (*MM* 113).[22]

Where essays like "Taos" and "Indians and an Englishman" "play it as farce" (*MM* 113), Lawrence's later writing about New Mexico generates what Newmark defines as "hybridizations born in place" (although I will argue in the following chapter that in some of that writing, at least, Lawrence still plays it as farce).[23] According to L. D. Clark, in the summer of 1924, at the Kiowa Ranch, Lawrence "brought together all that failed to coalesce in the southern Rockies in 1922 and 1923" into one of modern literature's "most outstanding achievements in response to place."[24]

Lawrence's outstanding achievement as a *poet*, *Birds, Beasts and Flowers*, was completed early in 1923 at the Del Monte Ranch, a little further down Lobo Peak from Kiowa. In line with Lawrence's own description of the book's trajectory—"begun in Tuscany, in the autumn of 1920, and finished in New Mexico in 1923"—*Birds, Beasts and Flowers* has been classified as traveling poetry, whether "a trip underground, a voyage of death and resurrection," in Sandra Gilbert's reading, or a poetic travelogue, in Keith Cushman's (*P* 656).²⁵ Read as a travel book, the place-names with which the individual poems are tagged are luggage labels, the collection as a whole the *carnet du voyage* of Lawrence's peripatetic postwar years. Although it is not among his examples, *Birds, Beasts and Flowers* proves the point Jahan Ramazani makes in *A Transnational Poetics* that "single-nation genealogies" cannot contain "the cross-national mobility" of poetry. Indeed, Lawrence's dynamic definitions of poetry as "transit," as a "journey of creation," and of "come-and-go, not fixity," anticipate Ramazani's vocabulary of poetic vectors and of modernism on the move (*P* 647).²⁶

But in mapping modernist mobilities, a transnational approach passes too quickly, perhaps, over the locations of modernism. "The World is Places," as Gary Snyder insists, and Lawrence was a dweller *in* places, as well as a traveler between them.²⁷ *Birds, Beasts and Flowers* is traveling poetry, but it is also what Snyder would call "place literate," a collection in which, Holly Laird notes, "[a]ll the verse is located geographically, and its order roughly corresponds to his travels eastward to the New World."²⁸ From Taormina to Taos, *Birds, Beasts and Flowers'* locational signatures underwrite what Gilbert, after Lawrence, defines as the poems' "acts of attention" (poetry, in Lawrence's definition, "makes a new effort of attention, and 'discovers' a new world within the known world" [*IR* 109]). In *Birds, Beasts and Flowers*, poetic acts of attention are also acts of emplacement.

Northern New Mexico would prove a temporary halting-point in what Lawrence called his savage pilgrimage of the postwar years, but it is the terminus of *Birds, Beasts and Flowers'* journey at least, and the final way station in the voyage through the underworld that shadows it (iv.375). In its cluster of New Mexico poems, *Birds, Beasts and Flowers* bears its clearest affinity with the localizing impetus of American poetic modernism. William Carlos Williams's *Spring and All*, Mary Austin's *The American Rhythm*, and Jean Toomer's *Cane* all appeared in 1923, each collection endorsing Michael Castro's point, that "[c]oming to grips with America as a place" was an imperative for its poets in the 1920s.²⁹ Published in the same year, Wallace Stevens's *Harmonium* is a more equivocal poetry of place, its poems revealing Stevens's attraction to the primordial Florida he encountered on business trips there, and his simultaneous recoil from its venereal soil. "The Comedian as the Letter C," the volume's centerpiece, offers a wry commentary on the local enthusiasms of Stevens's contemporaries, with the poem's hapless protagonist seeking a "blissful liaison, / Between himself and his environment" that, "For him, and not for him alone," is the "chief motive" of art. If his mock-epic dissents from the Williamsite credo that "his soil is man's intelligence," the quest of Stevens's emigrant poet-comedian, Crispin, is very like a parody, avant la lettre, of Lawrence's pilgrimage to the New World and his plans to establish a colony there.[30]

Notwithstanding his skepticism with regard to the localist project, Stevens's poetry, no less than that of Williams, is abundant proof that Atlantic-world modernism was not the monopoly of transpontines like Pound and Eliot. And via Lawrence, who in his roundabout fashion went the other way *to* the United States, we gauge the global dimensions of the homemade world of American poetic modernism.

This chapter goes on to trace the affiliative connections between Lawrence and American poets from Whitman to Williams. Those connections are copper-fastened by the special relationship between Lawrence and Whitman, but comprise a complex and expanded circuit of transmission and reception; Whitman's legacy is not entailed on Lawrence in a direct line of poetic descent. The relations between Lawrence and American poetry are better understood in the exogamous terms of reference adopted in theories of genre as world-system: indeed, the transactions between Lawrence's and American poetics offer a working model of what Margaret Cohen, in her analysis of "Traveling Genres," identifies as the ways in which "literary codes circulate and translate across distinct yet interrelated cultural and literary fields."[31] Genre "is not just a theory of classification but, perhaps even more crucially, a theory of interconnection," according to Wai Chee Dimock, who insists that interconnection is "not necessarily a genealogical connection, but, just as often, a broad spectrum of affinities," a "phenomenal field of contextually induced parallels [born] of the local circumstances that shape them."[32] In what follows, Lawrence's reception of, and in, American poetry is assessed within the broader contours of the transatlantic affinities and parallels between his poems and those of his U.S. precursors and contemporaries.

Lawrence, Whitman, H.D.

"I always write really towards America," Lawrence told Amy Lowell in 1921.[33] As Jeremy Hooker remarks, "*Birds, Beasts and Flowers* concludes with poems set in New Mexico, but Lawrence's thinking about America preceded this book, and also colours much of it."[34] A number of the *Birds, Beasts and*

Flowers poems that were composed in Europe in 1920 and 1921 are written "towards America," addressing the spirit of the place and Lawrence's own anxious anticipation about encountering it in person. "The Evening Land," which is located at Baden-Baden, is an apostrophe to America: "Shall I come to you"?, the poet asks. There is, he continues,

> Something in you which carries me beyond
> Yankee, Yankee,
> What we call human,
> Carries me where I want to be carried. . . .
>
> Or don't I?

(P 241, 243)

Lawrence, who admits that he is "half in love" with America, wonders "What am I in love with? / My own imaginings?" (P 244). His imaginings are of a "Dark, elvish, / Modern, unissued, uncanny America," the America of "nascent demon people / Lurking among the deeps of your industrial thicket" evoked in the first version of *Studies in Classic American Literature* (P 244). This imagined America is a last resort, the vital alternative to what the poem "Turkey-Cock" describes as the "dead letter" of the East and "Europe moribund" (P 323).

Together with "Turkey-Cock," the other "Birds" poems of *Birds, Beasts and Flowers*—"Humming-Bird," "Eagle in New Mexico," and "The Blue Jay"—constitute an American *aviarium*, although "Turkey-Cock" and "Humming-Bird" were both written in Europe. Lawrence analogizes the turkey-cock, with its quality of "aboriginality," to "a Red Indian darkly unfinished and aloof," and of course it is the potent wild turkey of pagan America, and not the official Thanksgiving or Turkey Day fowl, that is the emblem of the poet's arrival in the New World: "do you await us, wattled father, Westward?" (P 321, 323). Appropriately, Harriet Monroe printed "Turkey-Cock" and "The Evening Land" in *Poetry* magazine in November 1922, to mark Lawrence's arrival in the United States in September of that year.

Birds, Beasts and Flowers locates "Humming-Bird" at Española, New Mexico, but the poem was written in Italy, perhaps, Keith Sagar suggests, in June 1920, when Lawrence was revising his chapter on Crèvecoeur's *Letters from an American Farmer* for *Studies in Classic American Literature*. It is, Sagar remarks, "the only poem in the collection about a creature Lawrence had never seen. The actual encounter was Crèvecoeur's, not his." The implication is that the poem is a sleight-of-hand on Lawrence's part, a lapse in the respect that *Birds, Beasts and Flowers* elsewhere shows for "the otherness of the non-human creation."[35] The point may rather be that the poem is as much Lawrence's homage to Crèvecoeur as it is to the hummingbird. Lawrence's "little bit chipped off in brilliance" is itself a chip off what in *Studies* Lawrence praises as Crèvecoeur's "curiously sharp, hard bit of realisation," the description of the hummingbird as a "miniature work" of nature in his "Letter X" (*P* 324; *SCAL* 199).[36] Crèvecoeur, Lawrence writes in *Studies*, doesn't turn his birds "into 'little sisters of the air,' like St. Francis, or start preaching to them. He knows them as strange, shy, hot-blooded concentrations of bird-presence" (*SCAL* 37). By relocating the poem to New Mexico, where he saw hummingbirds himself for the first time, Lawrence is verifying the accuracy of the view of "actual nature" in the writing of Crèvecoeur, another transplanted European in the New World (*SCAL* 34).

"Humming-Bird," then, reveals the extent to which the *Birds, Beasts and Flowers* poems' acts of attention to animal and plant life are refracted: through the medium of language, and through the writing of the classic Americans, Crèvecoeur and Poe (the poems "Peace" and "Tropic" are dedicated to Poe's "unappeased spirit" [iii.630]) as well as Whitman. In *Studies in Classic American Literature*, Lawrence casts aspersions on Whitman's supposed "'splendid animality'" (149). The epilogue to *Birds, Beasts and Flowers*, "The American Eagle," duly identifies Whitman's "YAWP!!!" with the eagle's scream of the Yankee dollar, and Whitman's "DEMOCRACY. EN MASSE. ONE IDENTITY" with the national motto, *E PLURIBUS UNUM*, which the eagle in the Great Seal of the United States holds in its beak (*P* 365; *SCAL* 151). "The American Eagle" is the bitter end of the argument with Whitman—the poet who described himself as "stucco'd with quadrupeds and birds all over"— which animates *Birds, Beasts and Flowers*.[37]

Lawrence had been writing toward America, as a poet, for a decade prior to *Birds, Beasts and Flowers*' publication. Although his poems appear in five of the six volumes of the quintessentially English *Georgian Poetry* anthologies that were published between 1912 and 1922, from an early stage Lawrence sought to differentiate his work from the "skilled verse" of the Georgians. Tellingly, in a 1913 letter to the *Georgian Poetry* editor, Edward Marsh, he did so by invoking Whitman as an exemplar of the unconstricted possibilities of free verse. "Sometimes Whitman is perfect," Lawrence told Marsh (ii.61). Lawrence's growing allegiance to Whitman during the 1910s meant that he maintained a more-or-less neutral position in the English poetry wars of the period: loosely associated with the Georgians and with the Imagists, he aligned himself with neither faction. But if he resisted the dos and don'ts of Georgianism and of Imagism alike, Lawrence clearly absorbed elements both of the Georgians' milder innovations and of the modernists' more drastic attempts to renovate poetic vision and diction. Lawrence, as Laird so astutely describes him, was "attentive to the currents of his time even when he swims against them: few poets have been more conscious of the aesthetic climate in which they wrote or more deliberate in modifying or flouting its conventions."[38]

Among the affinities between Lawrence and the Georgian writers, Kim Herzinger identifies "the location of an authentic English tradition in the organic connection between man and nature" and a "sense of participation in the beginning of a 'new world'" of which the conclusion of *The Rainbow* is "perhaps the period's most potent expression."[39] In Lawrence's definition, *The Rainbow* constituted a "voyage of discovery," a voyage out from England and its narratives: "We are like Columbus, we have our back upon Europe, till we come to the new world" (ii.362). As Tony Pinkney has pointed out, *The Rainbow* (together with *Women in Love*) also represents Lawrence's "most far-reaching engagement with modernist aesthetics."[40] In Lawrence's fiction and poetry of the 1910s, that Georgian "new world" motif is placed under experimental pressures emanating, in the poems at least, from the influence of Whitman's proto-modernist New World poetics.

"New Heaven and Earth," for instance, puts into practice what Lawrence had proposed in the letter to Marsh, the substitution of Whitmanian prosodies for English metrical models. The poem was first printed in Amy Lowell's anthology *Some Imagist Poets 1917* as "Terra Nuova." That title partly invokes the *Vita Nuova*, but the poem itself revokes Dante's Platonic vision, refusing his sublimation of sexual passion to poetic vocation and celebrating instead a new world in which erotic and poetic discovery are conjoined. It is not Dante but the Whitman of "Children of Adam" who is the avatar of what Harold Bloom has deemed "the most profoundly Whitmanian poem not written by Walt."[41] The poem's debt to Whitman is as clear as it is considerable:

> Ah no, I cannot tell you what it is, the new world
> I cannot tell you the mad, astounded rapture of its discovery.
> I shall be mad with delight before I have done,
> and whosoever comes after will find me in the new world
> a madman in rapture. (*P* 213)

Lawrence had found the "clue" to this "new world," to what his essay "Poetry of the Present" would call the "terra incognita" of "the incarnate, carnal self," in "free verse: Whitman," the one being all but synonymous with the other for him (*P* 649). Later in 1917, "Terra Nuova" would be included, now titled "New Heaven and Earth," in *Look! We Have Come Through!*, the sequence in which Lawrence makes his first sustained experiment with free verse forms. The Futurist illustration on the jacket of the first edition of *Look!* flags the volume's avant-garde credentials, but by 1917 Lawrence had already located a more potent source of innovation than the Italian Futurists in the old American writers he had been reading so intensively that year.[42] By way of the classic Americans, Whitman in particular, Lawrence moves beyond the obsolescent "skill" of Georgian verse to a "carnal" poetic of embodiment that flouts sexual as well as metrical proprieties. *Look! We Have Come Through!*, which is defined as a "confession" in the foreword, likewise violates the Imagist principle of impersonality, Lawrence putting the *"carnal self"* into his poems (*P* 941, 647).

Lawrence's association with Imagism has been dismissed as nominal and expedient, yet it amounted to more than the regular if meager royalties he received from Amy Lowell's anthologies.[43] More valuable, for Lawrence, were the relationships he forged with a number of remarkable American women who, as poets or editors or both, were key players in the movement on both sides of the Atlantic, among them Lowell herself, Harriet Monroe, Alice Corbin Henderson, and H.D. (Hilda Doolittle). It was Amy Lowell who marketed him as an Imagist, but Lawrence's relationship to the poetics of Imagism was worked out by way of intertextual exchanges with H.D. that would continue after their personal friendship came to an end. In *Birds, Beasts and Flowers*, Lawrence carries on the conversation he had begun with H.D. and Imagism in 1916, while for decades after his death, H.D. would still invoke—and, in *Tribute to Freud* (1956), attempt to exorcize—Lawrence in her post-Imagist poem-sequences and palimpsests.

The two had met at one of Amy Lowell's London dinner parties in 1914, two years after Ezra Pound had launched "H.D. Imagiste" as the figurehead of the new poetic school that Lowell was now maneuvering to take over. Following their expulsion from Cornwall in the autumn of 1917, Lawrence and Frieda lodged for a time with H.D. in London in her flat in Mecklenburgh Square, where the three made up one of the triangulated relationships reconstructed in *Bid Me to Live* (1960), H.D.'s roman à clef of the war years. In her book, H.D. recollects that Lawrence "called her Persephone" because he "liked her flower poems" (he liked "Sea Iris" in particular, which would appear in Lowell's anthology *Some Imagist Poets, 1915* together with a number of the poems later included in Lawrence's *Look! We Have Come Through!*).[44] In *Bid Me to Live*, the Lawrence-figure plays Pluto—or Dis, in the Roman pantheon—to H.D.'s Persephone: "Dis of the under-world, the husband of Persephone. Yes, he was her husband."[45] Pluto, in the *Birds, Beasts and Flowers* poem "Purple Anemones," is "the dark, the jealous god, the husband" to a Persephone who, with her visits in season to his mother-in-law, is modeled in part on Frieda Lawrence, and in part on H.D., Lawrence's Persephone-poet (*P* 262):

> Look out, Persephone!
> You, Madame Ceres, mind yourself, the enemy is upon you.
> About your feet spontaneous aconite,
> Hell-glamorous, and purple husband-tyranny
> Enveloping your late-enfranchised plains

(*P* 263)

Susan Stanford Friedman has likened "the potent flowers in Lawrence's early novels and in Georgia O'Keeffe's flower paintings of the 1920s" to the flowers in H.D.'s *Sea Garden* (1916), which "pulsate with an ecstatic eroticism."[46] And yet when they exchanged manuscripts in 1916, H.D.'s judgment was that Lawrence's poems were "not sublimated: too much body and emotions"—the same charge levied in a review of *Georgian Poetry: 1911–1912* against his early and "hyper-erotic" flower poem, "Snap-Dragon" (iii.102; *P* 696). In turn, Lawrence criticized H.D.'s cool classicism and urged her to kick over the "graven images" and "frozen altars" of her early Imagism. She did so with a vengeance in "Eurydice," a poem published in 1917 and seemingly extrapolated from an Orpheus-Eurydice sequence, the Orpheus part of which H.D. had written for Lawrence. "Stick to the woman speaking," Lawrence had told her: "it is the intuitive woman-mood that matters."[47] Taking his advice, H.D. took the woman's part in more than one sense. Sticking to the woman speaking, H.D., as Eurydice, speaks back to Orpheus, the archetype of the male poet. Orpheus appears in her poem as a composite of Lawrence and Richard Aldington, H.D.'s unfaithful husband and fellow-Imagist:

> So for your arrogance
> and your ruthlessness
> I have lost the earth
> and the flowers of the earth

According to Friedman, H.D.-Eurydice translates her anger and abjection into a gendered affirmation of her own creative power:

> I have more light;
>
> and the flowers,
> if I should tell you,
> you would turn from your own fit paths
> toward hell,
> turn again and glance back
> . . . .
> At least I have the flowers of myself,
> and my thoughts, no god
> can take that[48]

In "Purple Anemones," in which Lawrence glances back at H.D.'s "Eurydice" through the related chthonic myth of Persephone, the autonomy of the "late-enfranchised" New Woman is trumped by phallic "mastery." Pluto puts "Poor Persephone and her rights for women" back in her underground place—a "*bit of husband-tilth*," the hell-queen is his to harrow (P 263, 264). Pluto even expropriates the principle of primavera embodied in Persephone, the rite of spring itself: as Charles Segal notes, the myth of Persephone entails "the rescue of the Maiden or Köre from the dark realm of death [and so] restores nature to life after a period of barrenness."[49] Her seasonal emergence from the underworld is heralded by the "Hell's husband-blossoms" that spring up in her tracks:

> When she broke forth from below,
> Flowers came, hell-hounds on her heels.

In the thrill of the chase, and prefiguring the "phallic 'hunting out' of Connie Chatterley," "Hell is up!" indeed, in the person of Persephone's "Flower-sumptuous-blooded" husband, a hutzpah Hades with a hard-on (P 262, 263).[50]

According to H.D.'s lover, Cecil Gray, Lawrence had, by 1917, "become the object of a kind of esoteric female cult, an Adonis, Atthis, Dionysos religion of which he was the central figure": in a letter to Gray refuting the charge, Lawrence told him that "my 'women'" represent "the threshold of a new world, or underworld, of knowledge and being" (iii. 179–80). As Carol Siegel notes, "Lawrence sees women as the unconscious repository of truth."[51] And yet, blurring hard-and-fast gender boundaries, H.D. acknowledged Lawrence as one of her principal male Initiators: he was the catalyst for the revisionary mythmaking, begun in "Eurydice," which became the signature mode of H.D.'s post-Imagist poetry. For his part, Lawrence would go on to make an American-born lost girl the heroine of "St. Mawr" (1925). Lawrence's novella is a New World and, arguably, a feminist recapitulation of the Persephone myth so movingly deployed in *Last Poems* like "Bavarian Gentians," in which "black lamps from the halls of Dis" lead the poet "even where Persephone goes" (*P* 610, 611).

"Purple Anemones" displays the carnal appetite, whetted by Whitman, that Lawrence had developed in his poetry in the course of the 1910s. But like *Birds, Beasts and Flowers*, his earlier poems are intertwined, too, with the botanical myths of Imagism. Compare Lawrence's "Hymn to Priapus," a revised version of which is included in *Look!*, with H.D.'s poem printed in *Poetry* in 1913 as "Priapus / Keeper-of-Orchards," and retitled "Orchard" for *Sea Garden*. Both are the fruit of *The Golden Bough*, the two poems drawing in equal measure, although to significantly different ends, on Sir James Frazer's compendium of vegetation rites and seasonal ceremonies associated with fertility deities like Priapus, protector of fruit-plants, of gardens, and of the male genitalia.

Lawrence's "Hymn to Priapus" is a paean to male procreativity and the penis resurgent. The singer of the hymn, whose "love lies underground," looks to the ithyphallic god not for the restoration of his lost lady (or of the poet's dead mother—John Middleton Murry reads the "Hymn" as an elegy for Lydia Lawrence) but for his own resurrection, a characteristically Lawrentian resurrection of the flesh.[52] When his "Desire comes up," the singer is not a risen Christ but a happy-go-lucky Orpheus who receives no "look / Of admonition" from the lover he leaves down there in the "Fields of death" (*P* 159–61). By contrast, H.D.'s "Orchard" is a *priape* designed to propitiate the god of vegetable love. The poem is a study in and of abjection, its first-person speaker in thrall to the phallic principle she attempts to appease. She leaves as a placatory "offering" at the autumn altar of the "rough-hewn" rustic deity a *nature morte* arrangement, tokens of the postcoital fruitfulness of the season: "fallen hazel-nuts, / stripped late of their green sheaths," and "pomegranates already broken, / and shrunken figs."[53] But her votive gift of broken pomegranates will not resolve the universal antinomies of Eros and Thanatos, sex and death—the pomegranate is a symbol of marriage, its seeds binding Persephone to her underworld lord and master and making her one with the seasonal cycle of decay and regeneration in nature. Indeed, in the "Fruits" poems of *Birds, Beasts and Flowers*, where Lawrence devotes himself to "the female part" instead of the phallus, the "fissure" or "crack" in the pomegranate and the fig is the entry into Persephone's "realm of Generation" (*P* 233, 231):⁵⁴

> The fissure, the yoni,
> The wonderful moist connectivity towards the centre.
>
> Involved,
> Inturned,
> The flowering all inward and womb-fibrilled;
> All but one orifice.
>
> (*P* 233)

Notwithstanding the gendered and provocative symbolism of "Figs," the "Flowers" and "Fruits" sequences of *Birds, Beasts and Flowers* also display what Gaston Bachelard describes as the "dynamic virtues of miniature thinking."⁵⁵ These virtues, which Bachelard attributes to the botanist, are also those of the Imagist poem ("Consider the way of the scientists," Pound had counseled in "A Few Don'ts by an Imagiste").⁵⁶ If Lawrence's 1910s poetry, written under the lax tutelage of Whitman, was in H.D.'s judgment "too much," then her own flower and fruit poems were, like Crèvecoeur's "glimpses of actual nature, not writ large," an object lesson for Lawrence in miniature thinking (*SCAL* 34). The votive quality of H.D.'s verse, however, its graven images and its altars, made it too static in its virtues for Lawrence, whose preference was for poetry "without any base and pediment," which goes to "the creative quick" of things (*P* 647, 646).

Birds, Beasts and Flowers' "Medlars and Sorb-Apples" is a myth-for-myth reply to H.D.'s "Eurydice," in which Lawrence assumes Orpheus's identity, both as *ur*-poet and as the first botanist. Unlike H.D.'s mouthy Eurydice, Lawrence's Eurydice confirms his determination, articulated in the foreword to *Sons and Lovers*, "not to allow the power of Utterance to Woman."⁵⁷ The Eurydice of "Medlars and Sorb-Apples" reverts to classical type, reiterating the parting ("*Jamque vale!*") spoken by Eurydice in book 4 of Virgil's *Georgics*. Lawrence's Eurydice's stock goodbye blends with the mellow "retorts" of the rotting fruits of autumn into the "exquisite odour of leave-taking," the "Orphic farewell" that Lawrence would reprise, at the end of his life, in "The Ship of Death":

Now it is autumn and the falling fruit
and the long journey towards oblivion

the apples falling like great drops of dew
to bruise themselves an exit from themselves.

And it is time to go, to bid farewell
to one's own self

(P 236–37, 630)

In his volume of the Cambridge biography, Mark Kinkead-Weekes represents Lawrence, in 1917, as an Orpheus descending into the hell of wartime England: *Look! We Have Come Through!* "was a tribute to his Eurydice (*not to be left behind*), and also a farewell to a whole phase of his life with her [Frieda]."58 In "Medlars and Sorb-Apples," Lawrence leaves another Eurydice, H.D., behind in the autumnal underworld of London in a time of war. In a London letter to Harriet Monroe written during the war, Lawrence told her that

> here the autumn of all life has set in, the fall: we are hardly more than the ghosts in the haze, we who stand apart from the flux of death. I must see America. I think one can feel hope there. I think that there the life comes up from the roots, crude but vital. Here the whole tree of life is dying. It is like being dead: the underworld. I must see America. I believe it is beginning, not ending. (ii.417)

Imagism and Indians

Lawrence's encounter with London Imagism, mediated though H.D., took place well after the original Imagiste moment had passed. Although he had known Ezra Pound since 1909, Lawrence's own Imagist poems would appear only in the anthologies produced in the post-1914 phase of the movement when, under Lowell's direction, Imagism had mutated into what Pound disparagingly termed "Amygism."59 In her mission to popularize (and Americanize) the New Poetry, Lowell had reversed Pound's earlier tactic of creating a mystique around Imagism, the "Doctrine" of which, much like the secret doctrine of theosophy, was revealed only to an inner circle of initiates or adepts. In making a broader church of that Imagist cenacle, Lowell had turned it, Pound complained, into a "democratic beer-garden." Lawrence was no democrat, but he was, according to Pound, an "*Amy*gist" who had never "accepted the Imagist program."⁶⁰ For his part, Lawrence came to regard Pound as a "mountebank," although his comments about Lowell would remain more diplomatic: "She is not a good poetess.... But she is a very good friend" (iii.61).⁶¹

Unsurprisingly, it was Lowell's brand of Imagism that had the greater impact in the United States, although she had her detractors there too. As editor and associate editor of the Chicago-based modernist magazine *Poetry*, Harriet Monroe and Alice Corbin Henderson had the prior claim on introducing Imagism to an American readership (through the offices of Pound, in his role as *Poetry*'s overseas correspondent). In her study of *Poetry*, Ellen Williams notes that throughout the Imagism-Amygism furor, Monroe remained "faithful" to Pound, despite Lowell's efforts to win her over.⁶² Later in the 1910s, however, Monroe and Henderson would compete with both Pound's and Lowell's versions by promoting Imagism in the pages of *Poetry* not only as an American poetic idiom but also as an indigenous product of the Southwest.

Lawrence, as a long-standing contributor to *Poetry* who was also an Amygist, would be drawn in to these turf wars. Soon after his arrival in New Mexico in the autumn of 1922, Lowell wrote to warn him that Santa Fe was "the nest of [her] enemies."⁶³ She meant Henderson, who had moved there from Chicago in 1916 to receive treatment for tuberculosis, and the poet Witter Bynner, a more recent arrival, at whose home off the Santa Fe Trail Lawrence had, as it happened, spent his first night in New Mexico. It was Bynner who had conferred the unkind moniker of "hippopoetess" on the ample Amy Lowell; he had been one of the perpetrators, too, of the notorious Spectra hoax of 1916 which, with Lowell as the prime target, had parodied Imagist and other avant-gardist pieties.⁶⁴ A year later, in *Tendencies in Modern American Poetry*, Lowell may well have Bynner in her own sights when she alludes to "those nefarious persons who endeavor to keep themselves before the public by means of a more or less clever charlatanism."⁶⁵ Post Spectra, Bynner would modify his views, not of Lowell—she reappears as "The Poetess" in Bynner's *Guest Book* (1935) who "would have ordered God from the front door, / If he had come in clothes that meant the back"—but of the poetic possibilities of the image as "a clearly seen picture of an idea."⁶⁶ Poems in Bynner's *A Canticle of Pan* (1920) like "In Shantung," which was written after his first visit to China in 1917, are reminiscent of Pound's Imagist chinoiseries:

A burnished magpie
Strutting in the sun
Claiming a path among furrows of rice—
But in the distance
The quiet trot
Of a blue-coated horseman.[67]

Helen Carr has suggested that Pound's redactions of Chinese poetry offered "a template by which Native American poetry could be approached" by white American admirers.[68] In Bynner's case, however, his turn to Native American and Hispanic traditions meant a return to more conventional prosody. "A Dance for Rain," from his New Mexico collection *Indian Earth* (1929), is an example:

These were the men, a windy line,
Their elbows green with a growth of pine.
And in among them, close and slow,
Women moved, the way things grow,
With a mesa-tablet on the head
And a little grassy creeping tread.

The rhyming couplets are Bynner's heavy-handed attempt to reproduce the rhythm of "the drum / Calling for the rain to come" at the July ceremonial at Cochiti.[69]

Mary Austin's more generous judgment was that Bynner's *Indian Earth* poems did indeed capture an authentic American rhythm. In the addenda to the second edition of her own collection, *The American Rhythm: Studies and Reëxpressions of Amerindian Songs*, Austin compares Bynner with Lawrence, describing both as poets who, "having given themselves to living on Indian earth, are willing to admit the influence on their own output, of so fresh and vigorous a poetic approach."[70] Lawrence would not have relished Austin's coupling of his work with Bynner's, with whom he had a testy relationship, and he took a hearty dislike to Austin herself when they met in person at Mabel Dodge Luhan's house in Taos in 1924.

"The American Rhythm," the extended essay that prefaces the first, 1923, edition of Austin's book, is a manifesto for an indigenous poetics, a homegrown and local American Imagism. Austin's thesis, predicated on her theory of the "landscape line," is that "verse forms are shaped by topography" and "are developed from the soil native to the culture that perfected them." The "union of artist and Indian through the land" was, Carr comments, a central tenet of American primitivism; that union allows Austin to argue that a direct relationship obtains "between aboriginal and later American forms," between what she calls "the beginning poetry and the becoming poetry of America."[71] More specifically, Austin suggests that "the aboriginal process approaches closest to what is called Imagism," or "glyphic" poetry. "Thunder Dance at San Ildefonso" is Austin's reëxpression of a song in the Tewa language:

> Slow cloud
> Low cloud
> Wing-hovering cloud
> Over the thirsty fields,
> Over the waiting towns
> Low cloud, slow cloud
> Let the rain down![72]

Castro observes that when translators like Austin "used imagist concepts and techniques to produce their English translations, the results were bound to bear a striking resemblance to imagist forms."[73] This happens in "Thunder Dance"; despite Austin's insistence that her glyphs are in "the mold of Amerind verse," the poem bears the typographical imprint of the quintessential Imagist poem, Pound's "In a Station of the Metro." In the version printed in *Poetry* in 1913, white space lends a calligrammatic definition to Pound's "Petals   on a wet, black   bough   ."[74]

Where Austin owes an unacknowledged debt to the techniques of Poundian Imagism, Alice Corbin Henderson's *Red Earth: Poems of New Mexico* (1920) displays a knowing and tactical redeployment of its tenets. "Listening" is the first in her *Indian Songs* sequence, adapted from Frances Densmore's translations of Chippewa songs:

> The noise of passing feet
> On the prairie—
> Is it men or gods
> Who come out of the silence?[75]

What comes out of the silence is an echo of Pound's "The Return," a poem published in his volume *Ripostes* in 1912 and reprinted both in his own 1914 anthology *Des Imagistes* and in Henderson's and Monroe's *The New Poetry* in 1917: "See, they return; ah, see the tentative / Movements, and the slow feet."[76] Adapting the compressed mythic method of Pound's poem, Henderson locates her "men or gods" on native ground, "On the prairie."

A number of Henderson's *Red Earth* poems, including "Listening," had first appeared in a 1917 issue of *Poetry* "almost entirely devoted to poems from American-Indian motives." Henderson's and Carl Sandburg's comments on "Aboriginal Songs," which appear in the same issue, anticipate aspects of Austin's defense of the autochthonous origins of American Imagism, Sandburg quipping that "the Red Man and his children committed plagiarism on the modern imagists and vorticists," and Henderson commenting that the Indian song, like the Imagist poem, is "content to give the image and not to talk about it."[77] The *Poetry* special issue, together with collections like Henderson's *Red Earth*, Bynner's *Indian Earth*, and Austin's *American Rhythm*, confirms Castro's contention that "[t]he red man, in effect, comes with the territory" for the American poet.[78]

Works like these also lay the New Mexico modernists open to the charges of essentializing or orientalizing the region, of dabbling in literary eugenics, and of "playing Indian."[79] Austin is found guilty on all counts in Leah Dilworth's study of Southwestern primitivism. Austin did indeed claim that there was a "genetic resemblance" between Native originals and her own reëxpressions of Amerindian songs, a resemblance that, Austin suggested, is equivalent to her "being an Indian."[80] Lawrence is playing Indian, too, although he takes the genetics out of the genetic fallacy, in his 1922 essay "Indians and an Englishman," when he describes himself as the "changeling son" of an "old red father" (*MM* 120).

The *Birds, Beasts and Flowers* poem "The Red Wolf," which was written, like the essay, in the autumn of 1922, is a more self-reflexive meditation on the relationship between Anglo writer and Indian earth. The poet surfaces from his underground journey through the Fourth Dimension, or what Gary Snyder calls the "mythological present," and emerges into the Third Space, the postcolonial contact zone of northern New Mexico.[81] Walking out of the twilight of the Old World idols, the poet obeys his own injunction, in "Turkey-Cock," to "Take up the trail of the vanished American / Where it disappeared at the foot of the crucifix" (*P* 323). On the plaza of Taos Pueblo, the poet meets his pagan guide to a new dispensation and a "new story":

Across the pueblo river
That dark old demon and I
Thus say a few words to each other.

(*P* 355)

The Indian embodies *Studies in Classic American Literature*'s demon of the continent. But the dark old demon is also the poet's own demon, whose task, as Lawrence defines it in his Note to the *Collected Poems*, is to "shake" his "real poems" out of him (*P* 655). A dark demon muse, the Indian is the poet's aboriginal alter ego, suggesting Lawrence's complicity in what Gayatri Chakravorty Spivak identifies as the "constitution of the Other as the Self's shadow."[82] A postcolonial politics of representation, Spivak observes, produces radically asymmetric relationships, in which "[t]he person who *knows* has all the problematics of selfhood. The person who is known seems not to have a problematic self."[83] This is the case in "The Red Wolf," in which the tribal elder is an archetypal "old father," while the poet belongs neither to the white world he has left behind nor to the community of the Taos Indians. The poet is not a prodigal or native son but a pariah, a "*stray from the pale-face*" who "Sniffs round your place. / Lifts up his voice and howls to the walls of the pueblo" (*P* 354).

Neil Roberts is nonetheless right to pick up on the "tacit slide," in the poem's title, "of the word 'red' from the Indian to the white man" that "signifies an at least aspirational kinship" with the Indian on Lawrence's part.[84] As the red *wolf*, Lawrence is again claiming kinship by changing kind—the red wolf was Lawrence's totem animal, according to the Taos Indians.[85] Maria DiBattista has argued that the "appeal of totemism for Lawrence" is that "it constitutes a system of relationships—animalistic, spiritual, and social—that honors the law of difference."[86] In "The Red Wolf," however, the poet takes on a totemic identity in order to interpolate himself into the tale of the tribe, into the animal lore and, perhaps, the trickster-myths of the American Indian, making up, maybe, for what Mary Austin notes is the "paucity of wolf myths in Pueblo lore." Like its cognate animal the coyote, Lawrence's wolf evinces the stubborn refusal to disappear that Gary Snyder ascribes to the New Mexico pueblos.[87]

Dilworth argues that "in the role of the mutable, mobile maker of meaning" the Anglo writer in the Southwest "retained the power of signification and subjectivity," whereas "the Indian was reduced to a set of appropriable signifiers and was not expected to engage in the mimesis of the civilized." "The Red Wolf" won't wear this blanket definition of "aesthetic 'playing Indian'" insofar as the power of signification appears to rest to some degree with the Indian, who names the poet:

I'm the red wolf, says the dark old father.
All right, the red-dawn-wolf I am.

(*P* 355)[88]

But whatever the Indian says, of course, he says in the words of the poet—as Spivak concludes, the subaltern cannot speak. In "The Red Wolf," Lawrence is playing Indian in wolf's clothing, conflating ethnic with animal otherness in order to insinuate himself into the signifying system of the pueblo. But, as a *"Thin red wolf of a pale-face,"* the poet is an interloper on Indian earth who, at the end of the poem, is left to stage his lonely sit-in within the pueblo's walls: "I'm going to sit down on my tail right here" (*P* 354, 355).

Lone wolf or lone lorn Englishman, Lawrence was nonetheless connected to the networks of northern New Mexico modernism. He was a frequent contributor to the local little magazine *Laughing Horse*, for instance, his close association with which is discussed in the following chapter. His work also appears in the first anthology of New Mexico poetry, Alice Corbin Henderson's *The Turquoise Trail* (1928), which reprints "The Red Wolf" together with two other *Birds, Beasts and Flowers* poems, "Men in New Mexico" and "Autumn at Taos."

Henderson begins her preface to *The Turquoise Trail* with an assertion of regional uniqueness that echoes Charles F. Lummis's promotion of New Mexico in the 1890s as "the United States which is *not* the United States":

> Ordinarily, state boundaries are not demarcations of separate and distinct poetic atmospheres; but the life in New Mexico represents an atmosphere and a world entirely different from that of any other part of the country.[89]

The New Mexico state line keeps at bay the standardizing influence of national, U.S.-America, and fosters a unique poetic microclimate or "atmosphere": as Jonathan Bate has argued, "[a] map divided according to bioregions will look very different from one bounded according to nation states."[90] "New Mexico Poetry," as it is represented in *The Turquoise Trail*, is an eclectic mix, ranging from cowboy ballads like Badger Clark's "High Chin Bob" and N. Howard Thorp's "What's Become of the Punchers?" to Indian songs like Bynner's "A Dance for Rain" and the jazzier "red-man syncopations" of Marsden Hartley's "The Festival of the Corn."[91] Henderson rounded up her contributors from Anglo émigrés to New Mexico (Austin, Bynner, Luhan, and Henderson herself), temporary residents (Lawrence and Hartley), and assorted visitors to the state like the unlikely trio of Yvor Winters, Carl Sandburg, and John Galsworthy. Lawrence, who had little time for Sandburg and less for Galsworthy, sits uneasily in their company, perhaps, albeit that in her preface, Henderson defines the New Mexican spirit of place in quintessentially Lawrentian terms:

> [T]he subliminal influence of soil and atmosphere inevitably affect the expression of any poet or artist who, consciously or unconsciously, is submerged in a new environment—particularly when that environment is as strange as it is new, as liberating as it is primal.[92]

In the first version of his essay "The Spirit of Place," Lawrence had suggested that European settlers in the New World

> walked a new earth, were seized by a new electricity, and laid in line differently. Their bones, their nerves, their sinews took on a new molecular disposition in the new vibration. (*SCAL* 177)

In its 1918 version in particular, "The Spirit of Place" is the product of World War I. The essay recodes as organic process the iron harvest of the war itself and the processes of industrial modernity—the Iron Age of technology—of which, in Lawrence's view, the war was the inevitable outcome:

> Even the buds of iron break into soft little flames of issue. So will people change. So will the machine-parts open like buds and the great machines break into leaf. Even we can expect our iron ships to put forth vine and tendril and bunches of grapes, like the ship of Dionysos in full sail upon the ocean. (*SCAL* 178)

In the late essay "New Mexico," "[t]he sky-scraper will scatter on the winds like thistledown, and the genuine America, the America of New Mexico, will start on its course again" (*MM* 181). Here, Lawrence is again reversing Ruskin's vision, in "The Work of Iron in Nature, Art, and Policy," of "a planet colonized by a horrifying steel-vegetation."[93] Likewise, in *Birds, Beasts and Flowers*, Lawrence's first postwar collection of poetry, "iron can put forth" and "break and bud" (*P* 259). Marsden Hartley's suggestion that the recourse of American artists to the "soil" and to "the localized expression we are free to call American in type" should also be understood as reactions to the war is borne out by Mabel Dodge Luhan's relocation from Manhattan to Taos in 1917 and the appearance in the same year of a special, Southwestern, issue of *Poetry* magazine.[94]

Lawrence, Whitman, Williams

Harriet Monroe had launched *Poetry* in 1912 expressly "to give the art of poetry an organ in America."[95] But almost from the outset, there were tensions as to its remit: "Are you for American poetry or for poetry?" Pound asked Monroe.[96] As overseas editor, Pound "wanted the magazine to be international, with American poets included when they reached an international standard"; Monroe and Henderson "wanted the magazine to be American with international connections."[97] "The Motive of the Magazine," as Monroe envisaged it, is explained in the first issue: poetry "is not a matter of direct creation, but a reciprocal relation between the artist and his public" of the kind that Whitman had envisaged in his preface to the 1855 edition of *Leaves of Grass*. Whitman's assertion, "To have great poets there must be great audiences too," would become *Poetry*'s motto.[98]

Whitman, who was also the "tutelary genius" of *Seven Arts*, was, Alan Trachtenberg observes, a touchstone for American "artists dedicated to 'making it new' from the turn of the century through the 1920s."[99] James Nolan goes further, hailing Whitman as a shamanic "Poet-Chief," an American Orpheus and the precursor of an Imagist poetic that Nolan, like Austin and Henderson, theorizes as a "Native" mode.[100] Whitman had himself addressed those he called the "Poets to Come" in an Inscription to *Leaves of Grass*, telling them he has written only "one or two indicative words for the future" and that he is "Expecting the main things from you." His own book Whitman would describe as a "*carte visite* to the coming generation of the New World."[101] Henderson had called on her contemporaries to fulfil Whitman's prophecy of a new "breed" or "gang" of poets in an early poem, "America," which appeared in *Poetry* in 1912:

> *I hear America singing* . . .
> And the great prophet passed
> . . . .
> When will the master-poet
> Rise, with vision strong,
> To mold her manifold music
> Into a living song?[102]

The trouble here is that Henderson molds Whitman's expansive vision into a rhymed quatrain; her poem hardly represents the kind of living song for which it calls and is clearly not the kind of verse William Carlos Williams had in mind when he suggested that "[t]he only way to be like Whitman is to write *unlike* Whitman."[103] Later in the 1910s, Van Wyck Brooks would blame the Genteel Tradition for blocking the transmission of a living tradition in American writing. Like Nolan, who finds in Whitman what Lawrence calls the "missing link" between the American who is merely a "recreant European" and the representative of the "the next era" (*SCAL* 11), Brooks attempts to restore the broken continuity of American poetry by identifying Whitman as a "precipitant" for the poets of his generation.[104] Even the expatriate Pound made "A Pact," if a grudging one, with Whitman, the "pig-headed father," in a poem first printed in *Poetry* in 1913. Addressing Whitman, Pound concedes that "It was you that broke the new wood," but tells him that "Now is a time for carving": Whitman, that is, is the lumberjack who has provided the raw materials with which Pound—the better craftsman, as Eliot called him—may now work.[105]

As Bloom insists, however, "the drama of influence and its discontents rarely is as rich and valuable as in Lawrence's agon with his American original."[106] Despite his evident frustration with the Whitman who "dumps us down cartloads of material, cartload after cartload," Lawrence was less concerned than some of his contemporaries with reconciling Whitman's expansiveness with the stringent poetic economy of Imagism (*SCAL* 369). His difficulty was not with the rough-hewn nature of Whitman's language experiment either—Lawrence had told Edward Marsh in 1913 that "instinct" in poetry is "finer than the skill of the craftsmen" (ii.61). Rather, Lawrence took issue with the philosophical and ideological corollary of Whitman's poetic innovation, the great experiment of American democracy (which, in its nineteenth- and twentieth-century manifestations at least, was likewise anathema to Pound, and differentiates both Pound and Lawrence from Williams, whose belief was that American poetry after Whitman "must be truly democratic").[107] David Ellis and Howard Mills have argued that, in consequence, Lawrence draws only on Whitman's "negative aid" in *Birds, Beasts and Flowers*, where an ethic of inviolate otherness is practiced in explicit opposition to the Whitmanian ethos of democratic merging.[108] "As soon as Walt *knew* a thing, he assumed a One Identity with it," Lawrence complains in *Studies in Classic American Literature*; by contrast, *Birds, Beasts and Flowers*' "things"—like the "Fish" in the poem of that title—"move in other circles" than the poet's cosmos (*SCAL* 151; *P* 293). In the *Birds, Beasts* poem "Bibbles," Lawrence's "Little black dog in New Mexico" is the proxy for his dispute with Whitman:

Oh Bibbles, oh Pips, oh Pipsey
You little black love-bird!
Don't you love *everybody!!!*
Just everybody.

You love 'em all.
Believe in the One Identity, don't you,
You little Walt-Whitmanesque bitch?

(*P* 345, 346)

Lawrence mimics Whitman's signature modes—the direct address to the reader, the rhetorical question—in order to mock his "mistake," his indiscriminate puppy love for all and sundry (*SCAL* 157).

A poem like "Bibbles," with its rebarbative assertion of singularity in the face of Whitmanian Oneness, seems to confirm the received notion of Lawrence himself as "a snarling outsider to the cultural milieu of his time."[109] Yet, because it *is* a dog-fight with Whitman, "Bibbles" belongs to what is a collective and, with the important exceptions of Lawrence himself and of Federico Garcia Lorca, an American, tradition: that of the Whitman response-poem. In this subgenre, which extends from Pound's "A Pact" through "A Supermarket in California," Allen Ginsberg's Cold War elegy for Whitman's "lost America of love," the Poets to Come invoke Whitman, and answer him back.

Ginsberg's poem is at once an homage to Whitman's freewheeling prosody and a troubled meditation on poetic transmission. The Whitman who is greeted as "father" and as "teacher" proves an unreliable compass to the American Century in which his fellow-travelers are trying to find their way. "Where are we going, Walt Whitman," Ginsberg asks, almost a century after the first edition of *Leaves of Grass*: "Which way does your beard point tonight?"[110] Crossing Charon's instead of Brooklyn's ferry, Whitman is represented as a latter-day American Virgil who, at the end of the poem, is left on the far bank not of the East River, but of the Lethe (the Acheron, in Virgil's *Aeneid*). Lawrence had anticipated Ginsberg's gentler misgivings in *Studies in Classic American Literature*, where Whitman is acknowledged as a "pioneer" but not as a pathfinder for "other wayfarers along the road." In Lawrence's judgment, Whitman made a wrong turn from the "open road" onto the "emotional highway of Love" (*SCAL* 155, 157); this has proved a "dead end," although "lots of new little poets" (Lawrence probably has Carl Sandburg in mind) are "camping on Whitman's camping ground now" (*SCAL* 155). Instead of producing a poetry *of* the present that is commensurate with Whitman's, Lawrence finds that poets *in* the present are merely peddling belated Whitmanesqueries.

In "Poetry of the Present," an essay written in 1919, Lawrence had called for a new poetry of "the urgent, insurgent Now" that, like Whitman's, is "near the quick" (*P* 647).¹¹¹ An homage to Whitman, the essay is also the closest Lawrence would come to producing a poetic manifesto, and as such, "Poetry of the Present" is at significant odds with Amy Lowell's *Tendencies in Modern American Poetry*, which Lawrence had read on its publication in 1917. Speaking on behalf of the cohort of Imagists represented in her anthologies, Lawrence included, Lowell states that "we oppose the cosmic poet" since "concentration is of the very essence of poetry."¹¹² As Nolan points out, however, "Whitman proclaims the cosmic and then incarnates the particulars," and in the view of American poets like Williams (who was himself one of *Des Imagistes*, in Pound's 1914 anthology of that title), Whitman anticipated the Imagist motive.¹¹³ Lawrence thought so too: as Stephen Tapscott notes, Lawrence would recall that "his first fascination with Whitman had coincided with his own Imagist phase," and in "Poetry of the Present" Lawrence praises Whitman's "sheer appreciation of the instant moment" (*P* 647).¹¹⁴

The Whitman who is hailed in "Poetry of the Present" as the poet of "life itself" (*P* 647) returns as the "post mortem" poet of *Studies in Classic American Literature* (151). But even at his most disaffected, in the "Whitman" chapter of *Studies*, Lawrence still concedes that among the "classic" American writers Whitman was "the first to break the mental allegiance." This makes Whitman the "first white aboriginal," a poet-chief indeed, with "the true rhythm of the American continent speaking out in him" (*SCAL* 156–57). Whitman achieves the "contact" between writer and environment, "between man and his circumambient universe, at the living moment," which for Lawrence, as for Wallace Stevens's Crispin, is the chief motive of art (*P* 646; *STH* 171).

"Contact" was likewise a keyword for American poets and painters like Williams and Marsden Hartley who regarded Whitman as the harbinger of an indigenous American modernism predicated on what Hartley called "the redman's contact."¹¹⁵ In 1920, the year "Poetry of the Present" appeared as the preface to the U.S. edition of Lawrence's *New Poems*, Williams had cofounded the little magazine called *Contact* on the premise that "[i]f Americans are to be blessed with important work it will be through intelligent, informed contact with the locality which alone can infuse it with reality."¹¹⁶ Later—and clearly influenced by *Studies in Classic American Literature*—Williams would equate what he called "the American subterfuge" with "the American lack of indigenous experience." He would call on the American artist to make "an intense effort to 'touch' the facts of the objective reality around him, to establish a contact with his immediate environment."¹¹⁷

Spring and All is the product of Williams's own effort to establish that local contact. His prose-and-poetry sequence was brought out by Contact Editions in 1923, the watershed year for an American poetic modernism that defined itself, in Williams's case explicitly and polemically, against the productions of American-born émigrés like Pound and Eliot. Williams would later complain that with the publication of *The Waste Land* in 1922, Eliot had "returned us to the classroom just at the moment when I felt that we were on the point of an escape to matters much closer to the essence of a new art form itself—rooted in the locality which should give it fruit."[118] The year after *The Waste Land*, Williams responds in *Spring and All* to that poem's vision of postwar decline by transplanting Eliot's aborted fertility myths from the killing fields of Europe to the local American scene.[119] In Williams's "new world naked," "spring approaches" as it should, *Spring and All* reaffirming the germinal properties of a seasonal cycle that has lost its restorative power in the waste land of the Old World.[120]

Williams had already announced his American difference from the Europhile Eliot in the prologue to *Kora in Hell*, a sequence of improvisations published in 1920. In the improvisations themselves, the myth of Persephone (Korë) is deployed in order to plumb the depths of what Williams described as his own "hell of repression."[121] The title of *Spring and All* tells us, in its laconic American way, that, unlike *Kora*, the 1923 sequence entails anabasis as well as katabasis, emergence from the chthonic realm, as well as the descent into it. Restoring the Persephone myth to its origins as a vegetation rite symbolizing the planting, germination, and harvesting of crops, *Spring and All* is an "expression of a re-awakened genius of *place*" of the kind for which Williams would continue to call in his *In the American Grain*.[122]

Williams's underworld mythography works like Lawrence's, Margot Louis suggests, in "reconnecting us with our physicality."[123] *Birds, Beasts and Flowers*, which opens with Persephone's "Pomegranate" in place of Eve's apple, recasts the fall, T. R. Wright observes, "as a willing enjoyment of the fruits of the earth" and figures "the descent into hell as a regeneration of energy."[124] In the Persephone-poems "Pomegranate" and "Purple Anemones," botanical myths replenish the sterile postwar environment, recovering what Williams, in *Spring and All*, calls the "vitality of the classics."[125]

The Spirit of Place and the Poetics of Space

Like Williams's, Lawrence's organicism is the outgrowth not of a belated Romanticism, but of a modernist aesthetic that, Anne Fernihough maintains, "lead[s] to a retrieval of the material world."[126] More specifically, and again like Williams and Marsden Hartley, Lawrence locates that material aesthetic—which he defines as "*physical* awareness," the "awareness of touch," and as a poetics of "*thereness*" as opposed to "nowhereness"—in the work of Whitman and of Paul Cézanne (*LEA* 207, 211, 197). In "Poetry of the Present" Lawrence notes that Whitman "pruned away his clichés," and in doing so showed us that "[w]e can get rid of the stereotyped movements and the old hackneyed associations of sound or sense" (*P* 648). In the same way, Cézanne's canvases break through "the mental consciousness stuffed full of clichés that intervene like a complete screen between us and life" (*LEA* 215).

Lawrence's "screen" is what Williams calls the "barrier between the reader and his consciousness of immediate contact with the world": to break through that barrier, Williams argues that the artist must do away with "strained associations" that "separate the work from 'reality.'"[127] In his *Adventures in the Arts* (1921)—which is dedicated to Stieglitz and, like *Studies in Classic American Literature*, served as a model for Williams's *In the American Grain*—Hartley argues that Whitman and Cézanne alike dispense with "jaded tradition," enabling the poets and artists to come to see what is "under our home eye."[128] Hartley hails Whitman and Cézanne as "the prophets of the new time"; the two "walk together out of a vivid past," teaching the artist and the poet of the present to strive

> toward actualities, toward the realization of beauty as it is seen to exist in the real, in the object itself, whether it be mountain or apple or human, the entire series of living things in relation to one another.[129]

Bram Dijkstra has suggested that it was Cézanne's "direct treatment of the 'Thing'" that, via Stieglitz and 291, introduced the tenets of Imagism to America in 1911, two years prior to the publication, in *Poetry* magazine, of F. S. Flint's and Pound's Imagist obiter dicta. Peter Halter likewise notes that, for the poets and painters of the Stieglitz circle, Cézanne was "a figure of the utmost importance," the "prime example of an artist who not only thought of the work of art as a creation instead of a 'reproduction,' but who also saw it as a product of 'direct expression of direct experience.'"[130]

Hartley's comments on Cézanne anticipate Lawrence's remarks, in "Introduction to These Paintings," on the appleyness of Cézanne's apple, which "is a great deal, more than Plato's Idea" (*LEA* 203). The difference between Cézanne's apple and Eve's—or between Persephone's pomegranate and Eve's apple—is what Lawrence elsewhere defines as "the difference between Pluto and Plato" (*FSLC* 64). Cézanne's apple, Lawrence says, means nothing less than the "fall" of Platonic and of Christian idealism; like the chthonic myths that dispace the Christian narrative in *Birds, Beasts and Flowers*, the painter's apple signifies "the collapse of our whole way of consciousness, and the substitution of another way" (*LEA* 212).[131] Cézanne's apple, like *Birds, Beasts and Flowers*' "Peach" or the plums in Williams's "This Is Just To Say," is "a real attempt to let the apple exist in its own separate entity" (*LEA* 201).[132] What Lawrence calls the *thereness* of the apple the philosopher Maurice Merleau-Ponty defines as Cézanne's "global 'locality,'" or what it means "when we say that a thing is *there*."[133]

In the commentary on Cézanne in "Introduction to These Paintings," Lawrence is drawing on the critique of mimesis in Jane Harrison's *Ancient Art and Ritual*, which he had read in the first instance in 1913 and that had also informed his 1924 New Mexico essay "Indians and Entertainment." According to Harrison, the Platonic artist "imitates natural objects, which are themselves in his philosophy but copies of a higher reality. All the artist can do is to make a copy of a copy, to hold up a mirror to Nature." It is "by studying those rudimentary forms of art that are closely akin to ritual," she proposes, "that we come to see how utterly wrong-headed is this conception." Among an "image-making people" like the Etruscans, Harrison says, the "abstract idea arises from the only thing it can possibly arise from, the concrete fact." "No ideas but in things," as Williams would so succinctly put it.[134]

Lawrence and Hartley both discovered an art akin to ritual in northern New Mexico. When he traveled there in 1918, Hartley found in Taos Pueblo a "proving ground" for his own artistic practice and for his theories of American expression.[135] The essay "Tribal Esthetics," which appeared in the *Dial* in that year, is the first of a series on Native American rituals in New Mexico, including the Fiesta of San Geronimo at Taos and the Corn Dance at Santo Domingo. These ceremonials are Lawrence's subjects in "Taos" and "The Dance of the Sprouting Corn" respectively, the latter ritual symbolizing what William York Tindall calls the "Easter ceremony of the resurrected vegetable," or what Lawrence calls the "green resurrection" of the corn, "the mystery of germination" in springtime (*MM* 72, 76).[136]

Lawrence's *Look! We Have Come Through!*, which concludes with a poem titled "Craving for Spring," is, as Mark Kinkead-Weekes notes, "a Persephone story of resurrection into new spring."[137] At the other end of the seasonal cycle, in the *Birds, Beasts and Flowers* poem "Autumn at Taos," the fall is coterminous with the coming-into-being of a new world. "Autumn at Taos" illustrates Gaston Bachelard's argument that poems are "acts of emergence":

> poetry puts language in a state of emergence, in which life becomes manifest through its vivacity. These linguistic impulses, which stand out from the ordinary rank of pragmatic language, are miniatures of the vital impulse. A micro-Bergsonism that abandoned the thesis of language-as-instrument in favor of the thesis of language-as-reality would find in poetry numerous documents on the intense life of language.[138]

"Poets and painters are born phenomenologists," Bachelard insists; in their work, "things 'speak to us,'" giving us "a contact with things."[139] In Lawrence's poem, northern New Mexico in the autumn, like a Cézanne landscape, "has its own weird anima, and to our wide-eyed perception it changes like a living animal under our gaze" (*LEA* 214):

> Over the rounded sides of the Rockies, the aspens of autumn
> The aspens of autumn,
> Like yellow hair of a tigress brindled with pine.
>
> (*P* 360)

Applying Jonathan Bate's theory of ecopoetics to "Autumn at Taos," the biota of the poem—the aspens and pines—comprise "the ecosystem of the text."[140] The poem is composed of "images of *felicitous space*," images of the kind that, in Bachelard's judgment, "deserve to be called topophila" or "eulogized space":[141]

> Down on my hearth-rug of desert, sage of the mesa,
> An ash-grey pelt
> Of wolf all hairy and level, a wolf's wild pelt.
>
> (*P* 360)

"Poetry," Martin Heidegger says, "first causes dwelling to be dwelling."[142] In contrast to his tentative and troubling occupation of Indian earth in "The Red Wolf," in "Autumn at Taos" the animistic landscape of northern New Mexico accommodates the poet:

> Make big eyes, little pony
> At all these skins of wild beasts;
> They won't hurt you.
>
> (*P* 361)

The birds and beasts of the bioregion through which the poet rides on his little pony furnish the living fabric of his environment:

> Pleased to be out in the sage and the pine fish-dotted foot-hills,
> Past the otter's whiskers,
> On to the fur of the wolf-pelt that strews the plain.
>
> (*P* 361)

"It may be D. H. Lawrence hocus-pocus, / But I prefer a room that's got a focus," Auden wrote in defense of the fireplace.[143] In "Autumn at Taos," the carpet of desert sage, gray like the pelt of the local Lobo wolf, is the poet's hearth-rug, and "the rounded sides of the squatting Rockies," the "leopard-livid slopes of America," form the walls of his New World home (*P* 361). "Autumn at Taos" thus captures what Bachelard calls the "intimate immensity" of the poetics of space.[144]

"The Blue Jay" is set in the more modest dimensions of the Del Monte Ranch on Lobo Peak, which was Lawrence's home for a period from early December 1922:

> The blue jay with a crest on his head
> Comes round the cabin in the snow.
>
> (*P* 326)

The poet's cabin is a New World equivalent of the "hut," defined by Bachelard as "the tap-root of the function of inhabiting."[145] The blue jay's adjacent home is in "the pine-tree that towers like a pillar of shaggy smoke / Immense above the cabin" (*P* 326). For Bachelard, nests are "primal images," and as such are "evidence of a cosmic situation" of the kind that Lawrence would later describe with reference to the "cosmic noises" to be heard at the Kiowa Ranch in the essay "Reflections on the Death of a Porcupine," and which the poet and his dog Bibbles, the "little black bitch in the snow," encounter as they approach the bird's home in the pine tree at Del Monte: "*Ca-a-a!* comes the scrape of ridicule out of the tree. // *What voice of the Lord is that, from the tree of smoke?*" (*RDP* 350; *P* 326). The "laughing" god manifested in the pine tree's pillar of cloud is not Jehovah, but the American Pan Lawrence would invoke in the essay "Pan in America," written in the summer of 1924 at the nearby Kiowa Ranch: "in the world of Pan," Lawrence remarks, "[t]he contact between all things is keen and wary: for wariness is also a sort of reverence, or respect" (*MM* 163). Atavistic as it is, Lawrence's New World version of pantheism commands respect for the quiddity, the constitutive essences of bird, animal, and plant life. In "The Blue Jay," while he chides the bird—"Whose boss are you, with all your bully way?"—Lawrence pays a keen tribute to the miniature materiality of this "bit of blue metal" (*P* 327, 326).

Modernism and phenomenology, Matt ffytche suggests, have a common "desire to heal the rift between words and things" and so recover "a primary 'this-ness,'" a direct apprehension of life.[146] *Birds, Beasts and Flowers* belongs to a tradition, both phenomenological and biocentric, that rejects mimesis in favor of the "celebration of unmediated experience."[147] This is the substance of "Snake": sloughing off its biblical connotations, Lawrence's snake, "earth-golden from the burning bowels of the earth," is an emissary from the realm of generation itself when it slips through the "fissure in the earth-wall" into the poet's garden (*P* 303).

There is, however, a fissure or "gap in connection" between word and thing in *Birds, Beasts and Flowers*, Amit Chaudhuri argues: Lawrence's snake "remains, to a large extent, textual and does not simply or unproblematically travel off the page towards life and the landscape."[148] As Marianne Moore put it, poetry can only "present // for inspection, 'imaginary gardens with real toads in them'" (or snakes, in Lawrence's case).[149] Although the snake comes into the poet's own garden (at the Villa Fontana Vecchia in Taormina), the poem can only present, or represent, the real in the environment of its own wordscape, or textual imaginary.

Lawrence concedes the point when he comments, in *Studies in Classic American Literature*, that "locality expresses itself perfectly, in its own flowers, its own birds and beasts" (178). Language, by comparison, is an imperfect medium, a proxy expression of the actuality to which it may aspire but can never attain. This makes the poet a "second-comer"—which is Lawrence's status in "Snake," when he waits his turn at the water-trough for his "guest" to finish drinking (*P* 303). A second comer, the poet is not the redeemer of a fallen world, but a pale imitation of the birds and beasts and flowers that, like the snake, are the authentic "lords / Of life" (*P* 305). Like Marianne Moore's *Observations* (1925), *Birds, Beasts and Flowers* is a bestiary, a book not a bioscape.

But, again like Moore, Lawrence still discovers, in poetry, "a place for the genuine," a verbal equivalent of Cézanne's visual aesthetic of *thereness*.[150] It is in its phenomenological poetics of place, or "global 'locality,'" that we discover *Birds, Beasts and Flowers*' closest affinity with American modernism.

3

Tales of Out Here

"St. Mawr," "The Princess," and "The Woman Who Rode Away"

Lawrence traveled to northern New Mexico in September 1922 at the invitation of Mabel Dodge Luhan. At first he considered working there with Jan Juta, who had provided the illustrations for *Sea and Sardinia*, on another "*amalgamate*" travel book (iv.138), before deciding to collaborate with Mabel herself on a work of fiction. Mabel envisaged that, as a writer-in-residence of kinds at her compound at Taos, Lawrence would produce "an American novel" that would transfigure "*my* experience, *my* material, *my* Taos . . . into a magnificent creation." Instead, she alleges, the book was "killed" in its infancy by a jealous Frieda Lawrence. Mabel, who "never even saw the chapter he did," speculates that Frieda "tore it up."[1] The seven-page manuscript did survive, and was published in 1971 as "The Wilful Woman."[2]

During his first period in New Mexico, initially as Mabel's guest in Taos and then some seventeen miles off in the foothills of the Rockies at the Del Monte Ranch, Lawrence wrote several articles, and he completed *Birds, Beasts and Flowers* and the revised version of *Studies in Classic American Literature*. But until he traveled to Mexico in March 1923 to begin work on *Quetzalcoatl*, the first version of *The Plumed Serpent* (the book Lawrence would later call his "real novel of America" (iv.457)), he produced no fiction other than the novel-fragment. Mabel, and the United States she embodied in which "[e]verything . . . goes by *will*," was to blame for the hiatus: "How can one write about it, save analytically," Lawrence complained (iv.310). In 1924, when he discovered that he could, after all, write fiction in and about the United States and New

Mexico, Lawrence drew upon the personality and experience of the woman who had stymied his earlier attempt to do so. Her biographer can with some justification argue that "Mabel's quest for spiritual and emotional redemption became the central theme of [Lawrence's] American fiction."[3] This chapter suggests that his New Mexico stories, "St. Mawr," "The Princess," and "The Woman Who Rode Away," may indeed be read as collaborations: between Lawrence and women—Catherine Carswell and Dorothy Brett, as well as Mabel—and between Lawrence and American literary genres and traditions.

Like Lawrence's later New Mexico fictions, "The Wilful Woman" is premised on a journey or a quest, that of "[a] woman travelling from New York to the South west, by one of the tourist trains" (*SM* 199). The opening sentence of the novel-fragment touches on the troubling proximity of tourism, colonialism, and pilgrimage in the Southwest, which is also Lawrence's subject in essays like "Indians and an Englishman" and "Just Back from the Snake-Dance—Tired Out." The wilful woman of the fragment, the Mabel-figure, is Sybil Mond; a worldly prophetess, as her name suggests, she is identified with the train in which she travels, "dangerous as the headlights of a great machine coming full at you in the night" (*SM* 199). Lawrence is reproducing here what Leo Marx would subsequently identify as the "metaphoric design which occurs everywhere in [American] literature from the 1840s on": the machine in the garden, the figure for the "contradiction between rural myth and technological fact" in which Marx locates "the root conflict" of American culture.[4]

Lawrence's portrait of Sybil Mond in "The Wilful Woman" is overdetermined: an emblem of industrial modernity, she is also a colonizer who achieves her own manifest "destiny" with her expedition into the "terra nova" of New Mexico (*SM* 203, 202). She is a force of nature, too, her "buffalo's force" connecting her to the Indian West, as well as a mythological figure, an American Isis who is searching for the lover she has "pitched . . . piecemeal away into the south-western desert" (*SM* 202, 201). Not long after they married in 1917, Mabel had dispatched her third husband, the artist Maurice Sterne, to the Southwest: writing to her from Santa Fe, Sterne told Mabel that he had found her "object in life": to "[s]ave the Indians, their art-culture—reveal it to the world!"[5] The proliferating representations of her in "The Wilful Woman" suggest that from the outset Mabel is straining the parameters of the novel Lawrence had begun to write around her, and with her. Although he would sketch scenarios for a further eleven chapters (charting Mabel's separation from Sterne, her attraction to Pueblo Indian culture, and her evolving relationship with Tony Lujan, the Taos Indian who would become her fourth and final husband), Lawrence's first attempt to write an American novel stalled with the "'train' episode" (iv.318). When he next attempted to write fiction in and about the U.S. Southwest, Lawrence would turn to the "fabulous-symbolic mode" of the tale instead.[6]

Lawrence's recourse to the "dehumanized" genres of romance and fable is often regarded as a symptom of the misanthropy inculcated in him during World War I. Chris Baldick, for instance, argues that his nightmarish experience of wartime England caused Lawrence to renege on "the commitment of the traditional novel to the sympathetic portrayal of human individuals within social relations."[7] But the rejection of social verisimilitude for the abstraction of romance also defines the American literary tradition, or at least the "classic" American canon as Lawrence conceived of it in the war years, when he was writing the first version of *Studies in Classic American Literature*.[8] The connection between Lawrence's American criticism and his creative practice in the United States is closer than his commentators have tended to appreciate, the three stories that make up his Southwestern trilogy all engaging with, and unsettling, American generic conventions. According to New Americanist Donald E. Pease, American romance and its related forms protect "the image repertoire productive of the US national community": the romance genre generates images that "interconnect an exceptional national subject (American Adam) with a representative national scene (Virgin Land) and an exemplary national motive (errand into the wilderness)."[9] Lawrence's borderlands stories not only decenter the national narrative but also expose the "resistant materialities" of race, class, and gender, those thorny realities that, Pease argues, the national narrative attempts to erase.[10] Lawrence's New Mexico tales, "St. Mawr," "The Princess," and "The Woman Who Rode Away," touch the three points of what Sylvia Rodriguez terms Taos's "triethnic triangle": the Anglo-American spiritual and material ambition to possess the land, and the colonization and dispossession of the Hispano-American and of the Indian.[11]

In February 1923, at the Del Monte Ranch, Lawrence had revised the proofs for a trio of tales published in London that March as *The Ladybird, The Fox, The Captain's Doll* and in New York the following month as *The Captain's Doll: Three Novelettes*. Con Coroneos and Trudi Tate have pointed out that these stories ("The Fox," "The Captain's Doll," and "The Ladybird") differ from the four other collections of his tales published in Lawrence's lifetime in that they were "designedly written" as a volume.[12] There is convincing internal evidence for this, too, the tripartite structure of the collection reflecting and reinforcing a dominant theme of the stories, that of the ménage à trois. Trinitarian configurations recur in Lawrence's fiction of the Americas and in his lived experience there (in *The Plumed Serpent*, Ramón, Cipriano, and Kate make up a threesome that displaces the Christian trinity and the conventional courtly love triangle alike). Although they would not be published as such, Lawrence thought of the three tales he composed in New Mexico in 1924 as "a book," too (v.136).[13] Each was a "story of out here," and together, Lawrence told his agent Curtis Brown, they would "make a vol. for America" (v.136; 270).

As Jahan Ramazani suggests, the work of migrant modernists like Lawrence cannot "be read as emblematic of single national cultures," and indeed, all three of his Southwestern stories germinated in Europe in the winter of 1923–24.[14] His patent unhappiness there—Lawrence likened himself in London to "a caged coyote" (iv.542)—revived his commitment both to the New World and to the mode of the tale: "I'm trying to amuse myself writing stories," he told Catherine Carswell (iv.564). The stories to which he refers are almost certainly the triplet comprising "Jimmy and the Desperate Woman," "The Border-Line," and "The Last Laugh": all were begun in February 1924 and would appear together in *The Woman Who Rode Away and Other Stories* (1928). As the editors of the Cambridge edition note, the three stories reflect Lawrence's "deep disillusionment with England and, on a more personal level, his complex relationship with [John Middleton] Murry," who is satirized in all three tales (xxv). Relations with Murry had been strained since 1916, when the Lawrences' attempt to live a communal life in Cornwall with Murry and Katherine Mansfield had ended in failure. Mansfield died in 1923, and in the same year Murry, who may also have had an affair at this time with Frieda Lawrence, became the lover of Dorothy Brett, the profoundly deaf English painter who would follow Lawrence back to New Mexico in 1924. Brett is the model for the female protagonist of "The Last Laugh" (Miss) "James," a Hampstead painter with bobbed hair who carries with her "a Marconi listening machine, for her deafness"; her companion, Marchbanks, is the Murry-figure in the tale (*WWRA* 123).

"The Last Laugh" belongs to what Patricia Merivale has identified as a "Pan cluster" in Lawrence's writings of the mid-1920s.[15] Lawrence gives himself a walk-on part at the beginning of the story as "Lorenzo," who, "grinning like a satyr," is by implication of the cohort of the great god Pan (*WWRA* 122). The "nymph-like" James is likewise a creature of Pan, welcoming the return of the god who transforms her fear of physical contact into a new "voluptuousness" (*WWRA* 125). Her sexual regeneration is part of a wider renovation of postwar London and, by extension, of the played-out Christian era. The Pan who was cast out at the dawn of that era now returns to wreak his revenge, unleashing the natural force of the wind that runs over the pipes of the organ in the Hampstead church "like pan-pipes" (*WWRA* 131). Pan's power proves fatal to the hypocritical Christian, Marchbanks, who with his "goat-like eyes" and "martyred expression" is "[a] sort of faun on the Cross, with all the malice of the complication" (*WWRA* 124, 123). Brett recognized something of that complication in Lawrence himself, it seems, since her account of their friendship repeatedly represents Lawrence both as a Christ-figure and as Pan, as "a God, the Lord of us all," and as "wicked and Pan-like"; indeed, an extraordinary double portrait she painted in Capri in 1926 depicts Lawrence in both roles at once.[16] Brett's memoir of him, which is written as a sustained address to Lawrence, describes the painting, which she named *The Man Who Died* after his story of that title:

> The picture is of a crucifixion. The pale yellow Christ hangs on the cross.... Before him, straddled across a rock, half curious, half smiling, is the figure of Pan, holding up a bunch of grapes to the dying Christ: a dark, reddish-gold figure with horns and hoofs. The head of Pan and of Christ are both your heads.[17]

Pan-power transfigures London in "The Last Laugh," yet the Lorenzo-figure in the story can only "ironically" celebrate the city as "'[a] new world!'": as in Arthur Machen's popular late Victorian tale "The Great God Pan," the megalopolis of London is not a propitious setting for the scene of pagan revival (*WWRA* 122). The stories Lawrence wrote on his return to the Southwestern United States involve a more radical transposition, in which the figure of Pan, and the mode of the tale, are translated into American terms.[18]

Lawrence left England in March 1924, relieved "to get away from the doom of Europe" (iv.600). On their return to New Mexico, Lawrence, Frieda, and Brett stayed for a short time with Mabel in Taos before relocating to the Kiowa Ranch on Lobo Peak. Lawrence set about renovating the cabins there, working alongside Indians from Taos Pueblo, among them Tony Lujan's nephew Trinidad Archuleta and his wife Rufina, and a Hispano-American carpenter, Pablo Quintano, known as Richard (see v.38). While the work on the ranch was still underway, Lawrence began to write "Pan in America," an essay that develops the premise of "The Last Laugh," that the pagan god who dies at the birth of Christianity "keeps on being re-born, in all kinds of strange shapes." Pan, who lurks in the "overgrown ridings of history," has an American propensity to recode history as nature and as myth. An "outlaw," Pan is identified with Lawrence himself, "the outlaw of modern

English literature" as Murry called him; Pan is also associated with Robin of Sherwood, the legendary outlaw of Lawrence's native Nottinghamshire and the descendant of the Green Man of English folklore, as well as with Robin Hood's American cousins, the desperados of the Wild West (*MM* 156, 155).[19] Pan has been travestied and emasculated in the Old World and its literature, even playing the part of Lucy Gray, the "sweet-and-pure" embodiment of Wordsworth's pantheism (*MM* 156).

Now, Pan has "crossed over to the young United States," Lawrence says, and it is in America, not in the Transcendentalists' pantheon but "among the Indians," that "the oldest Pan is still alive" (*MM* 157, 164). Lawrence identifies Pan with the aboriginal spirit of place he liked to attribute to the Kiowa Ranch itself, where the essay was written: in August 1924, he would change the name of the property from Lobo to Kiowa to acknowledge ancestral tribal ties to the land. The ponderosa pine tree growing beside Lawrence's cabin door there is "still within the allness of Pan," and the Pan-principle of "living relatedness" is celebrated by the local Pueblo Indians, who dance with "spruce twigs tied above their elbows" (*MM* 158, 159).

"Pan in America," which confects Pueblo Indian ritual with Frazer's account of Etrurian tree-worship, proposes a hybrid and transatlantic paganism for which, Lawrence was well aware, there was literary and historical precedent. In 1918, when he was working on *Studies in Classic American Literature*, Lawrence had consulted Nathaniel Hawthorne's *Twice-Told Tales* (1837), a collection of "good parables, and wonderful dark glimpses of early Puritan America," which includes "The Maypole of Merry Mount" (*SCAL* 98). Hawthorne's story evokes a paganism "rich with the old mirth of Merry England" that has been transplanted into "the wilder glee" of the Indian forest of New England. The "fauns and nymphs" of "ancient fable," along with assorted goat-men, green men, and Morris dancers, find refuge "in the fresh woods of the West" until they are routed by the Christian soldiers of Endicott's Puritan army.[20]

The historical source for Hawthorne's story is Thomas Morton's settlement at Merry Mount and Morton's own remarkable account of it in his *New English Canaan* (1637). Morton, long regarded as "a social, political and religious misfit in Puritan New England," had been recuperated in the more inclusive American historical scholarship of the 1920s: in 1924, for example, the year "Pan in America" was written, the *Proceedings of the Massachusetts Historical Society* published new material relating to "this most picturesque character in early New England history," including a description of the "seal affixed to his will," which bears the Morton device—a goat's head.[21] In the following year,

William Carlos Williams would devote a chapter to Morton and Merry Mount in his revisionist cultural history of the Americas, *In the American Grain*.

The Merry Mount community was an early and ill-fated American experiment in dissident utopianism that combined the revival of the May revels of old England with Native American rites. Richard Slotkin has argued that it was this commingling of English and Indian "blood myth and blood ritual" that fed Puritan fears "that the Indian would give strength to the pagan, the Dionysian elements in the English character and weaken or degenerate the power of order, authority, and Christianity."[22] The "quarrel" between these competing visions of the New World, Hawthorne writes, would determine the "future complexion of New England."[23] The felling of the phallic maypole (cut from the trunk of a pine tree) in Hawthorne's story is an assault on what Lawrence, in *Studies in Classic American Literature*, calls the Spirit of Place, and is an instance of the Puritan recoil from the sensuous properties of the New World environment. Nonetheless, in America, alone, Lawrence says, we may still "choose between the living universe of Pan, and the mechanical conquered universe of modern humanity" (*MM* 164).

Two Women and a Horse: "St. Mawr"

Making that choice is the subject of "St. Mawr," the "'novelette'" Lawrence had begun as he was completing "Pan in America" (v.91).[24] Both structurally and thematically "St. Mawr" is bilocated between the Old World and the New, between London and the Shropshire countryside where the story was conceived and its first stages are set, and the "little ranch under the Rocky Mountains" where it was written and its final episodes take place (*MM* 157). In early January 1924, Lawrence had traveled from London to Pontesbury in Shropshire, to visit the artist and mystic Frederick Carter: he had corresponded with Carter, with whom he shared an interest in the symbolism of the Book of Revelation, since 1922. It is Cartwright, the minor character in "St. Mawr" who is modeled on Carter, who confirms the story's American heroine's, Lou Carrington's, conviction that she can see Pan in her horse: the authentic Pan, he tells her, is the "God that is hidden in everything" (65). In the Roman period, the Pan the Arcadians had worshipped as a theriomorphic deity, half-man, half-goat, was translated into the universal principle of allness, or Cartwright's "everything." His own goat-like features—Cartwright has "the tilted eyebrows, the twinkling goaty look, and the pointed ears of a goat-Pan"—are proof that, in man, Pan is "over-visible: the old satyr: the fallen Pan" (*SM* 64, 65).[25]

Lou's husband, Henry (Rico) Carrington, epitomizes a lameness in the modern male that is made literal when he is thrown by her horse, St. Mawr, in the primordial landscape of the Shropshire Stiperstones. Rico's "eunuch" and "sterilising cruelty"—he determines to have the stallion gelded in revenge—is complemented by Flora Manby's "barren cruelty": Rico is a *castrato* Priapus and Flora a sterile version of the goddess of flowers and of fertility (*SM* 96). Unlike them, the horse, St. Mawr, has a "splendour that belonged to another world-age," a quality that cannot survive in our modern "eunuch civilisation" (*SM* 96). In a bid to *"preserve one last male thing,"* Lou takes the horse to America, where she puts St. Mawr to stud in Texas. Lou herself goes on to New Mexico in the company of her mother, Rachel Witt, and their part-Navajo servant, Phoenix (*SM* 97).

Lou "want[s] the wonder back again" (*SM* 62). Wonder, as Tony Tanner has defined it, is a quintessentially New World mode of apprehension, and in Lawrence's story it survives in the Old World only in the wonder horse, St. Mawr, and in "those places," like Shropshire and Cornwall, "where the spirit of aboriginal England still lingers" (73).[26] Elsewhere in the "hedged-and-fenced English landscape," Lou complains, "[e]verything enclosed, enclosed, to stifling" (*SM* 97). She eventually finds a place that is commensurate to her capacity for wonder in the wide open spaces of the American Southwest, which she surveys from the story's surrogate for the Kiowa Ranch:

> She felt a certain latent holiness in the very atmosphere, a young, spring-fire of latent holiness, such as she had never felt in Europe, or in the East. "For me," she said, as she looked away at the mountains in shadow and the pale-warm desert beneath, with wings of shadow upon it: "For me, this place is sacred. It is blessed." (*SM* 139–40)

Critics have often remarked on the duality of "St. Mawr"; James C. Cowan, for instance, argues that Lawrence deploys "dual methods, social satire and myth" in the story, to convey both "the moral waste land of contemporary life and a myth potent enough to transform it."[27] Yet the antinomies of "St. Mawr" are not wholly resolved by the recourse to myth in the long American coda that Lawrence added to the first, "English," version of the story. Rather, the tale, confounding Richard Chase's distinction between the British novel of manners and American Romance, keeps in play to the end the "double meaning" of its satirical and mythic methods, making the promise of regeneration in the wilderness more equivocal than it is in "Pan in America" (*SCAL* 12). Near the end of the story, Lou declares: "[a]nd I am here, right deep in America, where there's a wild spirit wants me, a wild spirit more than men." She has found her "mission" at the little ranch in the Rockies: "It saves me from cheapness," she tells her mother. But it is the mother, the aptly named Mrs. Witt, who has the last laugh, and the last word: her rejoinder, when Lou tells her that she has paid the princely sum of twelve hundred dollars for the dilapidated property, is "'[t]hen I call it cheap, considering all there is to it: even the name!'" (*SM* 155). The ranch in the story is called "Las Chivas," Spanish for female goats, the name signaling its former function as a goat farm. Lou's "dryad or faun look" connects her to Pan, but the place in which she pledges herself to his wild spirit may be too a tame a habitat, if a tempting one, for the great god, even in his randy and degenerate form as goat-god (*SM* 91).

In his astute review of the U.S. edition of *St. Mawr* (1925), Stuart Sherman insists that the "goat-ruined ranch in the mountains" makes it "obvious that this symbolical novel is intended to be mordantly satirical, as well." Likewise, Drew Milne finds that "St. Mawr"'s conclusion exposes "the illusions of narrative transcendence."[28] But how we interpret the ending of the tale is complicated by the interpolated history of the unnamed woman who lived at the ranch before Lou takes possession of it; her story, which halts the momentum of the quest-narrative, historicizes the "symbolical" quality of Lou's story.

To begin with, we are told, Lou's predecessor at the ranch had viewed her mountain environment as a "paradise on earth" (*SM* 150). To her, the ranch in the Rockies was a *locus amoenus* of the kind depicted in the American landscapes of Thomas Cole, the English-born artist who translated European philosophies of the sublime into American wilderness aesthetics. "Literary and artistic representations of natural sublimity came to be seen as an arm of American manifest destiny," Lawrence Buell observes; the New World sublime, that is, served as a psychological structure and sanction for domestic imperialism.[29] Like the pioneer women described by Annette Kolodny, who "claimed the frontiers as a potential sanctuary for an idealized domesticity," the woman in "St. Mawr" embodies the pastoral stage of the American historical process outlined in Frederick Jackson Turner's once-influential frontier thesis.[30] But "St. Mawr" involves a characteristically Lawrentian inversion of the providential narrative and of the Turner thesis, when the woman is driven out of the garden she has attempted to make out of the Southwestern wilderness by the pagan spirit of the place. The voice out of the ponderosa pine tree beside her cabin convinces here that "[t]here is no Almighty loving God. The God there is shaggy as the pine-trees" (*SM* 147). "It is almost arcadian,"

Lawrence wrote to Thomas Seltzer of the Kiowa Ranch. "But of course, the under-spirit in this country is never arcady" (v.46).

Jonathan Arac has argued that Lawrence's fiction calls for "a differentiated history of the sublime," rejecting as it does the onto-theological aesthetic of the Romantic sublime for the poetry of the immediate present.[31] In "St. Mawr," the sublime is imbricated with human history, as well as with the poetry of the present: the continental narrative of westward development may have been brought up short by the wild spirit of place, yet the derelict ranch—even the name, as Mrs. Witt says—bears witness nonetheless to the pathos of the all-too-human effort to tame the wilderness.

In his chapter on "Fenimore Cooper's Leatherstocking Novels" in *Studies in Classic American Literature*, Lawrence remarks that *The Last of the Mohicans* is "divided between real historical narrative and true 'romance.' For myself," he continues, "I prefer the romance. It has a myth-meaning, whereas the narrative is chiefly record" (61). The historical record of the Kiowa Ranch evidently interested him more than Cooper's novel's account of the Seven Years' War of 1757, since Lawrence would give a vivid summary of the history of the place, first settled in the 1800s under the provisions of the U.S. Homestead Act, in a letter to his niece:

> Forty years ago a man came out looking for gold, and squatted here. There was some gold in the mountains. Then he got poor, and a man called McClure had the place. He had 500 white goats here, raised alfalfa, and let his goats feed wild in the mountains. But the water supply is too bad, and we are too far from anywhere. So he gave up. (v.110–11)

In 1925, Lawrence would attempt to irrigate Kiowa from the Gallina cañon, some two miles off: "I go about with a hoe, irrigating—and for the time being am rancherito y nada mas" (v.254). At Kiowa, Lawrence experienced at firsthand something of "the business of ranching" (*RDP* 354), and he would assess the broader historical implications of that experience in 1929, in the introduction he wrote for Edward Dahlberg's novel, *Bottom Dogs*:

> It is not till you live in America, and go a little under the surface, that you begin to see how terrible and brutal is the mass of failure that nourishes the roots of the gigantic tree of dollars. And this is especially so in the country, and in the newer parts of the land, particularly out west. There you see how many small ranches have gone broke in despair, before the big ranches scoop them up and profit by all the back-breaking, profitless, grim labour of the pioneer. (*IR* 119)

Lawrence calls for the publication of "pioneer records and novels, the genuine unsweetened stuff" that is testimony to the "sheer brutality of the fight with that American wilderness" (*IR* 120, 119). In the light of this, Walter Benn Michaels's statement that the Southwestern location of "St. Mawr" "has nothing to do with American national or cultural identity" is unconvincing.[32] It is rather the case, as Tom Lynch suggests of Southwestern writing, that "[t]he stories we tell about ourselves and the land we inhabit influence how we think of and treat that land, simultaneously determining and revealing the degree to which we feel estranged or at home there."[33]

Like Lawrence's other tales of out here, "St. Mawr" is an American and New Mexican story in its mode, as much as in its setting and subject matter: the story gives an American signature to "the archetypal myth of the spiritual journey" that Keith Sagar identifies in it. Sagar likens Lou's horse to Bunyan's Evangelist, leading the pilgrim away from the City of Destruction, but what this leaves out is the story's relationship with hybrid, New World versions of quest romance. "St. Mawr" is, as Lawrence liked to call it, a "horse story" (v.133) and as such it has affinities with the Western; "St. Mawr" is surely a precursor for Cormac McCarthy's *Border Trilogy*, in which the horse is again the avatar of chthonic powers.

According to Leslie Fiedler, in the Western, and in the American pastoral tradition it typifies, the protagonist's journey into the wilderness is paradigmatic of the flight from the oppressions of the Old World to the spatial and spiritual potentialities of the New. In keeping with "classic," American-authored versions of wilderness romance, Lawrence's story renounces a social structure denominated as domestic and Christian in favor of a primal, pagan, and interracial space. But if "St. Mawr" confirms the generic conventions, it also confounds them: Lou's gender differentiates her quest from that of Cooper's Natty Bumppo, or Melville's Ishmael, or Twain's Huck Finn. Lou is looking, too, for a "far-away wild place" in which she might "make a good life" not only with her part-Navajo sidekick Phoenix but with her mother as well, the down-to-earth Demeter to Lou's more mystical Persephone in the story (*SM* 122). It may be the case, as Charles F. Lummis proposes in *The Land of Poco Tiempo*, that the "horse-loving" Navajo people were "inventors of the mother-in-law joke gray centuries before the civilized world awoke to it," but in "St. Mawr," the joke is on Phoenix. The mother-daughter dyad is the primary relationship in Lawrence's New Mexican reworking of the Persephone myth.

Carol Siegel suggests that "St. Mawr"—the novelette Lawrence had considered calling "Two Ladies and a Horse" (v.136)—should be read as a "radical and visionary feminist" document, a celebration of "the modern feminist dream of women's community."[34] "St. Mawr" does reconfigure the gendered and the generic conventions of American quest romance in suggestive ways. If the mother and daughter who search for "somewhere where we can be by ourselves" do not quite anticipate Siegel's feminist separatism, they do contest the male prerogative of American "bromance," giving a twist to the homosocial bent of American fiction first diagnosed in *Studies in Classic American Literature* (SM 133). New Americanists and eco-critics alike hold *Studies* responsible for the now discredited theory of American pastoral, propagated by Fiedler, according to which "wilderness in American writing serves as a liminal site for male self-fulfillment in recoil from adult responsibility associated with female-dominated culture in the settlements." Taking issue with Lawrence's and Fiedler's chauvinism, Lawrence Buell interprets the transmutation of wilderness into garden in female-authored frontier narratives as a gynocentric countertradition to the masculine version of wilderness romance.[35] The wilderness wins out over the garden in "St. Mawr," thus reversing the trajectory of "the morality play of westward expansion" in which "wilderness was the villain."[36] Yet, in his story, Lawrence feminizes the wilderness myth itself, much as Willa Cather does in her Southwestern fictions: in the New Mexico interlude in *The Professor's House* (1925) for instance, and in the Walnut Canyon episodes of *The Song of the Lark* (1915), a copy of which Cather sent to Lawrence shortly after she visited him at the Kiowa Ranch in the summer of 1925.

A feminist recuperation of "St. Mawr" has to contend, nonetheless, with Lou's abject self-fashioning as a "Vestal Virgin" attendant on a male spirit of place (138). As for the women's community Siegel locates in the story, Lawrence lampooned the New Mexico feminism of the day in *Altitude*, the unfinished Taos comedy he had started to sketch out in June 1924, when he was writing the first version of "St. Mawr." Here, Mary Austin, a vigorous proponent of the Mother-rule she attributed to Pueblo Indian culture, is pilloried for her belief in the coming of a female messiah who, it is intimated, may well be Austin herself. In *Altitude*, the New Mexico sublime is wholly synonymous with the ridiculous: Lawrence's playlet is a skit on the arty New Mexico hyped up by its Anglo doyennes, Austin and Mabel Dodge Luhan, for what the latter described as the "miraculous acceleration of awareness that climates and altitudes can accomplish in mortals."[37]

Lawrence abandoned *Altitude* after the first act, which was published posthumously in 1938 in the little magazine *Laughing Horse* (the editor, Spud Johnson, is among the play's dramatis personae). "St. Mawr," although it did not appear there, is the offspring of *Laughing Horse* and its agenda of "polemics, philippics, satire, burlesque."[38] Under Johnson's editorship, the magazine had transformed from its Californian beginnings "into a journal of, by and for New Mexicans." Its title, Johnson was pleased to discover, had a Southwestern resonance in a Navajo legend about "a turquoise horse on which the Sun-God travels . . . the Indians say, 'making the sun-noise,' which is a joyous neigh. For this beast, also, is a laughing horse."[39] Johnson's account of the Navajo myth appeared in the ninth, "Southwest Number" of the magazine, which Lawrence read in London early in January 1924. His response was printed in the next issue as "Dear Old Horse: A London Letter."

The London from which Lawrence is writing in the Letter resembles the cityscape of "The Last Laugh": there is "a bit of snow-brightness in the air," but Lawrence warns the "Dear old Horse" that it could "never be azure or turquoise here in London." "[L]et me get on your back," Lawrence pleads, "and ride away again to New Mexico" (*MM* 137). The "Pale Galilean . . . has triumphed over here," and "Great Pan is dead," but in the American Southwest "[i]t's a turquoise centaur who laughs, who laughs longest and who laughs last" (*MM* 138).[40] Like his American Pan, Lawrence's laughing horse recuperates the ribald energies of an older Europe, as Morton's May revels at Merry or Mare Mount had attempted to do.[41] The choice of America over England in "St. Mawr" and the "sardonic comedy" that F. R. Leavis finds in the story, are both prefigured in the "London Letter," in which Lawrence responds to biblical and Jungian horse symbolism alike with "a laugh, a loud, sensible Horse Laugh" (*MM* 139).[42] "St. Mawr" is a transatlantic confabulation of the English comedy of manners and that subspecies of the Western, the horse-opera. Transatlantic in its generic properties as well as in its theme, Lawrence's horse story is, as Stuart Sherman recognized, "a piece of symbolism" in the tradition of American Romance, symbolism spliced with English satire.[43] "St. Mawr" thus comports with Alastair Fowler's definition of the generic hybrid, in which "two or more complete repertoires are present in such proportions that no one of them dominates."[44] Riding roughshod over conventional distinctions between *stilus sublimus* (the "high" style of tragedy) and *stilus humilis* (the "low" style of comedy), "St. Mawr" is "comic opera played with solemn intensity," a mélange in the New Mexican mode Lawrence identified in his essay "Indians and an Englishman"(*MM* 113).

Between the Real World and Fairy-Land: "The Princess"

Like "St. Mawr," "The Princess" adopts and adapts American generic conventions, although to different ends. Hawthorne's 1844 tale "Rappaccini's Daughter" is the principal American intertext for Lawrence's story's exploration of what may be an incestuous father-daughter relationship. The supposedly royal blood that Dollie and Colin Urquhart share is a "secret" which renders her incapable "of intimacy with any other [man] than her father" (*SM* 161). Like Hawthorne's Beatrice, Dollie has been raised in a toxic "virgin zone," "in a sort of hot-house, in the aura of her father's madness" (*SM* 165).[45] Sharnaz Mollinger, who compares Lawrence with Hawthorne, finds that both "describe experience in terms of antitheses, of irreconcilable opposites that nevertheless must somehow be reconciled or transcended."[46] Mollinger is drawing here, of course, on Hawthorne's famous definition of American romance as "a neutral territory" between "the real world and fairy-land" in which "the Actual and the Imaginary may meet, and each imbue itself with the nature of the other."[47] It is from Hawthorne, too, that Richard Chase extrapolated his midcentury paradigm of American romance as an interstitial or "border" genre.[48] "The Princess," like the America evoked in *Birds, Beasts and Flowers*' "The Evening Land," has something of Hawthorne's "New England uncanniness," but the story has what the poem calls a "western brutal faery quality," too, which makes it "border" writing in a different sense from Chase's (*P* 243). In this tale of the Southwestern borderlands, the real world is not reconciled with fairy-land, but displaces it. From the first sentence of the story, the imaginary is undone by the actual: "To her father, she was The Princess. To her Boston aunts and uncles she was just *Dollie Urquhart, poor little thing*" (*SM* 159).

Written after "St. Mawr," in September and October of 1924, "The Princess" has been defined as "its shadow or negative."[49] Lou Carrington's pledge to "stay virgin" is a matter of choice, but the princess's, Dollie Urquhart's, wish "to keep herself intact, intact, untouched" is a neurosis (*SM* 139, 188). Like "St. Mawr," and like the princess herself, who is the child of a Scottish father and American mother, Lawrence's tale has both European and New World belongings. The basic storyline was suggested to Lawrence by Catherine Carswell, and he hoped that together they would develop her idea into a coauthored novel. Carswell recalls that

> [t]he theme had been suggested to me by reading of some savages who took a baby girl, and that they might rear her as a goddess for

themselves, brought her up on a covered river boat, tending her in all respects, but never letting her mix with her kind and leading her to believe that she was herself no mortal, but a goddess.

Lawrence's suggestion, like his advice to H.D. that she should stick to the woman speaking, was that Carswell should "get the woman character going" while he would "fill in the man."⁵⁰ In the event, when he wrote "The Princess," Lawrence supplemented Carswell's scenario (which he adapted for "The Woman Who Rode Away," too) with the Sleeping Beauty motif, derived from German fairy tale, which recurs in his fiction from *Sons and Lovers* through *Lady Chatterley's Lover*. The version of Sleeping Beauty in "The Princess" resembles early European renditions, in which the virginal princess is raped rather than kissed by her suitor.

"The Princess," like postcolonial American stories (Washington Irving's "Rip Van Winkle," for instance), grafts European folk and fairy tale onto an American theme and location. Dollie Urquhart, like Lou Carrington, is a transatlantic Persephone, with the difference that for Dollie, the New World and not England is her netherworld. Under the terms of her maternal grandfather's will, Dollie must live or, as she sees it, "be imprisoned" for six months of each year in the United States (*SM* 163). She is held captive there, in the mountains of northern New Mexico, by Domingo Romero, who, although he gives her the feeling that "death was not far from him," is more Pan than he is Hispano Hades. As such, and although he is an unlikely Romeo, Romero provides a male counterpart to Dollie's Persephone (*SM* 170); like Persephone who is dead to the earth in the winter, Pan revives when almond blossom appears on the boughs (as he does in Lawrence's story "The Last Laugh"). Fall is approaching, however, when Romero is shot and killed by the rangers who are searching for Dollie. After his death, the princess retreats to the East, where, we are told, "she married an elderly man," a father-substitute (*SM* 196). In the modern era, we are left to conclude, the Persephone-story, like the Pan myth, has lost its potency.

Leavis remarked that "St. Mawr" "has the Waste Land for theme": so too does "The Princess."⁵¹ But in "The Princess," the mythic method itself is subjected to the critique that myth makes of contemporary reality in Eliot's poem. Dollie Urquhart, we learn, has been raised by a father whose voice "came direct out of the hushed Ossianic past" (*SM* 159). The allusion here is to the contested authenticity of Scottish poet James Macpherson's late eighteenth-century "translations" of the ancient Celtic poems of Ossian. Kate, in

The Plumed Serpent, is an "Ossianic goddess" (60), but in "The Princess," the implication is that there may well be fakery, as well as self-delusion, in Colin Urquhart's claim that his child is of fairy stock, "the last of the royal race of the old people" (*SM* 161). In the American Southwest, Dollie imagines herself a fairy queen in her bower of bliss; what she finds there, however, is not the New Mexico that, since the 1890s, has been advertised as the "land of enchantment," but a "savage, heartless wildness" (*SM* 191). In an essay written a month before the story, "Just Back from the Snake Dance—Tired Out," Lawrence had demythologized the much-vaunted "Enchantment" of New Mexico and the hawking of Native American culture recycled as cheap entertainment for Anglo audiences: being at the Hopi Snake Dance, Lawrence wrote, was like "being right inside the circus-ring!" (*MM* 187). As Lynch has pointed out, tourism put pressures on "the Hispano agropastoral acequia culture of the region" as well.[52] "The Princess," the final scenes of which are set in the area known as the Enchanted Circle to the north of Taos, explores the correlation between enchantment and exploitation that is the subject of William DeBuys's fine study of the natural and human histories of the Sangre de Cristo Mountains region.

The northern New Mexico in which Dollie and Romero meet is an intercultural contact zone, a space in which interpersonal relations are premised on "conditions of coercion, radical inequality, and intractable conflict."[53] Romero's name is a local one. At the same time, his name (*domingo*: lord or master; *romero*: a pilgrim, one who visits a shrine) indicates that he, like Dollie, is of noble and perhaps even otherworldly descent—certainly, he is of the older, *nuevomexicano*, stock among the Hispanic residents of the region. There is an immediate "inter-recognition between them" (*SM* 170): "instantly she knew that he was a gentleman, that his 'demon,' as her father would have said, was a fine demon" (*SM* 169). Like Dollie again, although with different consequences, Romero is the last of his line: the "coming of the white man ... had finished the Romero family. The last descendants were just Mexican peasants" (*SM* 167). Romero is now employed as a guide at the New Mexico dude ranch where Dollie is staying as a paying guest.

The Rancho del Cerro Gordo is named after a battle in the Mexican-American War that proved a turning point in that conflict; in 1848, a year after this Thermopylae of the West, Mexico ceded vast tracts of land to the United States, including the territory of New Mexico, under the terms of the Treaty of Guadalupe Hidalgo. The Rancho, then, is metonymic of borderlands history and of the ongoing experience of the colonization and dispossession of the Mexicans who were the antecedent residents of a region that Rodolfo Acuna has defined as "Occupied America."[54]

Like the Kiowa Ranch essay "Reflections on the Death of a Porcupine," "The Princess" is evidence of Lawrence's growing acculturation, as a ranchero himself, to the precarious agrarian economy of the Sangre de Cristo region. The Hispanos of northern New Mexico were "a pastoral people," DeBuys observes, and were "among the poorest people in the world."[55] *Birds, Beasts and Flowers'* "Mountain Lion," which was written at the Del Monte Ranch in January 1923, is a lament for the "long slim cat, yellow like a lioness," trapped by local Lobo Valley *hispanoamericanos*. "I think in this empty world there was room for me and a mountain lion," Lawrence says; by killing the cougar, the hunters—"Mexicans, strangers"—have acted "foolishly" (*P* 351–52). His creaturely poetics, his closer identification with the mountain lion than with its human hunters, suggests that it is Lawrence who is the stranger in the scene—an "Anglo *estranjero*," as borderlands theorist Genaro Padilla describes him.[56] Indeed, Lawrence's poem may be read as an example of what Luc Ferry calls "Nazi Ecology."[57]

His New Mexico stories indicate Lawrence's greater understanding that the region in which he lived and wrote was a human environment, too, and, as DeBuys defines it, "an often tense cultural frontier."[58] When Dollie Urquhart makes up her mind to "go west, westwards" to the dude ranch, she is taking the tourist trail that retraces "the March of Empire." At the end of the story, when she retreats to the East, she follows the crowd of wealthy Eastern urbanites for whom the Southwest had, by the 1920s, become what Lawrence calls "a fine national playground" (*SM* 166; *MM* 187). Romero, we are told,

> had sold the ranch itself to the Wilkiesons, ten years before, for two thousand dollars. He had gone away: then reappeared at the old place. For he was the son of the old Romeros, the last of the Spanish family that had owned miles of land around San Cristobel. (*SM* 167)

The old Romero place has been converted into "a ranch for the rich," and Romero, who is now "working for white people," is dependent on the tourist economy for his living (*SM* 166, 167). Lawrence's Romero has fared less well than his namesake, the Margarito Romero discussed by DeBuys, who built his own dude ranch on land he owned in the foothills of the Organ Mountains, near Las Cruces.[59]

Lawrence's story reflects the dude ranch phenomenon in the American West and Southwest that peaked in the mid-1920s, when the Dude Ranch Association was formed: the fad was featured in newspapers and journals from the *New York Times* and the *Saturday Evening Post* to the *New Republic* and the *Ladies' Home Journal*.⁶⁰ The location of the Rancho del Cerro Gordo, which "lay by a stream on the desert some four miles from the foot of the mountains, a mile away from the Indian pueblo," indicates that it is modeled on Mabel Dodge Luhan's Taos estate (*SM* 166). In fact, later in the 1920s, Mabel would consider converting her hacienda into a dude ranch of the kind described in the story; she envisaged running the enterprise in partnership with Erna Fergusson, a Southwestern author and entrepreneur with hands-on experience of the local tourist trade. Lawrence wrote to Brett of his "horror" when he heard of the plan, although he did think that Mabel would suit the part of "Dude Rancheress" (vii.263).

Frederic Jameson has argued that the "situational consciousness" of a text is intrinsic to its meaning. Read in the borderlands context in and at least partly about which it was written, "The Princess" yields a politics of location that reinflects, if it cannot wholly redeem, the troubling sexual politics of the story.⁶¹ Romero's violation of Dollie following a single night of consensual sex is rape, and in that respect Lawrence's story feeds "the ever-present fear of the Mexican who did not know his place, and might become sexually aggressive toward white women."⁶² The story makes it clear, however, that Romero's determination to "conquer" the dudess-princess is a bid to regain his lost patrimony (*SM* 192). The cabin in the heart of the Rockies that is the scene of sex and rape and death in "The Princess" is the site of a miner's placer claim, bought by Romero's father, who failed to strike gold there. His actions are thus an extreme manifestation of the *machismo* that Chicana poet and theorist Gloria Anzaldúa diagnoses as "an adaptation to oppression and poverty and low self-esteem" on the part of the Chicano. According to Anzaldúa, the "loss of a sense of dignity and respect in the macho breeds a false machismo which leads him to put down women and even to brutalize them."⁶³

Anne McClintock, in her discussion of imperial uses of the female body as a boundary-marker, notes that

> If, at first glance, the feminizing of the land appears to be no more than a familiar symptom of male megalomania, it also betrays acute paranoia and a profound, if not pathological, sense of male anxiety and boundary loss.⁶⁴

Romero, of course, is himself the victim of U.S.-American imperialism, and he abuses Dollie in order to reassert his lost *derecho de pernada* or right of possession to the land. "The Princess" thus reverses the relationship between gender and geography in "St. Mawr," which also evokes a sexualized landscape but inverts the familiar trope of the American West as virgin land, ripe for penetration. Place, in "St. Mawr," is male, like the ithyphallic pine tree that is the guardian of the spirit of place in that story. In "The Princess," more predictably, Dollie is the lay of the land, like the frontier women who were prone "to sexual risk, to themselves being the territory that is explored and conquered by others."[65] But "The Princess" is also an exploration of what Rosa Linda Fregoso defines as the "gendered territoriality" of Hispano culture in the U.S. borderlands.[66] In Lawrence's story, the virgin land of American myth is an environment that bears the scars of Mexican-American experience and history, the borderlands an open wound, *"una herida abierta,"* in Anzaldúa's words, "where the Third World grates against the first and bleeds."[67]

The Victim and the Sacrificial Knife: "The Woman Who Rode Away"

"The Woman Who Rode Away" was written in the summer of 1924, when Lawrence was still working on "St. Mawr." If "St. Mawr" is, as Siegel suggests, a feminist document, "The Woman Who Rode Away," in Kate Millett's judgment, is Lawrence's "most impassioned statement of the doctrine of male supremacy."[68] Attempts to rehabilitate "The Woman Who Rode Away," however persuasive, have proved less effective than the devastating demolition job Millett performed on it in 1970, in her groundbreaking *Sexual Politics*. The story of an unnamed white "Woman" held captive by the male members of an Indian tribe and brought before the "phallic priest" who is "to plunge the phallic knife—penetrating the female victim and cutting out her heart" in the ultimate "death fuck"—Lawrence's tale could have been written to order for the gendered analysis to which Millett so wittily treats it.[69] Millett even preempts postcolonial attempts to recover and recode the story. Mark Kinkead-Weekes, for instance, argues that "The Woman Who Rode Away" should be read as a critique, not of female agency, but of U.S.-American neoimperialism. But according to Millett, the tale's putative anticolonialism is a blind for its author's sexual sadism, and the Indian a patsy, a proxy through whom Lawrence gives the wilful New Woman what she deserves:

> [t]he idea of leaving the emancipated woman to the "savage" to kill, delegating the butchery as it were, is really an inspiration; sexism can appear thereby to be liberal and anti-colonialist.

To prove her point, Millett remarks on the "inanities" of the story's "pseudo-Indian legend."[70]

But in "The Woman Who Rode Away" it is the Indians themselves who are "pseudo," not the sun legend in which they place their faith: as Neil Roberts argues, Lawrence's "account of the Chilchui world-view is plausible," if also "highly gendered."⁷¹ Like the Natcha-Kee-Tawara troupe in his 1920 novel *The Lost Girl*, the Chilchui tribe is an invention, although Lawrence had seen Huichole Indians—the probable source of his fictional Chilchuis—when he was traveling with Kai Götzsche in northern Mexico the winter before he wrote "The Woman Who Rode Away."⁷² The opening scenes of "The Woman Who Rode Away" are set in Mexico, in the Sierra Madre Occidental, but thereafter, as Mabel Dodge Luhan was quick to recognize, the story takes place in a thinly disguised "Mexican" version of Taos country.⁷³ "The Woman Who Rode Away," then, is a tale of out here, as much a New Mexico story as "St. Mawr" and "The Princess." The scene of the story's climax is the cave at Arroyo Seco, which was a landmark site on the informal tours of Taos and its environs to which Mabel treated her visitors; Lawrence went there with her in May 1924. Moreover, the story's scenario—minus the sacrifice—anticipates commercial tourist ventures like Indian Detours, which organized excursions into Indian country. The brainchild of Mabel's friend and prospective dude ranch partner, Erna Fergusson, Indian Detours would be introduced by the Santa Fe Railway, in association with the Fred Harvey Company, in May 1926. Advertisements for these tours off the beaten tourist track, placed in *Laughing Horse* and other local publications, enticed the visitor with "the lure of the real Southwest beyond the pinched horizons of your train window."⁷⁴ Lawrence's Woman makes her journey in order "to see" "wild Indians"; if she is the object of the male Indians' gaze, as Millett says, the Woman is herself implicated in a racialized erotics of spectatorship, as she sets off on what Roberts describes as her "journey of dangerous desire" (*WWRA* 45).⁷⁵ Lawrence's story is a satire on, not an instance of, the appropriation of the American Indian as a "'savage' stunt" for an Anglo audience (*SCAL* 41).

The relationship between its sexual politics and what Millett deems the faux anticolonialism of Lawrence's story is further complicated by the generic belongings of "The Woman Who Rode Away." Susan Howe notes in *The Birthmark*, her revisionary study of the uses of wilderness in American literary history, that the Indian captivity narrative is "the only literary-mythological form indigenous to North America."⁷⁶ The original New World captivity narrative, *The Captivity and Restoration of Mrs. Mary Rowlandson*, was printed in 1682 and recounts Rowlandson's experiences during the eleven weeks and five days she spent among the Narragansetts. Rowlandson's narrative, Kolodny explains, had profound symbolic significance "for a Puritan community that already tended to view itself as a suffering and embattled Old Testament Israel surrounded by enemies."[77] Nonetheless, Howe identifies a Lawrentian double meaning in Rowlandson's account of her captivity, an oscillation between the "RHYTHM OF THE OLD WORLD" (the piety the Puritan colonists brought across the Atlantic with them) and the "RHYTHM OF THE NEW" (the "mess of wheat" Rowlandson shares as a supper with Native Americans). "The trick of her text is its mix," Howe suggests.[78]

From its inception in Rowlandson's text, the Indian captivity narrative was a frontier genre, and one which, as the frontier moved westward and America exchanged its colonial status for nationhood, was subject to "generic alteration."[79] "The Woman Who Rode Away" samples, and unsettles, the conventions of the captivity narrative: the Woman leaves her home and her children to journey into the Indian wilderness, not through forced removal, but of her own volition. She actively seeks out "the God of the Chilchui," rather than seeking solace in her Christian faith, as Rowlandson had done (*WWRA* 51). The Woman's subsequent bondage, the story implies, is preferable to the "slavery" of her domestic life and marriage—her captivity with the Chilchui gives her a narcotic "release" (*WWRA* 40, 62). Where Rowlandson's tribulations are, at least ostensibly, providential, and her physical restoration a vindication of the spiritual mission of the New England colonies, Lawrence's woman must die in order to revivify a pagan cosmology.

According to Sheila Contreras, stories such as "The Woman Who Rode Away" are misinterpreted when "removed from their specific and historical and cultural contexts." It may indeed be the case, as Contreras concedes, that the story "enacts an all-too-familiar conjoining of racist and sexist assumptions," but it does so, nonetheless, "within an anti-Western, anti-imperialist framework that recognizes a history of expropriation and disenfranchisement of native peoples of the Americas."[80] As Paul Giles notes, Lawrence, in *Studies in Classic American Literature*, was attracted to "the ways in which symbolic forms fail entirely to coincide with their social settings."[81] Lawrence's own American fictions explore the slippage between American romance and American reality, and between genre and gender, and genre and ethnicity. "The Woman Who Rode Away," like Lawrence's other "tales of out here," tampers with the symbolic and ideological premises of national narrativity.

CONCLUSION

Wilful Women

Lawrence's Three Fates and Georgia O'Keeffe

Mabel Dodge Luhan, who read "The Woman Who Rode Away" in typescript in the summer of 1924, would subsequently refer to it as the story in which "Lawrence thought he finished me up."[1] Fiction may well have given Lawrence a vicarious means to satisfy his alleged desire to do away with Mabel, but the transactions between life and art in Lawrence's writing involve more than merely the transposition of the one into the other.

That Mabel read "The Woman Who Rode Away" as a revenge fantasy is understandable; that her defenders have done so is reductive, at best. If Mabel was indeed the woman who rode away, she would also live to ride another day—with a leg-up from Lawrence, to boot, who sent her a letter the October after he completed "The Woman Who Rode Away," encouraging Mabel to write her own life-story: "If you want to write your apologia pro vita sua—do it as honestly as you can—and if it's got the right thing in it, I can help you with it once it's done." Mabel didn't have the "restraint" required for "creative writing," Lawrence told her, but he thought that she might "make a document" (v.150–1). In 1926, Lawrence would write to Mabel from Italy to tell her that the document she had made constituted "the most serious 'confession' that ever came out of America, and perhaps the most heart-destroying revelation of the American life-process that ever has or ever will be produced. It's worse than *Oedipus* and *Medea*, and *Hamlet* and *Lear* and *Macbeth* are spinach and eggs in comparison" (v. 423). He is referring to the work that would be published in four volumes in the 1930s: *Background* (1933), *European Ex-*

periences (1935), *Movers and Shakers* (1936), and *Edge of Taos Desert* (1937). Despite Lawrence's warning, Mabel also wrote fiction: *Winter in Taos* (1935), in Margery Toomer's judgment, is the novel Mabel had wanted Lawrence to create out of "*my* experience, *my* material, *my* Taos."[2] *Winter in Taos* is a rejoinder both to Lawrence and to Oliver La Farge, whose short story "Hard Winter" (1933) is a distinctly unsympathetic portrayal of Mabel's relationship with Tony Lujan. In Mabel's treatment of it, her liaison with Tony amounts to much more than an Indian summer (with a hard winter to follow); in her novel, their union evolves in harmony with the seasonal cycle and the planting and harvesting of the land.[3]

Edge of Taos Desert, the final instalment of Mabel Dodge Luhan's memoir, covers the same ground as *Winter in Taos*, but here Mabel engages the conventions, not of the shepherd's calendar, but of the Indian captivity narrative. Her biographer, Lois Palken Rudnick, observes that the Anglo heroine (who is Mabel herself, of course) "does not symbolize *Judea capta* in the hands of the Indian antichrist," but reveals instead that the "light of true faith lies in the hands of the Pueblo Indians and is brought to the Anglo world by one of its own who has been captured and redeemed *within* the Indian world."[4] Rudnick's otherwise astute appraisal of the volume's genre politics perhaps overlooks what may have been Mabel's more specific design in *Edge of Taos Desert*: to refute the murderous uses to which Lawrence had put her in his foray into the captivity narrative genre in "The Woman Who Rode Away." Mabel redeems herself, in her book, from the abuses she endures as Lawrence's Woman; her journey into the Southwestern wilderness is not a fool's errand, according to Mabel, nor is the allure of the Land of Enchantment a fatal attraction. Unlike Lawrence's Woman, who must be put under the knife in a desperate bid to rejuvenate the Indians' failing fertility gods, Mabel affirms that she has found an abundant "new life" among the Pueblo Indian people of Taos.[5]

Lorenzo in Taos, Mabel's memoir of Lawrence, had appeared in 1933 and is addressed to the poet Robinson Jeffers, who had taken Lawrence's place in Mabeltown. Luhan's book is one of a spate of biographies—both hatchet-jobs and hagiographies—commissioned during the publishers' feeding frenzy that followed Lawrence's death in 1930. In T. S. Eliot's famous assessment of John Middleton Murry's *Son of Woman: The Story of D. H. Lawrence* (1931), "[t]he victim and the sacrificial knife are perfectly adapted to each other"—it was payback time for Murry, who, as Sydney Janet Kaplan notes, was "three times killed by Lawrence in imagination."[6] In comparison, Mabel got off lightly as the woman who rode away (although Rudnick points out that "she has been imagined dead in a greater variety of ways than any other woman in American literary history").[7] Like Murry's book, Mabel's exacts its revenge on the Lorenzo she had "called" from Italy to Taos, but who "did not do what I called him to do" once he got there. Twisting the knife, Mabel tells Jeffers that "you are the one who will, after all, do what I wanted him to do: give a voice to this speechless land."

In *Lorenzo in Taos*, Mabel styles herself very much as Lawrence saw her, as the epitome of the "will-of-the-American-woman." If she is a wilful woman, she is also a willing one, abject even in her readiness "to be put to his purpose."[8] In her book, Lorenzo—whose red beard shines in the sun "like the burning bush," and who is likened to John the Baptist when he bathes naked at the Manby Hot Springs—is the Author-God, and Mabel his handmaiden:

> To make the little dynamo inside begin to hum and discharge sparks, I had to have the living hand of the creator transmit to me its compelling authority. The hand of God, I suppose![9]

Mabel, as Rudnick so acutely describes her, was unable to reconcile the gendered empowerment of the New Woman with her belief in female subservience to male genius, a belief Lawrence confirmed in his prouncement that "Woman cannot take the creative lead, she can only give the creative radiation" (*SCAL* 248).[10]

Mabel appears in both aspects in "Ballad of a Bad Girl," a poem she had written to placate Lawrence on his return to New Mexico from Europe in the spring of 1924; the previous November he had written from Guadalajara to warn her that "[o]ne day I will come to you and take your submission" (iv.528). In the ballad, Mabel duly submits to his higher power: when she attempts to scale his creative heights, the bad girl is put down by "a very, very angry man / With blue, blue eyes and a red, red crest." A squib, although a disturbing one, "Ballad of a Bad Girl" encapsulates the testy exchanges that characterized the Lawrence-Luhan relationship, both on paper and in person. The poem, which is a riff on "Ballad of a Wilful Woman" in Lawrence's *Look! We Have Come Through!*, was printed in the tenth issue of *Laughing Horse* with illustrations by Lawrence, including his signature phoenix motif. By giving it his imprimatur, Lawrence is confirming the moral of the ballad, that "[t]his is no place for women here!"[11] But, because it was published as a collaborative effort, the poem also undermines Lawrence's privileged position as Author-God.

New Mexico in the modernist period was very much a place for women; Vera Norwood and Janice Monk have shown that it was a place that "liberated women's creativity and shaped their art."[12] As such, New Mexico was an unlikely enough environment for the Lawrence who, the month he arrived there, was hailed by Paul Rosenfeld in the *New Republic* as "the man who has appeared simultaneously with the individualizing, breeched, self-conscious women of the new century . . . the new complex, stubborn, recalcitrant female types" (to Lawrence's dismay, even his acolyte, Dorothy Brett, would adopt the breeches of the cowgirl when she followed him to New Mexico).[13] Although Taos competed as a cultural hub with Alice Corbin Henderson's Santa Fe, Norwood and Monk stress the connectedness of the Anglo women of northern New Mexico, whether permanent residents or visitors to the region. Lawrence's New Mexico writing, which was produced within this feminized matrix, would subsequently be reabsorbed into it, to be reconfigured by women writers and artists like Mabel, Brett, and Georgia O'Keeffe.

Recent scholarship in modernist studies has drawn attention to the composite nature of cultural production, and in particular to the work of women, both as authors in their own right and as often unacknowledged collaborators in the material creation and dissemination of texts in their roles as patrons, editors, or amanuenses.[14] Brett produced the typescripts of two of the stories Lawrence wrote at the Kiowa Ranch, "St. Mawr" and "The Woman Who Rode Away" (Lawrence tactfully gave the manuscript of "The Princess," in which Brett is the model for the neurotic Dollie, to Spud Johnson to type instead). Brett worked on the other stories on a typewriter borrowed from Mabel Dodge Luhan, the likely model for the Woman who rode away, until, in an attempt to clean it, Frieda Lawrence boiled and broke the Corona. Lawrence borrowed another typewriter from his Del Monte neighbour, Alfred Hawke, on which Brett completed "St. Mawr" (see v.126).

As Brett recalls in her memoir:

> I have started typewriting your story, "The Woman Who Rode Away." I am not good at typewriting, but I think I may save you some money, as the typists are so expensive. So I borrow a typewriter from Mabel and settle down to the job. You tear a few pages at a time out of your copybook—with some reluctance, as it spoils the book—but you write new pages every morning and it is the only way to manage.[15]

Her mistakes would make their way into the typescripts of Lawrence's work, where many of them remain; the editors of the Cambridge edition of *The Woman Who Rode Away and Other Stories*, who note that "Brett's typing led to many transmission errors," warn that "we cannot be certain of eliminating her influence on the texts" (lv). Typescripts are pre-texts in Gerard Genette's taxonomy of paratexts, and, according to a social theory of textual production like Jerome McGann's, to erase Brett's role in the process, were it possible to do so, would be to introduce distortions of another kind: literary works "remain human products," McGann insists. He argues that a "hypnotic fascination with the isolated author has served to foster an overdetermined concept of authorship, but (reciprocally) an underdetermined concept of literary work"—what Holly Laird describes as "the fiction of single authorship," and what Earl Ingersoll critiques as the "naive belief" on the part of his devotees "in a 'Lawrence' who exists as a kind of transcendental signifier within the grand narrative of his life."[16]

Brett's painting *Lawrence's Three Fates* (1958) reflects the hypnotic fascination described by McGann, but does so within a broader configuration of Lawrence, literary work, and women that deconstructs the myth of the author to which the picture subscribes (fig. 1). Lawrence's role in the painting is that of Zeus, the only god who can command the Fates; like Zeus, however, he is also bound to the Fates and to their intentions. In her canvas, Brett herself, Frieda Lawrence, and Mabel Dodge Luhan sit at a table in the domestic interior of the Lawrences' cabin at the Kiowa Ranch: Brett is typing, Mabel is signing a manuscript, and Frieda, with her habitual cigarette dangling from the corner of her mouth, is crossing her hands over a text that bears her signature. Of the three, only Frieda is garbed in the white robes of the Fates, perhaps in acknowledgement of her greater claim on Lawrence (although Brett told Alfred Stieglitz "I feel I am more his widow than Frieda," and took as the epigraph to the first part of her memoir of him Lawrence's dictum that "*Friendship is as Binding / As the Marriage Vow*").[17] Frieda's white dress may also indicate that, like Lawrence, she too has passed away: Frieda Lawrence died in 1956. Mabel wears pink and white, while Brett, at the other end of the color spectrum, sports a bright red shirt and, of course, breeches.

All three women had published competing memoirs of Lawrence in the early 1930s, and the painting represents the *tria Fata* weaving their strands of that intertextual skein, collectively controlling Lawrence's posthumous reputation or destiny. They are doing so in a more seemly manner than had been the case in 1935, when these would-be keepers of his flame fell out over the interring of Lawrence's ashes at the shrine built for the purpose by Frieda at Kiowa.[18] In Brett's picture, Lawrence himself is glimpsed through the open cabin door, sitting with his back against the trunk of the pine tree. He is writing, too, but his function in the painting is that of a muse; it is the women

Fig. 1. Dorothy Brett, *Lawrence's Three Fates*, 1958. By courtesy of Keith Sagar.

in the foreground who are authoring *him*. Brett's painting both realigns and reproduces the "asymmetric writing relationships" that obtained between Lawrence and the women of his circle.[19]

The ponderosa pine tree at Kiowa is the subject of Georgia O'Keeffe's remarkable 1929 painting, *The Lawrence Tree* (fig. 2). In a 1922 *Vanity Fair* article, Paul Rosenfeld had called O'Keeffe "a female counterpart to D. H. Lawrence," and in 1929 she visited Lawrence's ranch, staying there with Brett, who had moved back as a caretaker of kinds when the Lawrences left for Europe; O'Keeffe's painting was exhibited at Stieglitz's American Place gallery in 1930 as *Pine Tree with Stars at Brett's*.[20] Spiralling up into a ganglion-like mass of branches, her pine tree is every inch the "magnificent assertion" Lawrence had described in his essay "Pan in America," where "[t]he tree gathers

Conclusion | 107

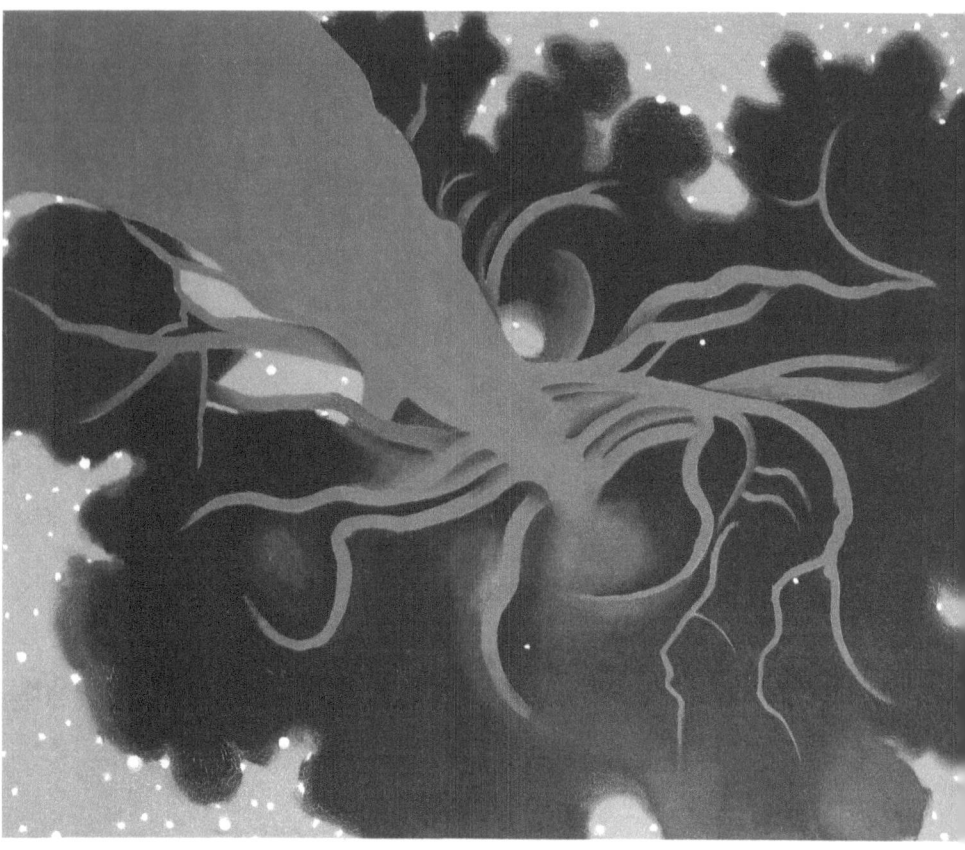

Fig. 2. Georgia O'Keeffe, *The Lawrence Tree*, 1929. Hartford (Conn.), Wadsworth Atheneum Museum of Art. Oil on canvas. 31 × 40 in. The Ella Gallup Sumner and Mary Catlin Sumner Collection Fund. 1981.23 © Georgia O'Keeffe Museum / DACS, 2014. Wadsworth Atheneum Museum of Art / Art Resource, N.Y. / Scala, Florence.

up earth-power from the dark bowels of the earth, and a roaming sky-glitter from above" (*MM* 158). The pine tree appears again in "St. Mawr," a story O'Keeffe admired for its evocation of the beauty and "the animosity of the spirit of place" (150).

Intermedial collaborations between Lawrence and women artists and writers in New Mexico would continue after he left Kiowa and America in September 1925. O'Keeffe worked on her first New Mexico still life from a bleached cranium she had picked up at the Kiowa Ranch. *Horse's Skull with Pink Rose* (1931) is her visual response to Lawrence's word-picture, in "St. Mawr," of "the bones strewing" the desert landscape:

Bones of horses struck by lightning, bones of dead cattle, skulls of goats with little horns: bleached, unburied bones. (*SM* 150)[21]

Appropriately, on leaving the ranch and America in 1925, Lawrence arranged for a copy of *Reflections on the Death of a Porcupine*, his "remarkable tribute to the life on the ranch" (*RDP* xli), to be sent to Alfred Stieglitz. "I . . . should have liked to see you," he told Stieglitz in a letter: "also to see Georgia O'Keefe [*sic*], and some of her things" (v.319).

In an interview with Edward Foster for *Talisman* magazine that is reprinted in her book *The Birth-mark*, poet-critic Susan Howe remarks that

> Sounds and spirits (ghosts if you like) leave traces in a geography. It's Lawrence's sense of the spirit of the place—"Never trust the artist. Trust the tale." The tale and the place are tied in a mysterious and profound way. How did the English Lawrence understand America so well? He did.[22]

Michael Bell provides an answer to Howe's question when he describes Lawrence as "in some measure, an adoptive American writer."[23]

"I can't write for America here in England. I must transfer myself" (iii.73): so Lawrence told his literary agent in 1917, when he was beginning to write what would become *Studies in Classic American Literature*. The years he spent in the United States between 1922 and 1925 would not make Lawrence into an "exuberant American," like French-born American farmer, Crèvecoeur (*SCAL* 32). Lawrence was not "a super-tourist" either, a "kodaker of spiritual knicknacks," which is how the *Saturday Review of Literature* described the author of *Mornings in Mexico* (lxix), nor was Lawrence the false prophet posthumously taken to task by T. S. Eliot in *After Strange Gods* for preaching "buncombe and false doctrine" imbibed from "capering redskins."[24] Instead, during his several extended residencies in New Mexico—which was "not the USA at all," as he saw it (v.277)—Lawrence was a working writer and a ranchero, a pro tem Americano who not only "brings 'Englishness' itself into question" but who also queries our definitions of American identity and of American literature.[25]

Far from setting a "classic" national canon, Lawrence, as an adoptive American or Americano, anticipates contemporary definitions of border writing and of U.S.-American writing as "world literature."[26] "If ever men had to think in world terms, they have to think in world terms today"—so Lawrence argued in "On Coming Home," an essay in which he identifies England as "the one really soft spot, the rotten spot in the empire" (*RDP* 183). But for all that he railed against English provincialism, Lawrence was alert, too, to the dangers of globalization, the early symptoms of which he would detect in his late article, "New Mexico":

> Superficially, the world has become small and known. Poor little globe of earth, the tourist trots around you as easily as they trot round the Bois or round Central Park. (*MM* 175)

The alternative to the global village, Lawrence argues, is the "living nodality" of place. It was an American place, the local America he encountered in northern New Mexico, that gave Lawrence what he would describe as "the greatest experience from the outside world that I have ever had" (*MM* 125, 176).

Notes

Introduction

1. Muthyala, *Reworlding America*, xiii.
2. Healey and Cushman, *Letters*, 104.
3. Sherman, "America Is Discovered," 208.
4. Ibid., 208–9.
5. Buell, *Environmental Imagination*, 33.
6. Giles, *Virtual Americas*, 89; Shumway, *Creating American Civilization*, 329.
7. Pease, *New American Exceptionalism*, 162, 164–65.
8. Dickstein, "The critic and society," 359. See Rahv, *Myth and the Powerhouse*.
9. Gross, "Transnational Turn," 378.
10. Sherman, "America Is Discovered," 208, 213.
11. Thompson, introduction to Lawrence, *Studies*, 9.
12. Aldington, *Portrait of Genius, But . . .*, 291.
13. Leavis, *D. H. Lawrence*, n.p.
14. North, *Reading 1922*, 11–12.
15. Clark, *Minoan Distance*, 307.
16. Lummis, *Land of Poco Tiempo*, 1.
17. Ibid., 3.
18. On the northern New Mexico meaning of *Americano* or *hispano-americano*, see Gonzalez-Berry and Maciel, *Contested Homeland*, 123–24.
19. See Lutz, *Cosmopolitan Vistas*, 55; Doyle, "Toward a Philosophy of Transnationalism," 5.
20. Jay, "The Myth of 'America,'" 167.
21. Pratt, *Imperial Eyes*, 6; Porter, "What We Know That We Don't Know," 510.
22. Giles, *Global Remapping*, 24.
23. Jameson, *Postmodernism*, 16.
24. Gross, for example, suggests that Bourne's "vision has a modern ring." "Transna-

tional Turn," 381. Mark Kinkead-Weekes suggests that Lawrence may have had "an eye on *Seven Arts*" as a potential venue for his essays on American literature. *Triumph to Exile*, 399.

25. Giles, *Global Remapping*, 22; Bertrand Russell alleged that Lawrence's beliefs "led straight to Auschwitz," "Portraits," 95.

26. Dimock, *Through Other Continents*, 3.

27. Ibid., 90, 108, 3–4.

28. Yépez, *Empire of Neomemory*, 155.

29. In a special issue of *American Literary History* devoted to the transnational paradigm, William J. Maxwell asserts that "[t]ransnationalism is no accessory of a postmodernism canceled after the fall of the World Trade Center—so pleads even the most rooted, down-home modernist writing, dependent on internationalizing forces from rapid capital flows to thin-soled anthropologists." "Global Politics," 362.

30. Dimock, *Through Other Continents*, 36, 7.

31. See Parrinder, *Nation and Novel*, 307, 341, and Levine, *Realistic Imagination*, 317–28.

32. Pease, "New Americanists," 11.

33. Hoffman, review, 496.

34. Lewis, *Paleface*, 111.

35. Marx, "Listen to the States!," 82. Marx comments on "how neatly the work of Messrs. Chase, Feidelson and Lewis fit together. In a sense they are all writing chapters of the same book," 82.

36. Goldsmith, *American Literary Criticism*, 151.

37. Marcus Cunliffe's remark that Fiedler reveals himself to be "a blood-brother of D. H. Lawrence" is featured on the jacket of the U.K. edition of Fiedler's *Return of the Vanishing American*. Christopher Castiglia has called on American Studies to re-evaluate its history; to recover the roots of our field, Castiglia argues, is not to go backwards. "Cold War Melancholy," n.p.

38. Pease, "New Americanists," 15; see Baker and Fiedler, *English Literature: Opening Up the Canon*.

39. Trachtenberg, "Myth and Symbol," 669.

40. Ibid., 670–71.

41. Marx, "Listen to the States!," 81.

42. Pease, *New American Exceptionalism*, 162, 164–65.

43. Sontag, *Literature Is Freedom*, n.p.

44. Gross, "Transnational Turn," 381, 384.

45. Ramazani, *A Transnational Poetics*, 63.

46. Laird, *Self and Sequence*, vii.

47. Howarth, *Cambridge Introduction*, 190–91.

48. Williams, *Imaginations*, 27.

49. Davie, "Two Ways Out of Whitman," 346.

50. For a revisionary assessment of the Georgians, see Howarth, *British Poetry in the Age of Modernism*.

51. Hooker, introduction to Lawrence, *Birds, Beasts and Flowers*, 8.

52. Ramazani, *A Transnational Poetics*, 81.
53. Castronovo, "Death to the American Renaissance," 190, 192.
54. Dimock, *Through Other Continents*, 74.
55. Herzinger, *D. H. Lawrence in His Time*, 18, 16.
56. Lawrence's use of the term "nodality" prefigures that of Soja in *Postmodern Geographies*, 149.
57. Bate, *Song of the Earth*, 280.
58. Jay, "Myth of 'America,'" 183–84.
59. Pease, "National Identities," 5.
60. Ibid., 3.
61. Slotkin, *Regeneration through Violence*, 466.
62. de Beauvoir, *Second Sex*, 253.
63. Feinstein, *Lawrence and the Women*, 9; Karrell, *Writing Together/Writing Apart*, xx, xxi.
64. According to Rudnick, "[m]ost Lawrence critics are contemptuous of Mabel and do their best to dismiss or downplay her influence on and relationship with Lawrence." *Mabel Dodge Luhan*, 348n2.
65. Ibid., 74, 120.
66. Williams, *Autobiography*, 138.
67. Luhan, *Intimate Memories*, 183–84.
68. Luhan, *Lorenzo in Taos*, 15.
69. The Taos art colony had been founded in 1898 by Bert Phillips and Ernest Blumenschein; from it emerged the Taos Society of Artists (ca. 1915–27), a group of painters who pursued a romantic-primitivist aesthetic. The precursors of the Taos Moderns, the generation of painters based there from 1940, were the modernist artists in Mabel Dodge Luhan's circle like Andrew Dasburg, Georgia O'Keeffe, and John Marin. See Witt, *Taos Moderns*.
70. Rudnick, *Mabel Dodge Luhan*, 240.
71. Cavitch, *D. H. Lawrence and the New World*, 57.
72. In his introduction to the Black Sparrow edition of *Birds, Beasts and Flowers*, Cushman comments that the poems mark "way-stations in the Lawrences' journey from Italy to Taos," ix.
73. Sagar, "How to Live," 209. For a contrary view of Rananim as a messianic fantasy propelled by Lawrence's estrangement from society at large, see Delany, *D. H. Lawrence's Nightmare*.
74. Merrild, *With D. H. Lawrence in New Mexico*, 73, 85.
75. See Moore, *Gurdjieff and Katherine Mansfield*, 3.
76. Gill established his first culture commune in Ditchling in Sussex in 1913; in 1924, following a schism, Gill's faction, which included the poet and artist David Jones, moved to the site of a derelict monastery at Capel-y-ffin, in the Welsh Marches.
77. Thomas Seltzer used only one of Merrild's designs for the jacket of his edition of *The Captain's Doll* (1923).
78. Tindall, *D. H. Lawrence and Susan His Cow*, 24.
79. Aldington, *Portrait of a Genius, But . . .* , 291.

Chapter 1. Hands-up, America!

1. Brooks, "The Critics and Young America," 117.

2. Nin, *D. H. Lawrence*, 93; see Harrison, *D. H. Lawrence and Italian Futurism*.

3. See Babbitt, *Literature and the American College*. An article published in Mencken's *American Mercury* in 1928, "Teaching American Literature in American Colleges," indicates that little had changed by the end of the decade, with only one in eleven undergraduate courses dedicated to teaching American literature (one in thirteen at postgraduate level). Vanderbilt, *American Literature and the Academy*, 268. See Graff, *Professing Literature*, and Renker, *Origins of American Literature Studies*.

4. Kurt L. Daniels remarks in his review of *Studies* that "Classic American Literature" is "a new phrase to most of us." "Mr. Lawrence on American Literature," 236.

5. Brooks, *Days of the Phoenix*, 17.

6. Brooks, *Sketches in Criticism*, 11.

7. The anonymous *Current Opinion* reviewer may have read Lawrence's article "Surgery for the Novel—or a Bomb," published in 1923, which speculates on what the future of fiction might be if "a bomb were put under the whole scheme of things" (*PH* 520).

8. See Roberts and Poplawski, *A Bibliography of D. H. Lawrence*, 91.

9. Pattee, "Call for a Literary Historian," 135.

10. Egan, "On the Sin of Being an American," 28; Weaver, "Narcissus and Echo," 327.

11. Raine, qtd. in Harper, *Wisdom of Two*, 44.

12. Lawrence describes his method in the preface to his *Fantasia of the Unconscious*: "I have found hints, suggestions for what I say here in all kinds of scholarly books . . . down to Frazer and his *Golden Bough*, and even Freud and Frobenius. Even then I only remember hints—and I proceed by intuition" (*PU* 62).

13. Pryse, *Apocalypse Unsealed*, 3, 39. According to Pryse's interpretation of the "symbolical language" of the Book of Revelation, the seven seals of the apocalypse are "the seven main chakras," 6.

14. Fernihough, *D. H. Lawrence*, 64.

15. Lawrence told Frederick Carter that he would confine his theory of the plexuses to his books on the unconscious. See Carter, *D. H. Lawrence*, 25.

16. Cavitch, *D. H. Lawrence and the New World*, 99.

17. Brock, "D. H. Lawrence Strings Some Literary Pearls," 9.

18. Sherman, "America Is Discovered," 208.

19. Sherman, "America Is Discovered," 213; "Lawrence Cultivates His Beard," 252.

20. Macy, "The American Spirit," 398–99. Macy had written the introduction for the unauthorized Modern Library edition of *Sons and Lovers* published in New York by Boni and Liveright in 1922.

21. Brooks, "On Creating a Usable Past," 337; Mencken, "Footnote on Criticism," 284.

22. Mencken, "Criticism of Criticism," 4; Spingarn, "Criticism in the United States," 290.

23. Spingarn, *Criticism in America*, n.p.

24. Two years later, Lawrence would read and apparently write a review of Mencken's *Americana*, although it seems that the review did not appear; in an October 1925 letter to

Alfred and Blanche Knopf, Lawrence discusses the reviews on which he is at work, noting that "the Mencken *Americana* is already done" (v.321). Peter Preston lists *Americana* among a number of Alfred A. Knopf books received for review by Lawrence in his *D. H. Lawrence Chronology*, 121.

25. Ezra Pound had placed Lawrence's story "The White Stocking" in the *Smart Set* in October 1914, the year Mencken assumed the editorship of the journal; Lawrence's poem "Violets" had appeared in the *Smart Set* the year before.

26. Lawrence also suggested to Sherman that he might contribute to the *New York Herald Tribune Books* the reflections on art and morality that he had begun in the versions of the "Whitman" chapter for *Studies*: in the event, his articles "Art and Morality" and "Morality and the Novel" appeared in 1925 in the *Calendar of Modern Letters*. Sherman died in an accident in 1926, and it was under his successor, Irita van Doren, that Lawrence's reviews (of Marmaduke Pickthall's *Saïd the Fisherman* and John Allen Krout's *The Origins of Prohibition*) appeared in the *New York Herald Tribune Books* on December 27, 1925, and January 21, 1926, respectively.

27. Frank, *Our America*, 135, 8–9.

28. Reising, *Unusable Past*, 50.

29. Boyd coined the phrase "Ku Klux Kriticism" in a 1923 article of that title that would be reprinted the following year in Spingarn's *Criticism in America*.

30. Mencken, "Criticism of Criticism," 5.

31. Mencken, "Paul Elmer More," 177–78.

32. Brooks, "On Creating a Usable Past," 337.

33. Kammen, *Mystic Chords*, 378.

34. Sherman, "America Is Discovered," 213.

35. Brooks, *Days of the Phoenix*, 106.

36. Seligmann, *D. H. Lawrence*, 72.

37. Professor of American Literature at Pennsylvania State College, Fred Lewis Pattee (1863–1950) was the author of the groundbreaking "Is There an American Literature?" (1896) and *A History of American Literature Since 1870* (1915). See Werner and Turner, "In Memoriam Fred Lewis Pattee."

38. Pattee, "Call for Literary Historian," 139–40.

39. Ibid., 134–35, 139–40. Pattee's article first appeared in Mencken's *American Mercury*, and would be reprinted as the first essay in Norman Foerster's influential *The Reinterpretation of American Literature* in 1928. In 1924, the most significant of the extant American literary histories was the four-volume *Cambridge History of American Literature*, edited by William Peterfield Trent, John Erskine, Stuart P. Sherman, and Carl Van Doren; published in New York by G. P. Putnam's Sons between 1917 and 1921, the work was reprinted between 1921 and 1925. Although it includes a cutting-edge chapter on "Non-English Writings," as well as an "Aboriginal" subsection contributed by Mary Austin, the Cambridge *History* did little to redress the longstanding neglect of writers like Melville, and Pattee critiques what he sees as its scattergun approach. Although its parent volume was the eighteen-volume *Cambridge History of English and American Literature* (1907–21), published by Cambridge University Press in the United Kingdom and by Putnam in the United States, Shumway has argued that the Cambridge *His-*

tory was nonetheless tantamount to a "declaration of the independence of American literary history." *Creating American Civilization*, 93.

40. Santayana, "Genteel Tradition," 86.

41. Lippmann, "Crude Barbarian," 70. Mary Austin's defense of Lawrence—which he dismissed as "boring"—appeared in the *New Republic* in the following month (iii.654). Correcting Lippmann, who had suggested that Lawrence should consult a map, Austin points out that Montezuma was indeed "born in what is now the United States," and she corroborates Lawrence's view of "root cultures in America." "Mrs. Austin Protests," 70. In his reply to Austin's reply to his own reply to Lawrence, Lippmann remarks that "[i]t did not occur to me that he [Lawrence] took the Back to Montezuma movement with such awful seriousness as Mrs. Austin does." "Mr. Lippmann Answers," 70. In 1920, the year in which Lawrence's "America, Listen to Your Own" appeared, William Carlos Williams asserted in the prologue to *Kora in Hell* that "[t]he New World is Montezuma." *Imaginations*, 24.

42. Fiedler, *Return of the Vanishing American*, 10.

43. Frank, *Our America*, 116n.

44. See Michaels, *Our America*, 136.

45. Williams, *In the American Grain*, 39.

46. Roberts, *D. H. Lawrence*, 70. Roberts is responding to Wayne Templeton's fiercer critique of Lawrence in "'Indians and an Englishman.'"

47. Williams, *In the American Grain*, 138.

48. Dimock, *Through Other Continents*, 178.

49. See Bergland, *The National Uncanny*.

50. Ellis, *Dying Game*, 76.

51. Lawrence, *Symbolic Meaning*, 9. Arnold's edition collects the eight *English Review* essays together with intermediate versions of Lawrence's American essays.

52. Pratt, *Imperial Eyes*, 6.

53. Thompson, introduction to Lawrence, *Studies*, 7.

54. Ellis, *Dying Game*, 58.

55. Ibid., 63.

56. Drohojowska-Philip, *Full Bloom*, 298. On Willa Cather and Tony Lujan, see Lewis, *Willa Cather: A Personal Record*, and Lee, *Willa Cather: A Life Saved Up*.

57. Aldington, *Portrait of a Genius, But* . . . , 335.

58. Sherman, "The National Genius," 246.

59. Wright, *D. H. Lawrence and the Bible*, 188.

60. The relationship between the homoerotic reading of American writing in *Studies in Classic American Literature* and the theme of *blutsbrüderschaft* in Lawrence's own fiction has been explored in Cowan's chapter on "The Artist as Myth-Maker" in his *D. H. Lawrence and the Trembling Balance*, 84–94, and in Ingersoll, "'A New Continent of the Soul.'"

61. See Ellis, *Dying Game*, 68.

62. Minter, "Fear of Feminization," 153, and Minter, "Great War," 96.

63. Melville, "To Ned," in *Selected Poems*, 16. Lawrence had stopped off at Rarotonga and Papeete on his voyage from Australia to San Francisco in 1922.

64. Lawrence read *Moby-Dick* in the 1907 Everyman's Library edition, which omits the epilogue in which Ishmael tells the reader that he has survived the wreck of the *Pequod*.

65. Bloom, *Anatomy of Influence*, 258, 256.

66. Brooks, "On Creating a Usable Past," 337, 339.

67. Miller, *T. S. Eliot*, 112–13.

68. Brooks, *Autobiography*, 510.

69. Eliot, *Selected Prose*, 22.

70. Brooks, "On Creating a Usable Past," 341, 337, 338, 340; Blake, *Beloved Community*, 236.

71. Williams, *Autobiography*, 174. Leavis, who considered Lawrence "the finest literary critic of his time," asserts that he "offers a serious 'classicism' a severer test than could have been divined." "D. H. Lawrence," 276. See Crick and DiSanto, "D. H. Lawrence 'An opportunity and a test.'"

Chapter 2. Under Our Home Eye

1. Richter, *Dada*, 83.

2. Williams "The American Background," 31–32.

3. Dijkstra, *Cubism, Stieglitz, and the Early Poetry of William Carlos Williams*, 108; Rosenfeld, "D. H. Lawrence," 126.

4. The reproduction of O'Keeffe's *Cross* (1929), one of a series, was probably the suggestion of Mabel Dodge Luhan, who arranged the *Survey Graphic* commission; a Penitente *morada* (chapel) abuts Mabel's hacienda in Taos (see *P* 359 and *MM* 114).

5. Grad, "Georgia O'Keeffe's Lawrencian Vision," 4.

6. Healey and Cushman, *Letters*, 76.

7. Plans for the New York exhibition were shelved due to fears that Lawrence's paintings would be confiscated by U.S. Customs; see vi.432–33, 505–6, and see Ellis, *Dying Game*, 425, 467.

8. Lynes, *O'Keeffe, Stieglitz and the Critics*, 27.

9. Dijkstra, *Cubism, Stieglitz, and the Early Poetry of William Carlos Williams*, 40.

10. Healey and Cushman, *Letters*, 54.

11. Sherman, *America and Allied Ideals*, 7.

12. Halter, *Revolution in the Visual Arts*, 132.

13. Michaels, *Our America*, 44.

14. Williams, *Imaginations*, 131, 11; Stevens, *Collected Poetry*, 302.

15. Muthyala, *Reworlding America*, xiii.

16. Williams, *In the American Grain*, 65.

17. Giles, "The Deterritorialization of American Literature," 45; Snyder, *Gary Snyder Reader*, 275. Eric White points out that Dewey's "Americanism and Localism" "prioritised 'discrete' things and places and resisted the totalising patina of 'national character.'" *Transatlantic Avant-Gardes*, 98.

18. See Newmark, "An Introduction to Neonativist Collectives."

19. Buell, *Environmental Imagination*, 253.

20. Luhan, *Lorenzo in Taos*, 88.

21. See Snyder, "'When the Indian was in Vogue.'"

22. See Worthen, "Lawrence's Theater of the Southwest."

23. Newmark, "An Introduction to Neonativist Collectives," 91.

24. Clark, *Minoan Distance*, 307.

25. Gilbert, *Acts of Attention*, 332; Cushman, introduction to *Birds, Beasts and Flowers*, ix.

26. Ramazani, *A Transnational Poetics*, 23.

27. Snyder, *Gary Snyder Reader*, 183. See Davis and Jenkins, *Locations of Literary Modernism*.

28. Snyder, *Gary Snyder Reader*, 262; Laird, *Self and Sequence*, 138.

29. Castro, *Interpreting the Indian*, 19.

30. Stevens, *Collected Poetry*, 27–29. The first version of "The Comedian as the Letter C" dates from 1921. See Strom, "Wallace Stevens's Revisions of Crispin's Journal."

31. Cohen, "Traveling Genres," 233.

32. Dimock, *Through Other Continents*, 74.

33. Healey and Cushman, *Letters*, 104.

34. Hooker, introduction to Lawrence, *Birds, Beasts and Flowers*, 8.

35. Sagar, *D. H. Lawrence: Poet*, 61, 52.

36. Crèvecoeur, *Letters from an American Farmer*, 170.

37. Whitman, *Complete Poetry*, 51.

38. Laird, *Self and Sequence*, 13.

39. Herzinger, *D. H. Lawrence in His Time*, 23, 40, 59, 98.

40. Pinkney, *D. H. Lawrence*, 100.

41. Bloom, *Anatomy of Influence*, 262.

42. Lowell took exception to *Look!*'s cover art, telling Lawrence that "a Futurist cover was too flippant an introduction to so serious a book": "the cover jars with the content of your book as though it were a sneer set in front of a sacrament." Healy and Cushman, *Letters*, 63. The dust jacket of the first, Chatto and Windus edition reproduces a drawing by the American avant-garde artist E. McKnight Kauffer.

43. An exception is Roberts, who has argued that "[t]he importance of Lawrence's association with the Imagist movement . . . tends to be underestimated." "Lawrence, Imagism and Beyond," 81.

44. H.D., *Bid Me to Live*, 141.

45. Ibid., 141.

46. Friedman, *Penelope's Web*, 58.

47. H.D., *Bid Me to Live*, 51, 62.

48. H.D., *Collected Poems*, 53–55.

49. Segal, *Orpheus*, 9.

50. Gilbert, *Acts of Attention*, xviii.

51. Siegel, *Lawrence among the Women*, 13. "Purple Anemones" suggests the influence of Leo Frobenius's *The Voice of Africa* (1913), which Lawrence had read in 1918, and from which he drew his ideas about the Etruscans and a lost Atlantean culture; according to Frobenius's symbolic order, the male principle consists in action, with the female as source, or what Anaïs Nin calls the "core." Nin, *D. H. Lawrence*, 42.

52. Laird, *Self and Sequence*, 90; see Murry, *Son of Woman*, 45.

53. H.D., *Collected Poems*, 29.
54. Gilbert, *Acts of Attention*, 336.
55. Bachelard, *Poetics of Space*, 150.
56. Pound, "A Few Don'ts," 203.
57. Kinkead-Weekes, *Triumph to Exile*, 64.
58. Ibid., 356.
59. Pound insisted that "Lawrence was never an Imagist. He was an *Amygist*." Quoted in Jones, *Imagist Poetry*, 25.
60. Ezra Pound, in Witemeyer, *Pound/Williams*, 100.
61. Lawrence, quoted in Hughes, *Imagism and the Imagists*, 170. See Litz, "Lawrence, Pound, and Early Modernism."
62. Williams, *Harriet Monroe*, 135.
63. Healey and Cushman, *Letters*, 110.
64. See Smith, *Spectra Hoax*.
65. Lowell, *Tendencies*, 238.
66. Bynner, *Selected Witter Bynner*, 114, 167.
67. Ibid., 46.
68. Carr, *Inventing the American Primitive*, 224.
69. Bynner, *Selected Witter Bynner*, 73.
70. Austin, *American Rhythm*, 68.
71. Carr, *Inventing the American Primitive*, 228.
72. Austin, *American Rhythm*, 118.
73. Castro, *Interpreting the Indian*, 22. On the politics and the praxis of translation from oral originals, see Swann, *On the Translation of Native American Literatures*, and Rothenberg, *Technicians of the Sacred*.
74. Austin, *American Rhythm*, 42; Pound, *Personae*, 251.
75. Monroe, "Aboriginal Songs I," 235.
76. Pound, *Personae*, 69.
77. Henderson, "Aboriginal Songs II," 256; Sandburg, "Editorial Comment," 255.
78. Castro, *Interpreting the Indian*, 19.
79. Dilworth, *Imagining Indians*, 175. See Deloria, *Playing Indian*; Auerbach, *Explorers in Eden*; and Trachtenberg, *Shades of Hiawatha*.
80. Austin, *American Rhythm*, 41.
81. Snyder, *Gary Snyder Reader*, 52.
82. Spivak, "Can the Subaltern Speak?," 280.
83. Ibid., 285; Spivak and Harasym, *Post-Colonial Critic*, 66.
84. Roberts, *D. H. Lawrence*, 80.
85. Brett suggests that the Taos Indians called Lawrence "Red Fox," but Bynner's recollection "is that it was 'Red Wolf,' a memory corroborated by his poem of that name." Brett, *Lawrence and Brett*, 89; Bynner, *Journey with Genius*, 8. Lawrence's knowledge of totemism was derived from Harrison's *Ancient Art and Ritual* (1913), J. G. Frazer's *Totemism and Exogamy* (1893), and from the discussion of "the mythic pedigree" of animal totemism and of zoolatry in Tylor's *Primitive Culture*, vol. 2, 213.

86. DiBattista, *Women in Love*, 77.

87. Austin, *Land of Journey's Ending*, 299. See Snyder, "The Incredible Survival of Coyote," in *Old Ways*, 67–93.

88. Dilworth, *Imagining Indians*, 208, 41.

89. Lummis, *Land of Poco Tiempo*, 1; Henderson, *Turquoise Trail*, vii.

90. Bate, *Song of the Earth*, 231.

91. Hartley, "Festival of the Corn," in Henderson, *Turquoise Trail*, 47.

92. Henderson, *Turquoise Trail*, xi.

93. Fernihough, *D. H. Lawrence*, 134.

94. Hartley, *Adventures in the Arts*, 55–56.

95. Monroe, "The Motive of the Magazine," 33; Monroe, *Poets and Their Art*, 251.

96. Pound, *Selected Letters*, 9. Although Monroe had been the first editor to publish his poems in the United States, Lawrence took issue with *Poetry*'s American bias in an anonymous piece, "A Britisher has a Word with Harriett [sic] Monroe," published in the Mexico-based little magazine *Palms* in 1923: "Oh what might not Milton have been, if he'd written under Calvin Coolidge!" (*STH* 159).

97. Scholes and Wulfman, *Modernism in the Magazines*, 9.

98. Monroe, "The Motive of the Magazine," 27; Whitman, *Complete Poetry*, 1082.

99. Trachtenberg, "Walt Whitman," 195. The November 1916 issue of *Seven Arts* declared that "[t]he spirit of Walt Whitman stands behind the SEVEN ARTS. What we are seeking, is what he sought." Quoted in Brooks, *Days of the Phoenix*, 22.

100. Nolan, *Poet-Chief*, 6.

101. Whitman, *Complete Poetry*, 175, 656.

102. Whitman, preface to *Leaves of Grass* (1855), in *Complete Poetry*, 5–26, 25; Corbin, "America," 81.

103. Williams, "America, Whitman, and the Art of Poetry," 31.

104. Brooks, *America's Coming-of-Age*, 109.

105. Pound explores his difficult relationship with Whitman in "What I feel about Walt Whitman" (1909) and in the essays of *Patria Mia* (1913). See Pound, *Selected Prose*, 145–46, 99–141.

106. Bloom, *Anatomy of Influence*, 258.

107. Williams, "America, Whitman, and the Art of Poetry," 29.

108. Ellis and Mills, *D. H. Lawrence's Non-Fiction*, 151.

109. Herzinger, *D. H. Lawrence in His Time*, 16.

110. Allen Ginsberg, *Collected Poems*, 136.

111. "Poetry of the Present" first appeared in *Playboy* 4/5 (1919) and would be reprinted as the foreword to the American edition of *New Poems* (1920), where Lawrence remarks that it should "have come as a preface to *Look! We Have Come Through!*," the earlier volume that is so profoundly indebted to Whitman (in spite of its title, *New Poems* is a collection of mostly older work) (*P* 649).

112. Lowell, *Tendencies*, 240. See Lowell, "Walt Whitman and the New Poetry," and Cederstrom, "Walt Whitman and the Imagists."

113. Nolan, *Poet-Chief*, 17.

114. Tapscott, *American Beauty*, 46.

115. Hartley, "America as Landscape," n.p. On Williams and Whitman, see Breslin, "Whitman and the Early Development of William Carlos Williams."

116. Williams, "Sample Critical Statement," 18.

117. Dijkstra, *Cubism, Stieglitz, and the Early Poetry of William Carlos Williams*, 136.

118. Williams, *Autobiography*, 174.

119. See North, *Reading 1922*.

120. Williams, *Imaginations*, 95. Pound's Persephone poems also symbolize "the power of renewal" and close "the gap between mythology and botany." Davenport, *Geography of the Imagination*, 143, 151.

121. Williams, *Imaginations*, 116. *Kora in Hell* is a reply to Pound's *Ripostes*, which is dedicated to Williams: the Propertian epigraph to Pound's volume reads *"Quos ego Persephonae maxima dona feram"* (which I may bring to Persephone [as] my most precious gift). Pound, *Personae*, 54.

122. Williams, *In the American Grain*, 216.

123. Louis, *Persephone Rises*, 112. See also Radford, *Lost Girls*, 224–73.

124. Wright, *D. H. Lawrence and the Bible*, 171.

125. Williams, *Imaginations*, 101. In the prologue to *Kora in Hell*, Williams had complained that "Hellenism, especially the modern sort, is too staid, too chilly, too little fecundative to impregnate my world," 12.

126. Fernihough, *D. H. Lawrence*, 9.

127. Williams, *Imaginations*, 88, 102.

128. Hartley, *Adventures in the Arts*, 37.

129. Ibid., 39, 36, 27.

130. Dijkstra, *Cubism, Stieglitz, and the Early Poetry of William Carlos Williams*, 23–24; Halter, *Revolution in the Visual Arts*, 82. See Altieri, *Painterly Abstraction*, and Fernihough, *D. H. Lawrence*. Lawrence's discussion of Cézanne in "Introduction to These Paintings" is a rebuttal of the theory of Significant Form in Roger Fry's *Cézanne* (1927).

131. Lawrence may be thinking of Cézanne's *Le Compotier* (1877), his *Still Life with Apples* (1895–98), or his *Apples* (1900–1901).

132. Williams, *Collected Poems*, 80.

133. Merleau-Ponty, *Primacy of Perception*, 180.

134. Harrison, *Ancient Art and Ritual*, 21–22, 71, 100; Williams, *Paterson*, 6.

135. Scott, *Marsden Hartley in New Mexico*, n.p.; see Tashjian, "Marsden Hartley and the Southwest."

136. Tindall, *D. H. Lawrence and Susan His Cow*, 109.

137. Kinkead-Weekes, *Triumph to Exile*, 356.

138. Bachelard, *Poetics of Space*, xxvii.

139. Ibid., xxviii.

140. Bate, *Song of the Earth*, 107.

141. Bachelard, *Poetics of Space*, xxxv.

142. Heidegger, *Poetry, Language, Thought*, 213.

143. Auden, *Collected Poems*, 89.
144. Bachelard, *Poetics of Space*, 183.
145. Ibid., 51.
146. ffytche, "Arduous Pain of Appearance," 201.
147. Norris, *Beasts of the Modern Imagination*, 3, 15.
148. Chaudhuri, *D. H. Lawrence*, 60.
149. Moore, *Poems*, 135.
150. Ibid., 135.

Chapter 3. Tales of Out Here

1. Luhan, *Lorenzo in Taos*, 59, 77, 85, 72.
2. Keith Sagar, who titled the novel-fragment "The Wilful Woman," published it in 1971 in his edition of *The Princess and Other Stories*.
3. Rudnick, *Mabel Dodge Luhan*, 199.
4. Marx, *Machine in the Garden*, 16, 354, 365.
5. Luhan, *Intimate Memories*, 184.
6. Coroneos and Tate, "Lawrence's tales," 112, 106.
7. Baldick, *Oxford English Literary History*, 230.
8. See Marx, *Machine in the Garden*, 342.
9. Pease, "National Identities," 4.
10. Ibid., 3.
11. Rodriguez, "Art, Tourism, and Race Relations in Taos," 87.
12. Coroneos and Tate, "Lawrence's tales," 104.
13. Lawrence wrote to his London agent Curtis Brown from Taos that "St. Mawr," together with "The Woman Who Rode Away" and "The Princess" "will make a book" (v.136), a suggestion he also made to his English publisher, Martin Secker (see *SM* xxvi, xxxii).
14. Ramazani, *A Transnational Poetics*, 25.
15. Merivale, *Pan the Goat-God*, 194.
16. Brett, *Lawrence and Brett*, 20–21, 56.
17. Ibid., 288. Brett partially destroyed the painting, but reworked it in 1963. The later version is reproduced in Hignett, *Brett*, n.p.
18. Ellis likens Pan-stories like "The Last Laugh" and "The Border-Line" not to Arthur Machen's "The Great God Pan" or E. M. Forster's "Story of a Panic," but to Poe's tales. Ellis, *Dying Game*, 163.
19. Murry, *Reminiscences*, 215.
20. Hawthorne, *Young Goodman Brown*, 134–35.
21. Banks, "Thomas Morton of Merry Mount," 160, 147, 159.
22. Slotkin, *Regeneration through Violence*, 58.
23. Hawthorne, *Young Goodman Brown*, 139.
24. The composition of "St. Mawr" is dated here according to the chronology provided in the Cambridge edition of the text in which the editor, Brian Finney, suggests that Lawrence probably wrote the story in early June 1924 (xi). Virginia Crosswhite Hyde, the editor of the

Cambridge edition of *Mornings in Mexico and Other Essays*, suggests that the revised version of "Pan in America" was written between May and June 1924, xvi.

25. Lawrence, who had read Gilbert Murray's *Four Stages of Greek Religion* in 1916, concurs with Murray's argument that the supposed evolution of the Greek god Pan from the theriomorphic to the anthropomorphic represented a decline. See Sagar, *D. H. Lawrence: Poet*, 51.

26. See Tanner, *Reign of Wonder*.

27. Cowan, *D. H. Lawrence's American Journey*, 81.

28. Sherman, "Lawrence Cultivates His Beard," 257; Milne, "Lawrence and the politics of sexual politics," 210.

29. Cole, "Essay on American Scenery," 102; Buell, *Environmental Imagination*, 35.

30. Kolodny, *Land Before Her*, xiii.

31. Arac, *Critical Genealogies*, 139, 143.

32. Michaels, *Our America*, 98.

33. Lynch, *Xerophilia*, 22.

34. Siegel, "'St. Mawr,'" 276–77.

35. Buell, *Environmental Imagination*, 25.

36. Nash, *Wilderness and the American Mind*, 24.

37. Luhan, "Georgia O'Keeffe in Taos," 407.

38. Johnson, et al., "Apologia," in Udall, *Spud Johnson and Laughing Horse*, 97. On *Laughing Horse*, see Fedirka, "'Our Own Authentic Wonderland.'"

39. Johnson, "Sun-Noise," in Udall, *Spud Johnson and Laughing Horse*, 153.

40. Lawrence's account of the death of the Pan, which he reprises in "Pan in America" and in his short story "The Overtone," probably derives from Elizabeth Barrett Browning's poem "The Dead Pan" (1844). Laughter, which is the mode of Pan in "The Last Laugh," is deemed an Indian attribute in Johnson's *Laughing Horse* article "The Last Laughers." See Udall, *Spud Johnson and Laughing Horse*, 124.

41. According to Williams, Morton erected his maypole in a ceremony to rename his habitation Merry or "Mare Mount." *In the American Grain*, 76. In the *Laughing Horse* "London Letter," Lawrence calls his laughing horse a "Hobby Horse," suggesting its connection to the unruly fertility symbol that survives into the modern era in May Day rituals in the Cornish village of Padstow, close to where the Lawrences lived for a time at Porthcorthan (*MM* 137).

42. Leavis, *D. H. Lawrence*, 226.

43. Sherman, "Lawrence Cultivates His Beard," 256.

44. Fowler, *Kinds of Literature*, 183.

45. Hawthorne, *Young Goodman Brown*, 290. The real-life model for Dollie Urquhart is Dorothy Brett, whose aristocratic pedigree Lawrence made much of, and who may herself have been the victim of childhood abuse. The journey Dollie makes with Romero in the story retraces the trip Lawrence made in late August 1924 to Columbine Lake in the Sangre de Cristo Mountains with Brett. Their neighbors at the Del Monte Ranch, William and Rachel Hawke, took paying guests, and Brett had ridden to Columbine Lake in the first instance with the Hawkes' "dudes." Dollie, like Miss James in "The Last Laugh," who is also modeled on Brett, is a painter who fears being touched by men.

46. Mollinger, "The Divided Self," 79.

47. Hawthorne, *Scarlet Letter*, 66.

48. Chase, *The American Novel*, 191.

49. Sagar, introduction to Lawrence, *Complete Short Novels*, 35.

50. Carswell, *Savage Pilgrimage*, 201.

51. Leavis, *D. H. Lawrence*, 225.

52. Lynch, *Xerophilia*, 53.

53. Pratt, *Imperial Eyes*, 6.

54. See Acuna, *Occupied America*.

55. DeBuys, *Enchantment and Exploitation*, 101, 211.

56. Padilla, "Imprisoned Narrative," 46.

57. Luc Ferry, quoted in Bate, *Song of the Earth*, 267.

58. DeBuys, *Enchantment and Exploitation*, 316.

59. Ibid., 141.

60. See Everts, "Dude Wranglers"; Rinehart, "Dude West"; Young's serial "Dude Ranch" articles; and Austin's "New Mexico Dude Life." Like "The Princess," Oliver La Farge's story "Country Boy," which was published in the *Saturday Evening Post* in 1938, is the story of a "dude wrangler" and an older, wealthier, woman. La Farge, *Yellow Sun, Bright Sky*, 107.

61. Jameson, "Third-World Literature," 338.

62. Delgado and Stefancic, "Minority Men," 217.

63. Anzaldúa, *Borderlands/La Frontera*, 83.

64. McClintock, *Imperial Leather*, 24.

65. Roberson, "American women and travel writing," 223.

66. Fregoso, "Re-Imagining Chicana Urban Identities," 76.

67. Anzaldúa, *Borderlands/La Frontera*, 25.

68. Millett, *Sexual Politics*, 286.

69. Ibid., 292. Siegel reads "The Woman Who Rode Away" as a stage in the journey toward the vision of cultural feminism that is realized, she contends, in "St. Mawr": Siegel argues that "Lawrence's women so often ride away because they are less suited by nature than men to conform to the dictates of our misnamed and misguided civilization." "'St. Mawr,'" 277.

70. See Kinkead-Weekes, "Gringo Senora"; Millett, *Sexual Politics*, 286.

71. Roberts, *D. H. Lawrence*, 108.

72. As the editors of the Cambridge Edition of *The Woman Who Rode Away and Other Stories* note, it was during the journey Lawrence made through northern Mexico with Kai Götzsche that he heard reports of "several wild Indian tribes living in the interior of Sonora and Chihuahua, the two northern states of Mexico bordering on the USA. The Huicholes, living further south, probably suggested the name for the Chilchuis," 390.

73. See Luhan, *Lorenzo in Taos*, 219.

74. *Laughing Horse* 13 (1926) and 14 (1927) carry advertisements for "The Indian Detour," designed for "those who wish to extend their trip off-the-beaten-path." The 1927 advertisement is reproduced in Udall, *Spud Johnson and Laughing Horse*, 138. On Indian Detours, see John Pen La Farge, *Turn Left at the Sleeping Dog*, and Padget, *Indian Country*. In "St. Mawr," "wild America" is only a car journey away from the commodified tourist mecca of Santa Fe. An advertising billboard welcomes "*Mr. Tourist*" to the town's annual fiesta, prompting Lou

Carrington to acknowledge her own connivance and that of her mother with the tourist trade (she "said in her own mind: 'Welcome Also Mrs and Miss Tourist!,'" 132, 133).

75. Roberts, *D. H. Lawrence*, 100.
76. Howe, *Birth-mark*, 89.
77. Kolodny, *Land Before Her*, 18.
78. Howe, *Birth-mark*, 126–27.
79. Kolodny, *Land Before Her*, 61.
80. Contreras, "'These Were Just Names to Her,'" 91, 100.
81. Giles, *Atlantic Republic*, 182.

Conclusion

1. Luhan, *Lorenzo in Taos*, 219.
2. Margery Toomer, letter to Mabel Dodge Luhan, Beinecke Rare Book and Manuscript Library, Yale University Library, Mabel Dodge Luhan Papers YCAL MSS 196.34, 993–94, n.d.
3. See La Farge, "Hard Winter" (1933), in his *Bright Sun, Yellow Sky*, 23–43.
4. Rudnick, introduction to Luhan, *Edge of Taos Desert*, xiii.
5. Luhan, *Edge of Taos Desert*, 331.
6. Eliot, review, 359; Kaplan, *Circulating Genius*, 199.
7. Rudnick, *Utopian Vistas*, 302.
8. Luhan, *Lorenzo in Taos*, 31, 45.
9. Ibid., 255, 67, 167, 73.
10. Rudnick, introduction to Luhan, *Edge of Taos Desert*, xiii.
11. Luhan, "Ballad of a Bad Girl," 299.
12. Norwood and Monk, *The Desert Is No Lady*, 2.
13. Rosenfeld, "D. H. Lawrence," 126.
14. See Miller, "Gender, sexuality and the modernist poem."
15. Brett, *Lawrence and Brett*, 107.
16. McGann, *Theory of Modern Textual Criticism*, 119, 122; Laird, *Women Coauthors*, 2; Ingersoll, *Lawrence, Desire, and Narrative*, 144.
17. Quoted in Hignett, *Brett*, 218; Brett, *Lawrence and Brett*, n.p.
18. Brett, Mabel, and the Taos Indians boycotted the opening ceremony of Lawrence's shrine at the Kiowa Ranch; Mabel allegedly plotted to steal the ashes and blow up the shrine. See Hignett, *Brett*, 224–28.
19. Laird, *Women Coauthors*, 2.
20. Quoted in Lynes, *O'Keeffe, Stieglitz and the Critics*, 46. With Alfred Stieglitz, O'Keeffe would act as the guardian of Lawrence's legacy in another sense, too, keeping on Brett's behalf her diaries, Lawrence's manuscripts, and her correspondence with Lawrence, a collection Brett willed to Stieglitz and O'Keeffe.
21. According to Drohojowska-Philip, when O'Keeffe moved permanently to the Ghost Ranch in Abiquiu in 1948, she identified with "St. Mawr"'s Lou in her quest for "self-acceptance and redemption" in northern New Mexico. *Full Bloom*, 299. Burke, however, argues that "O'Keeffe's vision" would "supplant Lawrence's." In her study of Mabel Dodge Luhan, primi-

tivism and place, Burke refers to a poster reproduction of Maria Chabot's well-known photograph of O'Keeffe on a motorbike in New Mexico. Captioned "Women Who Rode Away," the poster is proof, for Burke, that "Lawrence may have condemned to death the woman who rode away, but in the annals of popular culture, O'Keeffe has written a new ending. New Mexico is where women ride away, but they ride toward creative inspiration," 173. O'Keeffe's own *Lawrence Tree* is firmer and finer proof that the collaborations between Lawrence and women in New Mexico did not end with Mabel's murder sentence in "The Woman Who Rode Away."

22. Howe, *The Birth-mark*, 156.
23. Bell, "Lawrence and Modernism," 180.
24. Eliot, *After Strange Gods*, 60–61.
25. Chaudhuri, *D. H. Lawrence*, 163.
26. Hicks, *Border Writing*, xxliii.

Bibliography

Acuna, Rodolfo. *Occupied America: A History of Chicanos*. 6th ed. London: Longman, 2006.
Aldington, Richard. *Portrait of a Genius, But . . . : The Life of D. H. Lawrence, 1885–1930*. London: Heinemann, 1950.
Altieri, Charles. *Painterly Abstraction in Modernist Poetry: The Contemporaneity of Modernism*. Cambridge: Cambridge University Press, 1989.
Anon. "D. H. Lawrence Bombs Our Literary Shrines." *Current Opinion* (September 1923): 305–7.
Anzaldúa, Gloria. *Borderlands/La Frontera: The New Mestiza*. San Francisco: Aunt Lute Books, 1999.
Arac, Jonathan. *Critical Genealogies: Historical Situations for Postmodern Literary Studies*. New York: Columbia University Press, 1987.
Arnold, Armin. *D. H. Lawrence and America*. London: Linden Press, 1958.
———, ed. *The Symbolic Meaning: The Uncollected Versions of "Studies in Classic American Literature."* Fontwell: Centaur Press, 1962.
Auden, W. H. *Collected Poems*. Edited by Edward Mendelson. London: Faber and Faber, 1976.
Auerbach, Jerold S. *Explorers in Eden: Pueblo Indians and the Promised Land*. Albuquerque: University of New Mexico Press, 2008.
Austin, Mary. *The American Rhythm: Studies and Reëxpressions of Amerindian Songs*. Santa Fe: Sunstone Press, 2007.
———. *Land of Journey's Ending*. Tucson: University of Arizona Press, 1983.
———. "Mrs. Austin Protests." *New Republic* 25 (January 5, 1921): 70.
———. "New Mexico Dude Life." *New York Times* (June 8, 1941), sec. 10.8.
Babbitt, Irving. *Literature and the American College*. Boston: Houghton, Mifflin, 1908.
Bachelard, Gaston. *The Poetics of Space*. Translated by Maria Jolas. Boston: Beacon Press, 1994.
Baker, Houston A., Jr. and Leslie A. Fiedler, eds. *English Literature: Opening Up the Canon*. Baltimore: Johns Hopkins University Press, 1981.

Balbert, Peter, and Phillip L. Marcus, eds. *D. H. Lawrence: A Centenary Consideration*. Ithaca: Cornell University Press, 1985

Baldick, Chris. *The Oxford English Literary History Volume 10: 1910–1940. The Modern Movement*. Oxford: Oxford University Press, 2004.

Banks, Charles Edward. "Thomas Morton of Merry Mount." *Proceedings of the Massachusetts Historical Society* 58 (1924): 157–93.

Barthes, Roland. *Image-Music-Text*. Translated by Stephen Heath. New York: Hill and Wang, 1978.

Bate, Jonathan. *The Song of the Earth*. London: Picador, 2000.

Becket, Fiona. *D. H. Lawrence*. London: Routledge, 1972.

Bell, Michael. "Lawrence and Modernism." In Fernihough, *The Cambridge Companion to D. H. Lawrence*, 179–86.

Bendixen, Alfred, and Judith Hamera, eds. *The Cambridge Companion to American Travel Writing*. Cambridge: Cambridge University Press, 2009.

Bercovitch, Sacvan, ed. *The Cambridge History of American Literature: Volume Six, Prose Writing, 1910–1950*. Cambridge: Cambridge University Press, 2002.

Berger, Morris, Brian Wallis, and Simon Watson, eds. *Constructing Masculinity*. London: Routledge, 1995.

Bergland, René. *The National Uncanny: Indian Ghosts and American Subjects*. Hanover: University Press of New England, 2000.

Blake, Casey Nelson. *Beloved Community: The Cultural Criticism of Randolph Bourne, Van Wyck Brooks, Waldo Frank, and Lewis Mumford*. Chapel Hill: University of North Carolina Press, 1990.

Bloom, Harold. *The Anatomy of Influence: Literature as a Way of Life*. New Haven: Yale University Press, 2011.

Bourne, Randolph. "The War and the Intellectuals." *Seven Arts* (June 1917): 133–36.

Bourne-Taylor, Carole, and Ariane Mildenberg, eds. *Phenomenology, Modernism and Beyond*. Bern: Peter Lang, 2010.

Boyd, Ernest. "Ku Klux Kriticism." In Spingarn, *Criticism in America*, 309–20.

Bradshaw, Melissa. *Amy Lowell: Diva Poet*. Farnham: Ashgate, 2011.

Breslin, James E. "Whitman and the Early Development of William Carlos Williams." *PMLA* 82.7 (1967): 613–21.

Brett, Dorothy. *Lawrence and Brett: A Friendship*. Philadelphia: J. B. Lippincott Company, 1933.

Brock, Henry Irving. "D. H. Lawrence Strings Some Literary Pearls." *New York Times Book Review* (September 16, 1923): 9.

Brooker, Peter, and Andrew Thacker, eds. *The Oxford Critical and Cultural History of Modernist Magazines: Volume II: North America 1894–1960*. Oxford: Oxford University Press, 2012.

Brooks, Van Wyck. *America's Coming-of-Age*. New York: B. W. Huebsch, 1915.

———. *An Autobiography*. New York: E. P. Dutton and Company, 1965.

———. "The Critics and Young America." In Spingarn, *Criticism in America*, 116–51.

———. *Days of the Phoenix: The Nineteen-Twenties I Remember*. New York: E. P. Dutton and Company, 1957.

———. "On Creating a Usable Past." *Dial* (April 11, 1918): 337–41.

———. *Sketches in Criticism*. New York: E. P. Dutton and Company, 1932.
Buell, Lawrence. *The Environmental Imagination: Thoreau, Nature Writing, and the Formation of American Culture*. Cambridge, Mass.: Belknap Press of Harvard University Press, 1995.
———. *Writing for an Endangered World: Literature, Culture, and Environment in the US and Beyond*. Cambridge, Mass.: Belknap Press of Harvard University Press, 2001.
Burke, Flannery. *From Greenwich Village to Taos: Primitivism and Place at Mabel Dodge Luhan's*. Lawrence: University Press of Kansas, 2008.
Burwell, Rose Marie. "A Catalogue of D. H. Lawrence's Reading from Early Childhood." Special issue, "D. H. Lawrence's Reading." *D. H. Lawrence Review* 3.3 (1970).
Bynner, Witter. *Journey with Genius: Recollections and Reflections Concerning the D. H. Lawrences*. New York: John Day, 1951.
———. *The Selected Witter Bynner: Poems, Plays, Translations, Prose, and Letters*. Edited by James Kraft. Albuquerque: University of New Mexico Press, 1999.
Calderón, Héctor, and José David Saldívar, eds. *Criticism in the Borderlands: Studies in Chicano Literature, Culture, and Ideology*. Durham, N.C.: Duke University Press, 1991.
Carr, Helen. *Inventing the American Primitive: Politics, Gender and the Representation of Native American Literary Traditions, 1789–1936*. Cork: Cork University Press, 1996.
———. *The Verse Revolutionaries: Ezra Pound, H.D. and the Imagists*. London: Jonathan Cape, 2009.
Carswell, Catherine. *The Savage Pilgrimage: A Narrative of D. H. Lawrence*. Cambridge: Cambridge University Press, 1981.
Carter, Frederick. *D. H. Lawrence and the Body Mystical*. London: Denis Archer, 1932.
Castiglia, Christopher. "Cold War Melancholy, Cold War Hopes." Panel 423, "A Critical Past." Modern Language Association Convention (Boston, 2013).
Castro, Michael. *Interpreting the Indian: Twentieth-Century Poets and the Native American*. Norman: University of Oklahoma Press, 1983.
Castronovo, Russ. "Death to the American Renaissance: History, Heidegger, Poe." *ESQ: A Journal of the American Renaissance* 1.3 (2003): 179–92.
Cavitch, David. *D. H. Lawrence and the New World*. New York: Oxford University Press, 1969.
Cederstrom, Lorelei. "Walt Whitman and the Imagists." In Sill, *Walt Whitman of Mickle Street*, 205–23.
Chambers, Jessie. *D. H. Lawrence: A Personal Record*. Cambridge: Cambridge University Press, 1980.
Chase, Richard. *The American Novel and Its Tradition*. Baltimore: Johns Hopkins University Press, 1980.
Chaudhuri, Amit. *D. H. Lawrence and "Difference": Postcoloniality and the Poetry of the Present*. Oxford: Clarendon Press, 2003.
Clark, L. D. *Dark Night of the Body: D. H. Lawrence's The Plumed Serpent*. Austin: University of Texas Press, 1964.
———. *The Minoan Distance: The Symbolism of Travel in D. H. Lawrence*. Tucson: University of Arizona Press, 1980.
Clifford, James. *Routes: Travel and Translation in the Late Twentieth Century*. Cambridge, Mass.: Harvard University Press, 1997.

Cohen, Margaret. "Traveling Genres." In Manning and Taylor, *Transatlantic Literary Studies*, 232–35.

Cole, Thomas. "Essay on American Scenery." In McCoubrey, *American Art 1700–1960*, 98–110.

Contreras, Sheila. "'These Were Just Names to Her': Chilchui Indians and 'The Woman Who Rode Away.'" *D. H. Lawrence Review* 25.1–3 (1993–94): 91–103.

Corbin, Alice. "America." *Poetry* 1.3 (1912): 81.

Coroneos, Con, and Trudi Tate. "Lawrence's tales." In Fernihough, *Cambridge Companion to D. H. Lawrence*, 103–18.

Cowan, James C. *D. H. Lawrence and the Trembling Balance*. Philadelphia: Pennsylvania State University Press, 1990.

———. *D. H. Lawrence's American Journey: A Study in Literature and Myth*. Cleveland: Press of Case Western Reserve University, 1970.

Crick, Brian, and Michael DiSanto. "D. H. Lawrence 'An opportunity and a test': The Leavis-Eliot Controversy Revisited." *Cambridge Quarterly* 38.2 (2009): 130–46.

Cushman, Keith. Introduction to Lawrence, *Birds, Beasts and Flowers* (2007), vii–xiv.

———. "Lawrence and Knud Merrild: New Materials, New Perspectives." In Cushman and Ingersoll, *D. H. Lawrence: New Worlds*, 68–95.

Cushman, Keith, and Earl G. Ingersoll, eds. *D. H. Lawrence: New Worlds*. Madison: Fairleigh Dickinson University Press, 2003.

Dahlberg, Edward. *Can These Bones Live*. New York: New Directions, 1960.

Daniels, Kurt L. "Mr. Lawrence on American Literature." *New Republic* 36 (October 24, 1924): 236.

Davenport, Guy. *Geography of the Imagination*. London: Picador, 1984.

Davie, Donald. "Two Ways Out of Whitman." In Doyle, *William Carlos Williams*, 346–50.

Davis, Alex, and Lee M. Jenkins, eds. *The Cambridge Companion to Modernist Poetry*. Cambridge: Cambridge University Press, 2007.

———. *Locations of Literary Modernism: Region and Nation in British and American Modernist Poetry*. Cambridge: Cambridge University Press, 2000.

Day, Gary, and Brian Docherty, eds., *British Poetry, 1900–50: Aspects of Tradition*. London: St. Martin's Press, 1995.

de Beauvoir, Simone. *The Second Sex*. 1949. Translated by H. M. Parshley. Harmondsworth: Penguin, 1972.

DeBuys, William. *Enchantment and Exploitation: The Life and Hard Times of a New Mexico Mountain Range*. Albuquerque: University of New Mexico Press, 1985.

de Crèvecoeur, J. Hector St. John. *Letters from an American Farmer*. Oxford: Oxford University Press, 2009.

Delany, Paul. *D. H. Lawrence's Nightmare: The Writer and His Circle in the Years of the Great War*. New York: Basic Books, 1978.

Delgado, Richard, and Jean Stefancic. "Minority Men, Misery, and the Marketplace of Ideas." In Berger, Wallis, and Watson, *Constructing Masculinity*, 211–20.

Deloria, Philip J. *Playing Indian: Red Earth, White Lies*. New Haven: Yale University Press, 1999.

Dewey, John. "Americanism and Localism." *Dial* 68.6 (1920): 684–88.

DiBattista, Maria. *"Women in Love*: D. H. Lawrence's Judgment Book." In Balbert and Marcus, *D. H. Lawrence*, 67–90.

Dickstein, Morris. "The critic and society, 1900–1950." In Litz, Menand, and Rainey, *Cambridge History of Literary Criticism*, 322–76.

Dijkstra, Bram. *Cubism, Stieglitz, and the Early Poetry of William Carlos Williams: The Hieroglyphics of a New Speech*. Princeton: Princeton University Press, 1969.

Dilworth, Leah. *Imagining Indians in the Southwest: Persistent Visions of a Primitive Past*. Washington, D.C.: Smithsonian Institution Press, 1996.

Dimock, Wai Chee. *Through Other Continents: American Literature across Deep Time*. Princeton: Princeton University Press, 2009.

Dimock, Wai Chee, and Lawrence Buell, eds. *Shades of the Planet: American Literature as World Literature*. Princeton: Princeton University Press, 2007.

Doyle, Charles, ed. *William Carlos Williams: The Critical Heritage*. London: Routledge, 1980.

Doyle, Laura. "Toward a Philosophy of Transnationalism." *Journal of Transnational American Studies* 1.1 (February 2009).

Doyle, Laura, and Laura Winkiel, eds. *Geomodernisms: Race, Modernism, Modernity*. Bloomington: Indiana University Press, 2005.

Draper, R. P., ed. *D. H. Lawrence: The Critical Heritage*. London: Routledge, 1970.

Drohojowska-Philip, Hunter. *Full Bloom: The Art and Life of Georgia O'Keeffe*. New York: Norton, 2004.

Egan, Maurice Francis. "On the Sin of Being an American." *Literary Digest International Book Review* (September 1923): 28.

Eliot, T. S. *After Strange Gods: A Primer of Modern Heresy*. London: Faber and Faber, 1934.

——. *Selected Prose of T. S. Eliot*. Edited by Frank Kermode. London: Faber and Faber, 1975.

——. Review of *Son of Woman* by J. M. Murry. In Draper, *D. H. Lawrence*, 359–64.

Ellis, David. Introduction to Lawrence, *Complete Poems* (2002), i–xviii.

——. *D. H. Lawrence: Dying Game, 1922–1930*. Cambridge: Cambridge University Press, 1998.

——. "Poetry and science in the psychology books." In Ellis and Mills, *D. H. Lawrence's Non-Fiction*, 98–119.

Ellis, David, and Howard Mills. *D. H. Lawrence's Non-Fiction: Art, Thought and Genre*. Cambridge: Cambridge University Press, 1988.

Everts, Hal G. "Dude Wranglers." *Saturday Evening Post* (May 1, 1920): 32–34.

——. "More Tourists in West." *New York Times* (20 August 1923): 23.

Feidelson, Charles. *Symbolism and American Literature*. Chicago: University of Chicago Press, 1953.

Feinstein, Elaine. *Lawrence and the Women: The Intimate Life of D. H. Lawrence*. New York: HarperCollins, 1993.

Fedirka, Sarah A. "'Our Own Authentic Wonderland': The Modernist Geographical Imagination and 'Little Magazines' of the American West: *Gyroscope* (1929–30); *Troubadour* (1928–32); *Westward* (1927–34); *Laughing Horse* (1921–39); *New Mexico Quarterly* (1931–69); and *Intermountain Review* (1937–65)." In Brooker and Thacker, *Oxford Critical and Cultural History of Modernist Magazines*, 576–98.

Fernihough, Anne, ed. *The Cambridge Companion to D. H. Lawrence*. Cambridge: Cambridge University Press, 2001.

———. *D. H. Lawrence: Aesthetics and Ideology*. Oxford: Clarendon Press, 1993.

ffytche, Matt. "The Arduous Pain of Appearance: Phenomenology and its Uncertainties in the Work of George Oppen." In Bourne-Taylor and Mildenberg, *Phenomenology, Modernism and Beyond*, 189–204.

Fiedler, Leslie. *Love and Death in the American Novel*. Harmondsworth: Penguin, 1984.

———. *The Return of the Vanishing American*. London: Jonathan Cape, 1968.

Fishkin, Shelley Fisher. "Crossroads of Cultures: The Transnational Turn in American Studies." *American Quarterly* 57.1 (2005): 17–57.

Forster, E. M. *A Passage to India*. Harmondsworth: Penguin, 2005.

Fowler, Alastair. *Kinds of Literature: An Introduction to the Theory of Genres and Modes*. Oxford: Clarendon Press, 1982.

Frank, Waldo. *Our America*. New York: Boni and Liveright, 1919.

Frank, Waldo, Lewis Mumford, Dorothy Norman, et. al., eds. *America and Alfred Stieglitz: A Collective Portrait with 120 Illustrations*. New York: Literary Guild, 1934.

Franks, Jill, Eleanor H. Green, Sean Matthews, and Peter Preston, eds. *D. H. Lawrence: Return to Eastwood*. Nottingham: Critical, Cultural and Communications Press/D. H. Lawrence Research Centre, 2011.

Frazer, James George. *Totemism and Exogamy*. 1893. London: Forgotten Books, 2012.

Fregoso, Rosa Linda. "Re-Imagining Chicana Urban Identities in the Public Sphere, Cool Chuca Style." In Kaplan, Alarcón, and Moallem, *Between Woman and Nation*, 72–91.

Friedman, Susan Stanford. *Penelope's Web: Gender, Modernity, H.D.'s Fiction*. Cambridge: Cambridge University Press, 1990.

Fry, Roger. *Cézanne: A Study of His Development*. London: Hogarth Press, 1927.

Genette, Gerard. *Paratexts: Thresholds of Interpretation*. Translated by Jane E. Lewin. Cambridge: Cambridge University Press, 1997.

Gilbert, Sandra. *Acts of Attention: The Poems of D. H. Lawrence*. 2nd ed. Carbondale: Southern Illinois University Press, 1990.

Giles, Paul. *Atlantic Republic: The American Tradition in English Literature*. Oxford: Oxford University Press, 2006.

———. "The Deterritorialization of American Literature." In Dimock and Buell, *Shades of the Planet*, 39–61.

———. *The Global Remapping of American Literature*. Princeton: Princeton University Press, 2011.

———. *Virtual Americas: Transnational Fictions and the Transatlantic Imaginary*. Durham, N.C.: Duke University Press, 2002.

Ginsberg, Allen. *Collected Poems 1947–1980*. Harmondsworth: Penguin, 1987.

Goldsmith, Arnold L. *American Literary Criticism: 1905–1963*. Boston: Twayne, 1979.

Gonzalez-Berry, Erlinda, and David Maciel, eds. *The Contested Homeland: A Chicano History of the United States*. Albuquerque: University of New Mexico Press, 2000.

Goodman, Audrey. *Translating Southwestern Landscapes: The Making of an Anglo Literary Region*. Tucson: University of Arizona Press, 2002.

Grad, Bonnie L. "Georgia O'Keeffe's Lawrencian Vision." *Archives of American Art Journal* 38.3/4 (1998): 2–19.
Graff, Gerald. *Professing Literature: An Institutional History*. Chicago: University of Chicago Press, 2008.
Greenspan, Ezra, ed. *The Cambridge Companion to Walt Whitman*. Cambridge: Cambridge University Press, 1995.
Gross, Robert A. "The Transnational Turn: Rediscovering American Studies in a Wider World." *Journal of American Studies* 34.2 (2000): 373–93.
H.D. *Bid Me to Live*. London: Virago, 1984.
———. *Collected Poems 1912–1944*. Edited by Louis L. Martz. New York: New Directions, 1983.
Halter, Peter. *The Revolution in the Visual Arts and the Poetry of William Carlos Williams*. Cambridge: Cambridge University Press, 1994.
Harper, Margaret Mills. *Wisdom of Two: The Spiritual and Literary Collaboration of George and W. B. Yeats*. Oxford: Oxford University Press, 2006.
Harrison, Andrew. *D. H. Lawrence and Italian Futurism: A Study of Influence*. Amsterdam: Rodopi, 2003.
Harrison, Jane. *Ancient Art and Ritual*. London: Williams and Norgate, 1913.
Hartley, Marsden. *Adventures in the Arts*. Charleston: Bibliobazaar, 2007.
———. "America as Landscape." In *Marsden Hartley, New Mexico 1918–1920: An American Discovering America*, n.p. New York: Alexandre Gallery, 2003.
———. "The Festival of the Corn." In Henderson, *Turquoise Trail*, 44–51.
Hawthorne, Nathaniel. *The Scarlet Letter*. Harmondsworth: Penguin, 1970.
———. *Young Goodman Brown and Other Tales*. Edited by Brian Harding. New York: Oxford University Press, 1987.
Healey, E. Claire, and Keith Cushman, eds. *The Letters of D. H. Lawrence and Amy Lowell 1914–1925*. Santa Barbara, Calif.: Black Sparrow Press, 1985.
Heidegger, Martin. *Poetry, Language, Thought*. Translated by Albert Hofstadter. New York: Harper and Row, 1971.
Henderson, Alice Corbin. "Aboriginal Songs II." *Poetry* 9.5 (1917): 256.
———. "Indian Songs." *Poetry* 9.5 (1917): 235.
———. *Red Earth: Poems of New Mexico*. Santa Fe: Sunstone Press, 2003.
———, ed. *The Turquoise Trail: An Anthology of New Mexico Poetry*. Boston: Houghton Mifflin, 1928.
Herzinger, Kim A. *D. H. Lawrence in His Time: 1908–1915*. Lewisburg, Pa.: Bucknell University Press, 1982.
Hicks, D. Emily. *Border Writing: The Multidimensional Text*. Minneapolis: University of Minnesota Press, 1991.
Hignett, Sean. *Brett: From Bloomsbury to New Mexico*. London: Hodder and Stoughton, 1984.
Hoffman, Frederick J. Review of *D. H. Lawrence and America* by Armin Arnold. *American Literature* 31.4 (1960): 496–98.
———. *The Twenties: American Writing in the Postwar Decade*. New York: Viking Press, 1955.
Hooker, Jeremy. Introduction to Lawrence, *Birds, Beasts and Flowers* (2011), 7–13.

Howarth, Peter. *British Poetry in the Age of Modernism*. Cambridge: Cambridge University Press, 2005.

———. *The Cambridge Introduction to Modernist Poetry*. Cambridge: Cambridge University Press, 2012.

Howe, Susan. *The Birth-mark: Unsettling the Wilderness in American Literary History*. Hanover, Conn.: Wesleyan University Press, 1993.

Hughes, Glenn. *Imagism and the Imagists*. New York: Humanities Press, 1960.

Hyde, Virginia. "Mexican Cypresses: Multiculturalism in Lawrence's 'Novel of America.'" In Cushman and Ingersoll, *D. H. Lawrence*, 195–215.

Hyde, Virginia Crosswhite, and Earl G. Ingersoll, eds. *"Terra Incognita": D. H. Lawrence at the Frontiers*. Madison: Fairleigh Dickinson University Press, 2010.

———. *Windows to the Sun: D. H. Lawrence's "Thought-Adventures."* Madison: Fairleigh Dickinson University Press, 2009.

Ingersoll, Earl. *D. H. Lawrence, Desire, and Narrative*. Gainesville: University Press of Florida, 2001.

———. "'A New Continent of the Soul': Lawrence's Transcultural/Transhistorical Meeting with Herman Melville." In Hyde and Ingersoll, *Windows to the Sun*, 21–49.

Jameson, Fredric. *Postmodernism, Or, The Cultural Logic of Late Capitalism*. Durham, N.C.: Duke University Press, 1990.

———. "Third-World Literature in the Era of Multinational Capitalism." In *The Jameson Reader*, edited by Michael Hardt and Kathi Weeks, 315–39. Oxford: Blackwell, 2000.

Jay, Paul. "The Myth of 'America' and the Politics of Location: Modernity, Border Studies, and the Literature of the Americas." *Arizona Quarterly* 54.2 (1998): 165–92.

Johnson, Walter Willard. "Sun-Noise." In Udall, *Spud Johnson and Laughing Horse*, 153–54.

Jones, Peter, ed. *Imagist Poetry*. Harmondsworth: Penguin, 1972.

Kammen, Michael. *Mystic Chords of Memory: The Transformation of Tradition in American Culture*. New York: Vintage, 1993.

Kaplan, Caren, Norma Alarcón, and Minoo Moallem, eds. *Between Woman and Nation: Nationalisms, Transnational Feminisms, and the State*. Durham, N.C.: Duke University Press, 1999.

Kaplan, Sydney Janet. *Circulating Genius: John Middleton Murry, Katherine Mansfield and D. H. Lawrence*. Edinburgh: Edinburgh University Press, 2010.

Karrell, Linda K. *Writing Together/Writing Apart: Collaboration in Western American Literature*. Lincoln: University of Nebraska Press, 2002.

Kinkead-Weekes, Mark. *D. H. Lawrence: Triumph to Exile, 1912–1922*. Cambridge: Cambridge University Press, 1996.

———. "The Gringo Senora Who Rode Away." *D. H. Lawrence Review* 22.3 (1990): 251–65.

Kolodny, Annette. *The Land Before Her: Fantasy and Experience of the American Frontiers, 1630–1860*. Chapel Hill: University of North Carolina Press, 1984.

———. *The Lay of the Land: Metaphor as Experience and History in American Life and Letters*. Chapel Hill: University of North Carolina Press, 1975.

La Farge, John Pen. *Turn Left at the Sleeping Dog: Scripting the Santa Fe Legend, 1920–1955*. Albuquerque: University of New Mexico Press, 2001.

La Farge, Oliver. *Yellow Sun, Bright Sky: The Indian Country Stories of Oliver La Farge*. Edited by David L. Caffey. Albuquerque: University of New Mexico Press, 1988.

Laird, Holly. *Self and Sequence: The Poetry of D. H. Lawrence*. Charlottesville: University Press of Virginia, 1988.

———. *Women Coauthors*. Urbana: University of Illinois Press, 2000.

Lawrence, D. H. *Apocalypse and the Writings on Revelation*. Edited by Mara Kalnins, Cambridge: Cambridge University Press, 1980.

———. *Birds, Beasts and Flowers*. Edited by Keith Cushman. Jaffrey, N.H.: Black Sparrow Books, 2007.

———. *Birds, Beasts and Flowers*. Exeter: Shearsman, 2011.

———. *Complete Poems*. Edited by Vivian de Sola Pinto and F. Warren Roberts. Harmondsworth: Penguin, 1977.

———. *Complete Poems of D. H. Lawrence*. Edited by David Ellis. Ware, U.K.: Wordsworth Editions, 2002.

———. *The Complete Short Novels*. Edited by Keith Sagar and Melissa Partridge. Harmondsworth: Penguin, 1982.

———. *The First and Second Lady Chatterley Novels*. Edited by Dieter Mehl and Christa Jansohn. Cambridge: Cambridge University Press, 1999.

———. *Introductions and Reviews*. Edited by N. H. Reeve and John Worthen. Cambridge: Cambridge University Press, 2005.

———. *Kangaroo*. Edited by Bruce Steele. Cambridge: Cambridge University Press, 1994.

———. *Late Essays and Articles*. Edited by James T. Boulton. Cambridge: Cambridge University Press, 2004.

———. *Letters of D. H. Lawrence. Volume I. September 1901–May 1913*. Edited by James T. Boulton. Cambridge: Cambridge University Press, 1979.

———. *Letters of D. H. Lawrence. Volume II. June 1913–October 1916*. Edited by George J. Zytaruk and James T. Boulton. Cambridge: Cambridge University Press, 1981.

———. *Letters of D. H. Lawrence. Volume III. October 1916–June 1921*. Edited by James T. Boulton and Andrew Robertson. Cambridge: Cambridge University Press, 1984.

———. *Letters of D. H. Lawrence. Volume IV. June 1921–March 1924*. Edited by Warren Roberts, James T. Boulton, and Elizabeth Mansfield. Cambridge: Cambridge University Press, 1987.

———. *Letters of D. H. Lawrence. Volume V. March 1924–March 1927*. Edited by James T. Boulton and Lindeth Vasey. Cambridge: Cambridge University Press, 1989.

———. *Letters of D. H. Lawrence. Volume VI. March 1927–November 1928*. Edited by James T. Boulton and Margaret Boulton, with Gerald M. Lacy. Cambridge: Cambridge Press, 1991.

———. *Letters of D. H. Lawrence. Volume VII. November 1928–February 1930*. Edited by Keith Sagar and James T. Boulton. Cambridge: Cambridge University Press, 1993.

———. *Letters of D. H. Lawrence. Volume VIII. Previously Letters and General Index*. Edited by James T. Boulton. Cambridge: Cambridge University Press, 2000.

———. *Mornings in Mexico and Other Essays*. Edited by Virginia Crosswhite Hyde. Cambridge: Cambridge University Press, 2009.

———. *Phoenix: The Posthumous Papers of D. H. Lawrence*. Edited by Edward D. McDonald. London: Heinemann, 1936.

―――. *Phoenix II: Uncollected, Unpublished, and Other Prose Works by D. H. Lawrence*. Edited by Warren Roberts and Harry T. Moore. New York: Viking Press, 1970.

―――. *The Plays*. Edited by Hans-Wilhelm Schwarze and John Worthen. Cambridge: Cambridge University Press, 1999.

―――. *The Plumed Serpent*. Edited by L. D. Clark. Cambridge: Cambridge University Press, 1987.

―――. *The Princess and Other Stories*. Edited by Keith Sagar. Harmondsworth: Penguin, 1971.

―――. *Psychoanalysis and the Unconscious and Fantasia of the Unconscious*. Edited by Bruce Steele. Cambridge: Cambridge University Press, 2004.

―――. *Quetzalcoatl*. Edited by N. H. Reeve. Cambridge: Cambridge University Press, 2011.

―――. *The Rainbow*. Edited by Mark Kinkead-Weekes. Cambridge: Cambridge University Press, 1989.

―――. *Reflections on the Death of a Porcupine and Other Essays*. Edited by Michael Herbert. Cambridge: Cambridge University Press, 1988.

―――. *Sketches of Etruscan Places and Other Italian Essays*. Edited by Simonetta de Filippis. Cambridge: Cambridge University Press, 1992.

―――. *St. Mawr and Other Stories*. Edited by Brian Finney. Cambridge: Cambridge University Press, 1983.

―――. *Studies in Classic American Literature*. Edited by Ezra Greenspan, Lindeth Vasey, and John Worthen. Cambridge: Cambridge University Press, 2003.

―――. *Studies in Classic American Literature*. Edited by Jon Thompson. Exeter, U.K.: Shearsman, 2011.

―――. *Study of Thomas Hardy and Other Essays*. Edited by Bruce Steele. Cambridge: Cambridge University Press, 1985.

―――. *Twilight in Italy*. Edited by Paul Eggert. Cambridge: Cambridge University Press, 1994.

―――. *The Woman Who Rode Away and Other Stories*. Edited by Dieter Mehl and Christa Jansohn. Cambridge: Cambridge University Press, 1995.

―――. *Women in Love*. Edited by David Farmer, John Worthen, and Lindeth Vasey. Cambridge: Cambridge University Press, 1987.

Lawrence, Frieda. *Not I, But the Wind. . . .* London: Granada, 1983.

Leavis, F. R. "D. H. Lawrence and Professor Irving Babbitt." *Scrutiny* 1.3 (1932): 273–79.

―――. *D. H. Lawrence: Novelist*. London: Chatto and Windus, 1955.

Lee, Hermione. *Willa Cather: A Life Saved Up*. London: Virago, 1989.

Levine, George. *The Realistic Imagination: English Fiction from Frankenstein to Lady Chatterley*. Chicago: University of Chicago Press, 1981.

Lewis, Edith. *Willa Cather: A Personal Record*. New York: Knopf, 1953.

Lewis, R.W.B. *The American Adam: Innocence, Tragedy, and Tradition in the Nineteenth Century*. Chicago: University of Chicago Press, 1955.

Lewis, Wyndham. *Paleface: The Philosophy of the "Melting-Pot."* London: Chatto and Windus, 1929.

Lippmann, Walter. "The Crude Barbarian and the Noble Savage." *New Republic* 25 (December 15, 1920): 70–71.

———. "Mr. Lippmann Answers." *New Republic* 25 (January 5, 1921): 70.

Litz, A. Walton. "Lawrence, Pound, and Early Modernism." In Balbert and Marcus, *D. H. Lawrence*, 15–28.

Litz, A. Walton, Louis Menand, and Lawrence Rainey, eds. *Cambridge History of Literary Criticism: Volume VII, Modernism and the New Criticism*. Cambridge: Cambridge University Press, 2006.

Louis, Margot K. *Persephone Rises, 1860–1927: Mythography, Gender, and the Creation of a New Spirituality*. Farnham, U.K.: Ashgate, 2009.

Lowell, Amy. *Tendencies in Modern American Poetry*. New York: Macmillan, 1917.

———. "Walt Whitman and the New Poetry." *Yale Review* 16 (1927): 502–19.

Luckhurst, Roger, ed. *Late Victorian Gothic Tales*. Oxford: Oxford University Press, 2005.

Luhan, Mabel Dodge. "Ballad of a Bad Girl." In Udall, *Spud Johnson and Laughing Horse*, 298–301.

———. "A Bridge between Cultures." *Theatre Arts Monthly* 9 (1925): 297–301.

———. *Edge of Taos Desert*. Albuquerque: University of New Mexico Press, 1987.

———. "Georgia O'Keeffe in Taos." *Creative Arts* 8.6 (1931): 407–10.

———. *Intimate Memories: The Autobiography of Mabel Dodge Luhan*. Edited by Lois Palken Rudnick. Albuquerque: University of New Mexico Press, 1999.

———. *Lorenzo in Taos: The Story of D. H. Lawrence in New Mexico*. London: Martin Secker, 1933.

———. *Winter in Taos*. Albuquerque: University of New Mexico Press, 2007.

Lummis, Charles F. *The Land of Poco Tiempo*. Albuquerque: University of New Mexico Press, 1952.

Lutz, Tom. *Cosmopolitan Vistas: American Regionalism and Literary Value*. Ithaca: Cornell University Press, 2004.

Lynch, Tom. *Xerophilia: Ecocritical Explorations in Southwestern Literature*. Lubbock: Texas Tech University Press, 2008.

Lynes, Barbara Buhler. *O'Keeffe, Stieglitz and the Critics, 1916–1929*. Ann Arbor: UMI Research Press, 1989.

McClintock, Anne. *Imperial Leather: Race, Gender, and Sexuality in the Imperial Contest*. London: Routledge, 1995.

McCoubrey, John, ed. *American Art 1700–1960: Sources and Documents*. Englewood Cliffs, N.J.: Prentice-Hall, 1965.

McGann, Jerome. *A Theory of Modern Textual Criticism*. Chicago: University of Chicago Press, 1983.

McWilliams, John. "The Rationale for 'The American Romance.'" In Pease, *Revisionary Interventions into the Americanist Canon*, 71–82.

Macy, John. "The American Spirit." *Nation* 117 (October 10, 1923): 398–99.

Manning, Susan, and Andrew Taylor, eds. *Transatlantic Literary Studies: A Reader*. Edinburgh: Edinburgh University Press, 2007.

Marx, Leo. "Listen to the States!" *Critical Quarterly* 3 (1961): 81–83.

———. *The Machine in the Garden: Technology and the Pastoral Ideal in America*. New York: Oxford University Press, 1964.

Maxwell, William J. "Global Politics and State-Sponsored Transnationalism: A Reply to Jahan Ramazani." *American Literary History* 18.2 (2006): 360–64.

Melville, Herman. *Selected Poems of Herman Melville*. Edited by F. O. Matthiessen. Norfolk, Conn.: New Directions, 1972.

Mencken, H. L. "Criticism of Criticism of Criticism." In *Prejudices: A Selection*, edited by James T. Farrell, 3–11. New York: Vintage, 1959.

———. "Footnote on Criticism." In Spingarn, *Criticism in America*, 261–86.

———. "Paul Elmer More." In *Prejudices: Third Series*, 177–78. London: Jonathan Cape, 1923.

Merivale, Patricia. *Pan the Goat-God: His Myth in Modern Times*. Cambridge, Mass.: Harvard University Press, 1969.

Merleau-Ponty, Maurice. *The Primacy of Perception and Other Essays on Phenomenological Psychology, the Philosophy of Art, History, and Politics*. Translated by James M. Edie. Chicago: Northwestern University Press, 1964.

Merrild, Knud. *With D. H. Lawrence in New Mexico*. London: Routledge and Kegan Paul, 1965.

Michaels, Walter Benn. *Our America: Nativism, Modernism, and Pluralism*. Durham, N.C.: Duke University Press, 1995.

Miller, Cristanne. "Gender, sexuality and the modernist poem." In Davis and Jenkins, *Cambridge Companion to Modernist Poetry*, 68–84.

Miller, James E. *T. S. Eliot: The Making of an American Poet, 1888–1922*. Philadelphia: Pennsylvania State University Press, 2005.

Millett, Kate. *Sexual Politics*. London: Virago, 1971.

Milne, Drew. "Lawrence and the politics of sexual politics." In Fernihough, *Cambridge Companion to D. H. Lawrence*, 197–215.

Minter, David. "The Fear of Feminization and the Logic of Modest Ambition." In Bercovitch, *Cambridge History of American Literature*, 151–59.

———. "The Great War and the Fate of Writing." In Bercovitch, *Cambridge History of American Literature*, 89–101.

Mollinger, Sharnaz. "The Divided Self in Nathaniel Hawthorne and D. H. Lawrence." *Psychoanalytical Review* 66 (1979): 79–102.

Monroe, Harriet. "Aboriginal Songs I." *Poetry* 9.5 (1917): 251.

———. "The Motive of the Magazine." *Poetry* 1.1 (1912): 33.

———. *Poets and Their Art*. New York: Macmillan, 1926.

Moore, Harry T. *The Priest of Love: A Life of D. H. Lawrence*. Harmondsworth: Penguin, 1974.

Moore, James. *Gurdjieff and Katherine Mansfield*. London: Routledge and Kegan Paul, 1980.

Moore, Marianne. *Poems of Marianne Moore*. Edited by Grace Schulman. Harmondsworth: Penguin, 2003.

Murry, John Middleton. "Religion and Christianity." *Adelphi* (January 1924): 666–74.

———. *Reminiscences of D. H. Lawrence*. London: Jonathan Cape, 1933.

———. *Son of Woman: The Story of D. H. Lawrence*. London: Jonathan Cape, 1931.

Muthyala, John. *Reworlding America: Myth, History, and Narrative*. Athens: Ohio University Press, 2006.

Nash, Roderick. *Wilderness and the American Mind*. New Haven: Yale University Press, 1982.

Nelson, Cary, and Lawrence Grossberg, eds. *Marxism and the Interpretation of Culture.* Urbana: University of Illinois Press, 1988.

Newmark, Julianne. "An Introduction to Neonativist Collectives: Place, Not Race, in Cather's *The Professor's House* and Lawrence's *The Plumed Serpent.*" *Arizona Quarterly* 66.2 (2010): 89–120.

———. "Sensing Re-Placement in New Mexico: Lawrence, John Collier, and (Post) Colonial Textual Geographies." In Hyde and Ingersoll, *"Terra Incognita,"* 157–82.

Nin, Anaïs. *D. H. Lawrence: An Unprofessional Study.* Berkeley: University of California Press, 1961.

Nolan, James. *Poet-Chief: The Native American Poetics of Walt Whitman and Pablo Neruda.* Albuquerque: University of New Mexico Press, 1994.

Norris, Margot. *Beasts of the Modern Imagination: Darwin, Nietzsche, Kafka, Ernst, and Lawrence.* Baltimore: Johns Hopkins University Press, 1985.

North, Michael. *Reading 1922: A Return to the Scene of the Modern.* New York: Oxford University Press, 1999.

Norwood, Vera, and Janice Monk, eds. *The Desert Is No Lady: Southwestern Landscapes in Women's Writing and Art.* Tucson: University of Arizona Press, 1987.

Olson, Charles. *Collected Prose.* Edited by Donald Allen and Benjamin Friedlander. Berkeley: University of California Press, 1997.

———. *Selected Writings.* Edited by Robert Creeley. New York: New Directions, 1950.

Padget, Martin. *Indian Country: Travels in the American Southwest, 1840–1935.* Albuquerque: University of New Mexico Press, 2004.

Padilla, Genaro. "Imprisoned Narrative? Or Lies, Secrets and Silence in New Mexico Women's Autobiography." In Calderón and Saldívar, *Criticism in the Borderlands,* 43–60.

Parrinder, Patrick. *Nation and Novel: The English Novel from its Origins to the Present Day.* Oxford: Oxford University Press, 2006.

Pattee, Fred Lewis. "Call for a Literary Historian." *American Mercury* (May–August 1924): 134–40.

Pease, Donald E. "National Identities, Postmodern Artifacts, and Postnational Narratives." *boundary 2* 19.1 (1992): 1–13.

———. *The New American Exceptionalism.* Minneapolis: University of Minnesota Press, 2009.

———. "New Americanists." In Pease, *Revisionary Interventions,* 1–36.

———, ed. *Revisionary Interventions into the Americanist Canon.* Durham, N.C.: Duke University Press, 1994.

Peterfield, William, et al., eds. *Cambridge History of American Literature.* 4 vols. New York: G. P. Putnam's Sons, 1917–21.

Pinkney, Tony. *D. H. Lawrence.* Hemel Hempstead, U.K.: Harvester Wheatsheaf, 1990.

Porter, Carolyn. "What We Know That We Don't Know: Remapping American Literary Studies." *American Literary History* 3 (1994): 467–526.

Pound, Ezra. "A Few Don'ts by an Imagiste." *Poetry* 1.6 (1913): 200–206.

———. *Personae.* Edited by Lea Baechler and A. Walton Litz. New York: New Directions, 1990.

———. *Selected Letters of Ezra Pound, 1907–1944*. Edited by D. D. Paige. London: Faber and Faber, 1950.

———. *Selected Prose 1909–1965*. Edited by William Cookson. New York: New Directions, 1975.

Pratt, Mary Louise. *Imperial Eyes: Travel Writing and Transculturation*. London: Routledge, 2002.

Preston, Peter. *A D. H. Lawrence Chronology*. London: St. Martin's Press, 1994.

Pryse, James Morgan. *Apocalypse Unsealed: Being an Esoteric Interpretation of the Initiation of Ionnes Commonly Called The Revelation of St. John*. LaVergne, Tenn.: Kessinger, 2010.

Radford, Andrew. *Lost Girls: Demeter-Persephone and the Literary Imagination, 1850–1930*. Amsterdam: Rodopi, 2007.

Rahv, Philip. *The Myth and the Powerhouse*. New York: Farrar, Straus and Giroux, 1965.

———. "Redskin and Paleface." *Kenyon Review* 1.3 (1939): 251–56.

Ramazani, Jahan. *A Transnational Poetics*. Chicago: University of Chicago Press, 2009.

Reising, Russell J. *The Unusable Past: Theory and the Study of American Literature*. New York: Methuen, 1986.

Renker, Elizabeth. *The Origins of American Literature Studies: An Institutional History*. Cambridge: Cambridge University Press, 2010.

Richter, Hans. *Dada: Art and Anti-Art*. London: Thames and Hudson, 1997.

Rinehart, Mary Roberts. "Dude West." *Ladies' Home Journal* (April 1929): 14–15.

Roberson, Susan L. "American women and travel writing." In Bendixen and Hamera, *Cambridge Companion to American Travel Writing*, 214–27.

Roberts, Neil. *D. H. Lawrence, Travel and Cultural Difference*. Basingstoke: Palgrave Macmillan, 2004.

———. "Lawrence, Imagism and Beyond." In Day and Docherty, *British Poetry, 1900–50*, 81–93.

Roberts, Warren, and Paul Poplawski. *A Bibliography of D. H. Lawrence*. 3rd ed. Cambridge: Cambridge University Press, 2001.

Rodriguez, Sylvia. "Art, Tourism, and Race Relations in Taos: Toward a Sociology of the Art Colony." *Journal of Anthropological Research* 45.1 (1989): 77–99.

Rohman, Carrie. *Stalking the Subject: Modernism and the Animal*. New York: Columbia University Press, 2008.

Rosenfeld, Paul. "D. H. Lawrence." *New Republic* (September 27, 1922): 125–26.

Rothenberg, Jerome, ed. *Technicians of the Sacred: A Range of Poetries from Africa, America, Asia, Europe, and Oceania*. 3rd ed. Berkeley: University of California Press, 1985.

Rudnick, Lois Palken. Introduction to Luhan, *Edge of Taos Desert*, vii–xviii.

———. *Mabel Dodge Luhan: New Woman, New Worlds*. Albuquerque: University of New Mexico Press, 1984.

———. *Utopian Vistas: The Mabel Dodge Luhan House and the American Counterculture*. Albuquerque: University of New Mexico Press, 1998.

Russell, Bertrand. "Portraits from Memory, III: D. H. Lawrence." *Harper's Magazine* (February 1953): 95.

Sagar, Keith. Introduction to Lawrence, *The Complete Short Novels*, 11–45.

———. *D. H. Lawrence and New Mexico*. Paris: Alyscamps Press, 1995.

———. *D. H. Lawrence: Poet*. Penrith, U.K.: Humanities-Ebooks, 2007.

———. "How to Live?—The End of Lawrence's Quest." In Hyde and Ingersoll, *Windows to the Sun*, 207–23.

Sandburg, Carl. "Editorial Comment: Aboriginal Poetry." *Poetry* 9.5 (1917): 255.

Santayana, George. "The Genteel Tradition in American Philosophy." In *Selected Critical Writings of George Santayana*, vol. 2, edited by Norman Henfrey, 85–107. Cambridge: Cambridge University Press, 1968.

Scholes, Robert, and Clifford Wulfman. *Modernism in the Magazines*. New Haven: Yale University Press, 2010.

Scott, Gail R. *Marsden Hartley, New Mexico, 1918–1920: An American Discovering America*. New York: Alexandre Gallery, 2003.

Segal, Charles. *Orpheus: The Myth of the Poet*. Baltimore: Johns Hopkins University Press, 1989.

Seligmann, Herbert J. *D. H. Lawrence: An American Interpretation*. New York: Thomas Seltzer, 1924.

Sherman, Stuart P. *America and Allied Ideals: An Appeal to Those Who Are Neither Hot Nor Cold*. War Information Series, no. 12. Washington D.C.: Government Printing Office, 1918.

———. "America Is Discovered." In Draper, *D. H. Lawrence*, 208–13.

———. *Americans*. New York: Charles Scribner's Sons, 1923.

———. "Lawrence Cultivates His Beard." In Draper, *D. H. Lawrence*, 250–57.

———. "The National Genius." In Spingarn, *Criticism in America*, 228–60.

Shumway, David R. *Creating American Civilization: A Genealogy of American Literature as an Academic Discipline*. Minneapolis: University of Minnesota Press, 1994.

Siegel, Carol. *Lawrence among the Women: Wavering Boundaries in Women's Literary Traditions*. Charlottesville: University of Virginia Press, 1991.

———. "'St. Mawr': Lawrence's Journey Toward Cultural Feminism." *D. H. Lawrence Review* 26.1/3 (1997): 275–86.

Sill, Geoffrey M., ed. *Walt Whitman of Mickle Street: A Centennial Celebration*. Knoxville: University of Tennessee Press, 1994.

Slotkin, Richard. *Regeneration through Violence: The Mythology of the American Frontier 1600–1860*. Norman: University of Oklahoma Press, 1973.

Smith, Henry Nash. *Virgin Land: The American West as Symbol and Myth*. Cambridge, Mass.: Harvard University Press, 1974.

Smith, William Jay. *The Spectra Hoax: The Poetry Deception of the Century*. 2nd ed. Ashland, Ore.: Storyline Press, 2000.

Snyder, Carey. "'When the Indian was in Vogue': D. H. Lawrence, Aldous Huxley, and Ethnological Tourism in the Southwest." *Modern Fiction Studies* 53.4 (2007): 662–96.

Snyder, Gary. *The Gary Snyder Reader: Prose, Poetry, and Translations, 1952–1998*. Washington D.C.: Counterpoint, 1999.

———. *The Old Ways*. San Francisco: City Lights, 1977.

Soja, Edward. *Postmodern Geographies: The Reassertion of Space in Critical Social Theory*. London: Verso, 1989.

Sontag, Susan. *Literature Is Freedom: The Friedenspreis Acceptance Speech*. Falls Village, Conn.: Winterhouse Editions, 2003.

Spingarn, J. E. "Criticism in the United States." In Spingarn, *Criticism in America*, 287–308.

———, ed. *Criticism in America: Its Function and Status*. New York: Harcourt Brace and Company, 1924.

Spivak, Gayatri Chakravorty. "Can the Subaltern Speak?" In Nelson and Grossberg, *Marxism and the Interpretation of Culture*, 271–313.

Spivak, Gayatri, and Sarah Harasym. *The Post-Colonial Critic*. London: Routledge, 1990.

Stevens, Wallace. *Collected Poetry and Prose*. Edited by Frank Kermode and Joan Richardson. New York: Library of America, 1997.

Strom, Martha. "Wallace Stevens's Revisions of Crispin's Journal: A Reaction Against the 'Local.'" *American Literature* 54 (1982): 258–76.

Swann, Brian, ed. *On the Translation of Native American Literatures*. Washington D.C.: Smithsonian Institution Press, 1992.

Swigg, Richard. *Lawrence, Hardy and American Literature*. New York: Oxford University Press, 1972.

Tanner, Tony. *The Reign of Wonder: Naivety and Reality in American Literature*. Cambridge: Cambridge University Press, 1965.

Tapscott, Stephen. *American Beauty: William Carlos Williams and the Modernist Whitman*. New York: Columbia University Press, 1984.

Tashjian, Dickran. "Marsden Hartley and the Southwest: A Ceremony for Our Vision, a Fiction for the Eye." *Arts Magazine* 54.8 (1980): 127–31.

Templeton, Wayne. "'Indians and an Englishman': Lawrence in the American Southwest." *D. H. Lawrence Review* 25.1–3 (1993–94): 14–34.

Thompson, Jon. Introduction to Lawrence, *Studies in Classic American Literature* (2011), 7–36.

Tindall, William York. *D. H. Lawrence and Susan His Cow*. New York: Columbia University Press, 1939.

Toomer, Margery. Letter to Mabel Dodge Luhan, n.d. Beinecke Rare Book and Manuscript Library. Yale University Library. Mabel Dodge Luhan Papers YCAL MSS 196.34, 993–94.

Trachtenberg, Alan. "Myth and Symbol." *Massachusetts Review* 25.4 (1984): 667–73.

———. *Shades of Hiawatha: Staging Indians, Making Americans, 1880–1930*. New York: Hill and Wang, 2004.

———. "Walt Whitman: Precipitant of the Modern." In Greenspan, *Cambridge Companion to Walt Whitman*, 194–207.

Tuan, Yi-Fu. *Topophilia: A Study of Environmental Perceptions, Attitudes, and Values*. New York: Columbia University Press, 1990.

Turner, Frederick Jackson. *The Frontier in American History*. New York: Henry Holt and Company, 1935.

Tylor, E. B. *Primitive Culture*. 2 vols. London: John Murray, 1871.

Udall, Sharyn R., ed. *Spud Johnson and Laughing Horse*. Albuquerque: University of New Mexico Press, 1994.

Vanderbilt, Kermit. *American Literature and the Academy: The Roots, Growth, and Maturity of a Profession*. Philadelphia: University of Pennsylvania Press, 1986.

Weaver, R. M. "Narcissus and Echo." *Bookman* 57 (November 1923): 327–28.

Werner, W. L., and Arlin Turner. "In Memoriam Fred Lewis Pattee." *American Literature* 22.4 (1951): 573–74.

White, Eric. *Transatlantic Avant-Gardes: Little Magazines and Localist Modernism*. Edinburgh: Edinburgh University Press, 2013.

Whitman, Walt. *Complete Poetry and Collected Prose*. New York: Library of America, 1982.

Williams, Ellen. *Harriet Monroe and the Poetry Renaissance: The First Ten Years of Poetry, 1912–22*. Urbana: University of Illinois Press, 1977.

Williams, William Carlos. "The American Background." In Frank et al., *America and Alfred Stieglitz*, 31–32.

———. "America, Whitman, and the Art of Poetry." *The Poetry Journal* viii.i (1917): 27–39.

———. *The Autobiography of William Carlos Williams*. New York: New Directions, 1967.

———. *Collected Poems*. 2 vols. Edited by A. Walton Litz and Christopher MacGowan. London: Paladin, 1991.

———. *Imaginations*. New York: New Directions, 1970.

———. *In the American Grain*. New York: New Directions, 1956.

———. *Paterson*. Edited by Christopher MacGowan. New York: New Directions, 1992.

———. "Sample Critical Statement." *Contact* 4 (1921): 18.

Wilson, Rob. *American Sublime: The Genealogy of a Poetic Genre*. Madison: University of Wisconsin Press, 1991.

Witemeyer, Hugh, ed. *Pound/Williams: Selected Letters of Ezra Pound and William Carlos Williams*. New York: New Directions, 1996.

Witt, David L. *Taos Moderns: Art of the New*. Santa Fe: Red Crane Books, 1992.

Worthen, John. "Lawrence's Theater of the Southwest." In Cushman and Ingersoll, *D. H. Lawrence: New Worlds*, 243–57.

Wright, T. R. *D. H. Lawrence and the Bible*. Cambridge: Cambridge University Press, 2000.

Yépez, Heriberto. *The Empire of Neomemory*. Translated by Jen Hofer, Christian Nagler, and Brian Whitener. Oakland, Calif.: Chainlinks, 2013.

Young, Stark. "Dude Ranch I." *New Republic* 52 (1927): 43–44.

———. "Dude Ranch II." *New Republic* 55 (1928): 250–51.

———. "Dude Ranch III." *New Republic* 55 (1928): 279–80.

Index

Page numbers in italics refer to illustrations.

A

Aaron's Rod (Lawrence), 44
Abiquiu, N. Mex., 21, 125n21
"Aboriginal Songs II" (Henderson), 67
Acuna, Rodolfo, 97
Adventures in the Arts (Hartley), 76
Aeneid (Virgil), 73
After Strange Gods (Eliot), 109
Aldington, Richard, 25, 40, 59
Altitude (Lawrence), 92–93
America, 10, 11, 108, 109. See also *Studies in Classic American Literature* (Lawrence)
"America" (Henderson), 71
"America, Listen to Your Own" (Lawrence), 13, 36, 116n41
"America Is Discovered" (Sherman), 33
Americana (Mencken), 114n24
"Americanism and Localism" (Dewey), 117n17
American Language, The (Mencken), 31
American Literary History, 112n29
American Mercury, 114n3, 115n39
Americano (term), 6, 7
American Place, An, 48
American Rhythm, The: Studies and Reëxpressions of Amerindian Songs (Austin), 15, 53, 65–66, 67
Americans (Sherman), 32
"American Spirit, The" (Macy), 114n20
American studies, 3–4, 8, 26, 27, 31–32, 46, 112n37
America's Coming-of-Age (Brooks), 35
Ancient Art and Ritual (Harrison), 77, 119n85
"'A New Continent of the Soul'" (Ingersoll), 116n60
Anzaldúa, Gloria, 98, 99
Apocalypse (Lawrence), 30
Apocalypse Unsealed, The (Pryse), 30
Apples (Cézanne), 121n131
Arac, Jonathan, 90
Archuleta, Rufina, 85
Archuleta, Trinidad, 85
Armory Show, 20, 47
Arnold, Armin, 38, 116n51
Arroyo Seco, 100
"Art and Morality" (Lawrence), 115n26
Art-Nonsense and Other Essays (Gill), 23–24

Auden, W. H., 1, 79
Austin, Mary: on Bynner's *Indian Earth*, 65; and *Cambridge History of American Literature*, 115n39; as émigré to New Mexico, 69; and Imagism, 66, 67, 71; and Indians and Indian culture, 66, 67, 68, 92; and Lawrence, 65, 92, 116n41; and modernism, 7, 51; scholarship on, 67; works by, 15, 53, 65–66, 67
Australia, 11, 116n63
"Autumn at Taos" (Lawrence), 77–78

B

Babbitt, Irving, 27, 33, 34, 46
Bachelard, Gaston, 18, 62, 78, 79
Background (Luhan), 102
Baker, Houston A., Jr., 13
Baldick, Chris, 83
"Ballad of a Bad Girl" (Luhan), 104
"Ballad of a Wilful Woman" (Lawrence), 104
Bate, Jonathan, 17, 69, 78
Beauvoir, Simone de, 18
Bell, Michael, 109
"Benjamin Franklin" (Lawrence), 40
Bergland, René, 37
"Bibbles" (Lawrence), 72–73
Bid Me to Live (H.D.), 58, 59
Birds, Beasts and Flowers (Lawrence): America in, 18, 29, 54–55, 62, 75, 77–79, 94; and American poetic modernism, 15, 16, 17; analysis of, 16, 52–53, 54–56, 58, 59, 61, 80; editions of, 113n72; Indians in, 67; as Lawrence's first postwar poetry collection, 70; locality in, 80; "Mountain Lion" essay in, 97; poems reprinted from, 69; scholarship on, 54, 55, 72, 75; and Whitman, 72–73; writing of, 16, 24, 55, 67, 81, 97
Birth-mark, The (Howe), 100, 109
Black Atlantic, The (Gilroy), 14
Black Mountain School, 15
Blithedale Romance, The (Hawthorne), 22
Bloom, Harold, 45, 57, 72

"Blue Jay, The" (Lawrence), 79, 80
Blumenschein, Ernest, 113n69
Boni and Liveright, 114n20
Bookman, 28
Book of Revelation, 30, 44, 87, 114n13
"Border-Line, The" (Lawrence), 84, 122n18
Border Trilogy (McCarthy), 91
Bottom Dogs (Dahlberg), 90
Bourne, Randolph, 8, 49, 50
Boyd, Ernest, 33, 115n29
Boy in the Bush, The (Lawrence and Skinner), 18
Brett, Dorothy: and Alfred Stieglitz, 125n20; childhood of, 123n45; and D. H. Lawrence, 22, 24, 25, 82, 84, 85, 98, 105–6, 119n85, 123n45; and D. H. Lawrence's ashes and shrine, 106, 125n18; and Frieda Lawrence, 22, 24, 25, 106; and Georgia O'Keeffe, 25, 107, 125n20; and John Middleton Murry, 24, 84; and Mabel Dodge Luhan, 85; in Mexico, 25; as model for Lawrence protagonists, 84, 105, 123n45; in New Mexico, 22, 24, 25, 84, 85; painting of Lawrence by, 106–7
Brill, A. A., 25
"Britisher has a Word with Harriett Monroe, A" (Lawrence), 120n96
Brock, Henry Irving, 31
Brook Farm, 22, 23
Brooks, Van Wyck: and literary criticism, 26, 27, 31, 32, 35, 45, 46, 71–72; and *Seven Arts* magazine, 49
Brown, Curtis, 84, 122n13
Browning, Elizabeth Barrett, 123n40
Buell, Lawrence, 3, 89, 92
Burke, Flannery, 125n21
Bursum, Holm O., 38
Bursum Bill, 38
Bynner, Witter, 24, 64–65, 67, 69, 119n85

C

Calendar of Modern Letters, 115n26
"Call for a Literary Historian" (Pattee), 34

Call Me Ishmael (Olson), 27
Cambridge Edition of the Letters and Works of D. H. Lawrence, 19
Cambridge History of American Literature (Trent, et al.), 115n39
Cambridge History of English and American Literature, 115n39
Cambridge Introduction to Modernist Poetry (Howarth), 15
Cambridge University Press, 115n39
Camera Work, 47
Cane (Toomer), 53
Can These Bones Live? (Dahlberg), 27
Canticle of Pan, A (Bynner), 64–65
Cantos, The (Pound), 9
Capel-y-ffin, Wales, 113n76
Captain's Doll, The (collection, Lawrence), 83, 113n77
"Captain's Doll, The" (short story, Lawrence), 49, 83
Captivity and Restoration of Mrs. Mary Rowlandson, The, 100–101
Carey, John, 15
Carnegie, Andrew, 32, 40
Carr, Helen, 65, 66
Carswell, Catherine, 19, 24, 58, 82, 94–95
Carter, Frederick, 87, 114n16
Castiglia, Christopher, 12, 112n37
Castro, Michael, 66, 67
Castronovo, Russ, 16
Cather, Willa, 21, 37, 39, 92
Cavitch, David, 22, 31
"Certain Americans and an Englishman" (Lawrence), 38
Cézanne (Fry), 121n130
Cézanne, Paul, 47, 76–77, 78, 80, 121n130, 121n131
Chabot, Maria, 125n21
Chapala, Mex., 24
Chase, Richard, 3, 12, 13, 88, 94, 112n35
Chatto and Windus, 118n42
Chaudhuri, Amit, 80
Chicago, Ill., 64
"Children of Adam" (Whitman), 57

Chippewa Indians, 66
Clark, Badger, 69
Clark, L. D., 6, 52
Cohen, Margaret, 54
Cold War, 3
Cole, Thomas, 89
Collected Poems (Lawrence), 68
Collier, John, 38
Columbine Lake, 123n45
"Comedian as the Letter C, The" (Stevens), 53, 118n30
Contact Editions, 75
Contact magazine, 74
Contreras, Sheila, 101
Cooper, James Fenimore: characters created by, 91; depictions of Indians by, 36, 39; as inspiration for Lawrence, 10, 28; Lawrence on, 37, 39, 41–42, 44, 90; works by, 36
Cornwall, Eng., 23, 26, 49, 84, 88, 123n41
"Country Boy" (La Farge), 124n60
Cowan, James C., 19, 88, 116n60
Crèvecoeur. *See* St. John de Crèvecoeur, Hector
Criticism in America: Its Function and Status (Spingarn), 32, 115n29
"Criticism of Criticism of Criticism" (Mencken), 33
Cross (O'Keeffe), 48, 117n4
Cunliffe, Marcus, 13, 112n37
Current Opinion, 28
Cushman, Keith, 19, 53, 113n72
"Cypresses" (Lawrence), 29

D

Dahlberg, Edward, 27, 90
Dana, Richard Henry, 28, 43, 46
"Dance for Rain, A" (Bynner), 69
"Dance of the Sprouting Corn, The" (Lawrence), 77
Dante Alighieri, 57
Dasburg, Andrew, 21, 113n69
Davie, Donald, 16
"Dead Pan, The" (Browning), 123n40

"Dear Old Horse: A London Letter" (Lawrence), 93
Death Comes for the Archbishop (Cather), 39
DeBuys, William, 96, 97
De la Mare, Walter, 16
Delius, Frederick, 22
Del Monte Ranch. *See under* Lawrence, D. H., in New Mexico
"Democracy" (Lawrence), 5
Demuth, Charles, 48
Densmore, Frances, 66–67
Des Imagistes (Pound), 66, 74
Dewey, John, 51, 117n17
D. H. Lawrence (Seligmann), 34
"D. H. Lawrence and Professor Irving Babbitt" (Leavis), 46
D. H. Lawrence and the Trembling Balance (Cowan), 116n60
"D. H. Lawrence Bombs Our Literary Shrines," 28
D. H. Lawrence: Novelist (Leavis), 5
Dial magazine, 21, 32, 49, 77
DiBattista, Maria, 68
Dijkstra, Bram, 49, 76
Dilworth, Leah, 67, 68
Dimock, Wai Chee, 9–10, 17, 37, 54
Ditchling, Sussex, Eng., 113n76
Dodge, Mabel. *See* Lawrence, D. H., and Mabel Dodge Luhan; Luhan, Mabel Dodge
Doolittle, Hilda (H.D.), 58–60, 61, 63, 95
Dove, Arthur, 47, 48
Doyle, Laura, 7
Drohojowska-Philp, Hunter, 125n21
Dude ranches, 97–98, 123n45
Dunne, J. W., 10
Dying Game (Ellis), 19

E

Edge of Taos Desert (Luhan), 103
Egan, Maurice Francis, 28
Eliot, George, 5
Eliot, T. S.: as critic, 46, 103; as émigré, 54, 75; on Ezra Pound, 72; influences on, 46; and Lawrence, 109; and tradition, 46; Van Wyck Brooks on, 45; and William Carlos Williams, 75; works by, 45, 75, 95
Ellis, David, 19, 38, 72
Emerson, Ralph Waldo, 9, 10, 28
Enchanted Circle, N. Mex., 96
England, 2, 5, 110, 113n76. *See also* Cornwall, Eng.; London, Eng.
English Canaan (Morton), 86
English Review, 11, 14, 28, 29, 31, 41, 116n51
Equivalents (Stieglitz), 51
Erskine, John, 115n39
European Experiences (Luhan), 102–3
"Eurydice" (H.D.), 59–60, 61, 62
Evans, John, 22
"Evening Land, The" (Lawrence), 55, 94
Everyman's Library, 28
"Experiment with Time, An" (Dunne), 10

F

Fable genre, 83
Fantasia of the Unconscious (Lawrence), 5, 30, 32, 114n12
Feidelson, Charles, 3, 12, 13, 112n35
Feinstein, Elaine, 19
"Fenimore Cooper's Anglo-American Novels" (Lawrence), 41
"Fenimore Cooper's Longstocking Novels" (Lawrence), 42
Fergusson, Erna, 98, 100
Fernihough, Anne, 75–76
Ferry, Luc, 97
"Festival of the Corn, The" (Hartley), 69
ffytche, Matt, 80
Fiedler, Leslie, 3, 12–13, 36, 91, 92, 112n37
Finney, Brian, 122n24
Flint, F. S., 76
Flying-Heart Ranch. *See* Lawrence, D. H., in New Mexico: at Kiowa Ranch
Foerster, Norman, 115n39
Ford, Henry, 40
Forster, E. M., 122n18
Foster, Edward, 109

Four Stages of Greek Religion (Murray), 123n25
Fowler, Alastair, 93
"Fox, The" (Lawrence), 83
Frank, Waldo, 11, 32, 33, 36, 49
Frankenstein, 30
Franklin, Benjamin, 27, 28, 30, 40–41
Frazer, James George, 9, 30, 61, 86, 114n12, 119n85
Fred Harvey Company, 100
Freeman, Bessie, 22
Fregoso, Rosa Linda, 99
Freud, Sigmond, 25, 30, 114n12
Friedman, Susan Stanford, 59, 60
Frobenius, Leo, 30, 114n12, 118n51
Fry, Roger, 121n130
Fuller, Margaret, 43

G

Galsworthy, John, 69
Garsington Manor, 22
Gender, 14, 39, 43, 92, 104
Genette, Gerard, 106
Genteel Tradition, 35, 71
Georgian Poetry, 56
Georgian Poetry: 1911–1912, 59
Georgians, 56, 57, 58
Georgics (Virgil), 62
Gilbert, Sandra, 53
Giles, Paul, 3, 4, 8, 50–51, 101
Gill, Eric, 23, 24, 113n76
Gilroy, Paul, 14
Ginsberg, Allen, 73
Global Remapping of American Literature, The (Giles), 4
Golden Bough, The (Frazer), 9–10, 61
Goldsmith, Arnold, 12
Götzsche, Kai, 22, 23, 24, 100, 124n72
G. P. Putnum's Sons, 115n39
Grad, Bonnie, 48
Gray, Cecil, 60
"Great God Pan, The" (Machen), 85, 122n18
Green Man (folklore figure), 86
Grey, Zane, 37, 38

Gross, Robert A., 14, 111n24
Guadalajara, Mex., 6, 24, 104
Guardian, 13
Guest Book (Bynner), 64
Gurdjieff, George Ivanovich, 23

H

Halter, Peter, 49, 76
"Hard Winter" (La Farge), 103
Hardy, Thomas, 5
Harmonium (Stevens), 15, 53–54
Harrison, Jane, 77, 119n85
Hartley, Marsden, 47, 48, 69, 70, 74, 76
Hawke, Alfred, 105
Hawke, Rachel, 123n45
Hawke, William, 123n45
Hawke family, 22
Hawthorne, Nathaniel: and American romance genre, 10, 94; Lawrence on, 27, 32, 37, 42–43, 46, 86; Lawrence's initial reading of, 28; works by, 10, 22, 32, 42–43, 86, 87, 94
H.D. *See* Doolittle, Hilda
Heidegger, Martin, 78
Henderson, Alice Corbin: Amy Lowell on, 64; as anthology editor, 17, 69–70; health of, 64; and Imagism, 58, 64, 66–67, 71; and Indian culture, 7, 21, 66–67; and New Mexico modernism, 7, 51, 66–67; and *Poetry* magazine, 67, 71; and Santa Fe, 21, 64, 105
Herman Melville: Man, Mariner and Mystic (Weaver), 28
Herzinger, Kim, 17, 57
"High Chin Bob" (Clark), 69
Hispanics and Hispano-Americans, 7, 83
Hispano culture, 98, 99
History of American Literature Since 1870, A (Pattee), 115n37
Hoffman, Frederick J., 11
Homestead Act, 90
Hooker, Jeremy, 16, 54
Horse's Skull with Pink Rose (O'Keeffe), 108–9

Howarth, Peter, 15
Howe, Susan, 100, 101, 109
Huebsch, Benjamin, 28
Huichole Indians, 100, 124n72
Hyde, Virginia Crosswhite, 19, 122n24
"Hymn to Priapus" (Lawrence), 61

I

Imagism and Imagists: Alfred Stieglitz and, 76; Alice Corbin Henderson and, 64, 66–67; Amy Lowell and, 57, 58, 63, 64; Carl Sandburg and, 67; Cézanne and, 76; characteristics of, 62; Ezra Pound and, 62, 63–66; Harriet Monroe and, 64; H.D. (Hilda Doolittle) and, 58, 63; and Indian culture, 64, 66–67; Mary Austin and, 64; Stuart Pratt Sherman and, 40; and Whitman, 71, 72; Witter Bynner and, 64
"In a Station of the Metro" (Pound), 66
Indian captivity narratives, 100–101, 103
"Indian Detour, The," 124n74
Indian Detours, 100
Indian Earth (Bynner), 65, 67
Indians: Benjamin Franklin and, 40, 41; culture of, 10, 65, 77, 82, 93, 96; dispossession of, 83; in fiction, 88, 91, 123n40; James Fenimore Cooper and, 36; Lawrence and, 35–36, 39, 41, 55, 85, 86, 87, 99–100, 119n85, 125n18; Mabel Dodge Luhan and, 103; Mary Austin and, 66, 67, 68, 92; in Mexico, 124n72; in New Mexico, 7, 38, 77; as poetry subjects, 66–69; in *Studies in Classic American Literature*, 35–36, 37, 38, 39, 40, 41, 42, 68. See also *Studies in Classic American Literature* (Lawrence): Indians in
"Indians and an Englishman" (Lawrence), 52, 67, 82, 93, 116n46
"Indians and Entertainment" (Lawrence), 77
Ingersoll, Earl, 19, 106, 116n60
Institute for the Harmonious Development of Man, 23
Intellectuals and the Masses, The (Carey), 15

In the American Grain (Williams): Indians in, 37; Lawrence on, 37, 50; models for, 76; place in, 75; scholarship on, 8, 27; and *Studies in Classic American Literature*, 8, 50; Thomas Morton and Merry Mount in, 87
Intimate Gallery, 48
"Introduction to These Paintings" (Lawrence), 76–77, 121n130
Irving, Washington, 95
"Is There an American Literature?" (Pattee), 115n37
Italian Futurism, 27, 58
Italy: Lawrence in, 5, 16, 51, 52, 55, 80, 102; Mabel Dodge Luhan in, 20

J

Jalisco, Mex., 24
Jameson, Fredric, 8, 98
Jay, Paul, 7–8, 18
Jeffers, Robinson, 21, 103, 104
"Jimmy and the Desperate Woman" (Lawrence), 84
Johnson, Walter Willard ("Spud"), 17, 24, 93, 105, 123n40
Jones, David, 113n76
Journal of Transnational Studies, 7
"Just Back from the Snake-Dance--Tired Out" (Lawrence), 82, 96
Juta, Jan, 81

K

Kammen, Michael, 33
Kangaroo (Lawrence), 5, 24, 51
Kaplan, Sydney Janet, 103
Karrell, Linda, 19
Kauffer, E. McKnight, 118n42
Kinkead-Weekes, Mark, 63, 77, 99, 111n24
Kiowa Ranch. *See under* Lawrence, D. H., in New Mexico
Knopf, Alfred, 114n24
Knopf, Blanche, 114n24
Kolodny, Annette, 89, 100

Kora in Hell (Williams), 75, 116n41, 121n121, 121n125
Koteliansky, S. S., 48
Krout, John Allen, 115n26

L

Ladies' Home Journal, 98
Ladybird, The (collection, Lawrence), 83
"Ladybird, The" (short story, Lawrence), 49, 83
Lady Chatterley's Lover (Lawrence), 10, 34, 48, 95
La Farge, Oliver, 103, 124n60
Laird, Holly, 15, 53, 57, 106
Land of Poco Tiempo, The (Lummis), 7, 91
Las Cruces, N. Mex., 97
"Last Laugh, The" (Lawrence), 84–85, 95, 122n18, 123n40, 123n45
Last of the Mohicans, The (Cooper), 36, 90
Last Poems (Lawrence), 61
Laughing Horse: advertisements in, 100, 124n74; editor of, 17, 93, 123n40; Lawrence and, 17, 69, 93, 104, 123n41; Mabel Dodge Luhan and, 104
Lawrence, D. H.: and Alfred Stieglitz, 48, 109; and American audience, 54–55, 56; and American literature, 1–2; on Americans, 71–72; and Amy Lowell, 1, 10, 26, 28, 48, 54, 64; ashes of, 106, 125n18; on belief systems, 10; biographies, memoirs, and scholarship on, 17, 34, 40, 48, 49–50, 51, 63, 103, 106; and British literature, 1; and Carl Sandburg, 69, 73; and Cézanne, 76–77, 121n130, 121n131; characteristics of, 6; as critic, 49–50, 114n24, 115n26, 117n71; death of, 23, 103; and Dorothy Brett, 22, 24, 25, 82, 84, 85, 98, 105–6, 119n85, 123n45; in England, 2, 5, 11, 22, 23, 24, 26, 49, 58, 63, 83, 84, 85, 87, 93, 109; and Ezra Pound, 63–64; and Frederick Carter, 87; and Frieda Lawrence, 43; and Georgians and Georgianism, 57, 58, 59; and Georgia O'Keeffe, 109; and H.D. (Hilda Doolittle), 58–59, 61, 62, 63, 95; and Imagists and Imagism, 17, 40, 57, 58, 59, 61, 63–64, 76, 118n43, 119n59; impact of America on, 10–11; and Indians and Indian culture, 39, 52, 119n85; influences on, 16–17, 118n51; in Italy, 1, 5, 51, 52, 55, 80, 102; and John Galsworthy, 69; and John Middleton Murry, 84, 103; literature read by, 117n64, 123n25; and Mary Austin, 65, 92, 116n41; in Mexico, 1, 6, 11, 24, 25, 81, 104, 124n72; as modernist, 49–50; as painter, 117n7; in painting by Dorothy Brett, 106–7; Paul Giles on, 4; Paul Rosenfeld on, 105; on poetry, 53; and *Poetry* magazine, 55, 64, 120n96; prosecution of, 48; and Rananim, 11, 22, 23, 24, 113n73; on ranching, 90; as reviewer, 32, 33, 37, 50; and *Seven Arts* magazine, 8, 49; and Stuart Pratt Sherman, 49, 115n26; and Tony Lujan, 39; travels of, 11, 23, 24, 55, 85, 87, 116n63, 123n45; and understanding of America, 8; Whitman as influence on, 10, 16–17, 28, 45, 54, 56, 57, 58, 61, 72, 74, 120n111; and Willa Cather, 92; William Carlos Williams on, 48; and Witter Bynner, 65; on women, 60–61; working-class origins of, 31; and World War I, 5, 11, 23, 48–49, 51, 63, 70, 83
Lawrence, D. H., and Mabel Dodge Luhan: and *Altitude*, 92; and "Ballad of a Girl," 104; and "Ballad of a Wilful Woman," 104; correspondence between, 19, 21, 102, 104; falling out between, 21, 22; and "Hard Winter," 103; initial meeting of, 20; and Lawrence on Luhan as dude ranch owner, 98; and Lawrence's ashes, 125n18; and Lawrence's New Mexico tales, 19, 81–82, 98, 100, 102, 103–4, 105; and Lawrence's stays in New Mexico, 19, 21–22, 24, 38, 52, 65, 81, 85, 100; and Luhan/Lujan relationship, 21, 38, 39, 42, 82–83, 103, 104; and Luhan's memoir of Lawrence, 20, 52, 103, 104, 106; scholarship on, 19–20, 113n64; and *Studies in Classic American Literature*, 38, 39, 42, 43; and "Taos," 52; and "The Wilful Woman," 81, 82–83, 104

Lawrence, D. H., in New Mexico: activities in, 7; arrival in, 38, 51, 64; at Del Monte Ranch, 22, 23, 24, 52, 79, 81, 83, 97, 105, 123n45; departure from, 108, 109; at Kiowa Ranch, 22, 23, 24, 25, 85, 86, 87, 89–90, 92, 105, 108, 109; length of stays in, 1; return to, 104; Stuart Pratt Sherman on, 4, 6; in Taos and environs, 21, 24, 81, 85, 100; works written in, 2, 6, 14, 16, 17, 18, 19, 51–52, 85, 86, 97, 105

Lawrence, Frieda: death of, 106; and D. H. Lawrence, 43; and Dorothy Brett, 106; and H.D. (Hilda Doolittle), 58; and John Middleton Murry, 84; and Lawrence's ashes, 106; in Lawrence's works, 59, 63; and Mabel Dodge Luhan, 25, 43, 81, 105, 106; as memoirist, 106; in Mexico, 24, 25; in New Mexico, 22, 23, 24–25, 85; in painting by Dorothy Brett, 106–7; and World War I, 48, 49

Lawrence, Lydia, 61
Lawrence's Three Fates (Brett), 106, 122n17
Lawrence Tree, The (O'Keeffe), 25, 48, 107–8, 125n21
Leaves of Grass (Whitman), 71, 73
Leavis, F. R., 5, 12, 46, 93, 95, 117n71
Le Compotier (Cézanne), 121n131
Letters from an American Farmer (Crèvecoeur), 6, 29, 40–41, 55
Lewis, R.W.B., 3, 12, 13, 112n35
Lewis, Wyndham, 12
Lindsay, Vachel, 38
Lippmann, Walter, 36, 116n41
"Listening" (Henderson), 67
"Listen to the States!" (Marx), 13
Literary Digest International Book Review, 28
Literary studies, American. *See* American studies
Lobo Peak, 22, 79, 85
Lobo Ranch. *See* Lawrence, D. H., in New Mexico: at Kiowa Ranch
Lobo Valley, 97
London, Eng.: D. H. Lawrence in, 24, 58, 84, 87, 93; fictional depictions of, 84, 85; Frieda Lawrence in, 24, 58; H.D. (Hilda Doolittle) in, 58, 63; publication of Lawrence's works in, 83

"London Letter" (Lawrence), 123n41
Look! We Have Come Through! (Lawrence): Amy Lowell and, 118n42; jacket of, 58, 118n42; Lawrence on, 120n111; Mark Kinkead-Weekes on, 63, 77; publication of, 16; specific works in, 16, 58, 59, 61, 77, 104; and Whitman, 16, 120n111
Lorca, Federico Garcia, 73
Lorenzo in Taos (Luhan), 103, 104
Lost Girl, The (Lawrence), 100
Louis, Margot, 75
Love and Death in the American Novel (Fiedler), 12
Lowell, Amy: as anthology editor, 57, 58, 59, 74; and correspondence with Lawrence, 1, 10, 26, 28, 54; on cover of *Look!*, 118n42; and financial support for Lawrence, 48; and Imagists and Imagism, 58, 63, 64; Lawrence on, 64; on *Seven Arts* magazine, 49; and Witter Bynner, 64
Loy, Mina, 12
Luhan, Mabel Dodge: biography of, 20–21, 103–4, 113n64; and Erna Fergusson, 98, 100; and Frieda Lawrence, 25, 81, 106; and Georgia O'Keeffe, 117n4; as hostess, 65; in Lawrence's works, 43; marriages of, 39, 42, 82–83; and modernism and modernists, 15, 113n69; in New Mexico, 49, 69; in New York City, 49; in painting by Dorothy Brett, 106–7; ranch of, 98, 117n4; and Robinson Jeffers, 103, 104; scholarship on, 19–20, 125n21; and "The Woman Who Rode Away," 100, 102, 105, 125n21; works by, 51, 102–4, 106. *See also* Lawrence, D. H., and Mabel Dodge Luhan
Lujan, Antonio (Tony), 20, 21, 38, 42, 82, 85
Lummis, Charles F., 7, 18, 69, 91
Lutz, Tom, 7
Lynch, Tom, 91, 96

M

Machen, Arthur, 85, 122n18
Macpherson, James, 95
Macy, John, 31, 114n20
Mansfield, Katherine, 23, 24
Man Who Died, The (Brett), 85
Marble Faun, The (Hawthorne), 32
Marin, John, 47, 48, 113n69
Marsh, Edward, 56, 57, 72
Marshall Plan, 13
Marx, Leo, 12, 13, 82, 112n35
Maxwell, William J., 9, 112n29
McCarthy, Cormac, 91
McClintock, Anne, 98
McClure (previous owner of Kiowa Ranch), 90
McGann, Jerome, 106
"Medlars and Sorb-Apples" (Lawrence), 62–63
Melville, Herman, 10, 27, 43–44, 45, 46, 91, 115n39
Memoir of Maurice Magnus (Lawrence), 51
Mencken, H. L., 31, 32, 33, 114n3, 114n24, 115n39
Merivale, Patricia, 84
Merleau-Ponty, Maurice, 77
Merrild, Knud, 22, 23, 24, 113n77
Merry Mount [now Mass.], 86, 87, 93, 123n41
Mexican-American War, 7, 96
Mexico: connotation of *Americano* in, 6; D. H. Lawrence in, 1, 6, 11, 24, 25, 81, 104, 124n72; Frieda Lawrence in, 24, 25; publications from, 120n96; and United States, 96
Mexico City, Mex., 24
Michaels, Walter Benn, 8, 37, 50, 51, 91
Millett, Kate, 99, 100
Mills, Howard, 72
Milne, Drew, 89
Minter, David, 43
Moby-Dick (Melville), 6, 10, 28, 43, 44, 117n64

Modernism: Alfred Stieglitz and, 8, 15, 20, 34, 47–48, 49, 76; Alice Corbin Henderson and, 7, 51, 66–67; American, 15, 16, 17, 33; European, 27, 47; Ezra Pound and, 9, 54; Georgia O'Keeffe and, 113n69; Lawrence and, 15, 16, 17, 49–50; Mabel Dodge Luhan and, 15, 113n69; in New Mexico, 7, 51, 66–67, 113n69; in New York City, 15; Stuart Pratt Sherman and, 33; William Carlos Williams and, 54
Modern Library, 114n20
Mollinger, Sharnaz, 94
Monk, Janice, 104, 105
Monroe, Harriet: as anthology editor, 66; correspondence with, 63; and Imagism, 58, 64; and Lawrence, 120n96; and *Poetry* magazine, 55, 64, 70–71, 120n96
Monte Cassino, 51
Montezuma, 116n41
Moore, Marianne, 80
"Morality and the Novel" (Lawrence), 115n26
More, Paul Elmer, 27, 32, 33, 34
Mornings in Mexico and Other Essays (Lawrence), 17, 25, 109, 122n24
Morrell, Ottoline, 22
"Mortal Coil, The" (Lawrence), 49
Morton, Thomas, 86–87, 93, 123n41
Mountsier, Robert, 28
Movers and Shakers (Luhan), 103
Murray, Gilbert, 123n25
Murry, John Middleton, 23, 24, 61, 84, 86, 103
Muthyala, John, 1, 50
Myth and the Powerhouse, The (Rahv), 3
"Myth of 'America' and the Politics of Location, The" (Jay), 7–8

N

Narragansett Indians, 100
Nation, 31, 32
Nation and Athenaeum, 44
Native Americans. *See* Indians
Navajo Indians, 91, 93

Index | 153

New American studies. *See* American studies
New Critics, 35
"New Heaven and Earth" (Lawrence), 57–58
New Humanism, 27
Newmark, Julianne, 19, 51, 52
New Mexico: Alice Corbin Henderson on, 69–70; as borderland, 4, 6, 7; Carl Sandburg in, 69; Charles F. Lummis on, 6–7; connotation of *Americano* in, 6, 7; Dorothy Brett in, 84, 105; economy in, 97; Frieda Lawrence in, 22, 23, 24–25, 85; Georgia O'Keeffe in, 21, 125n21; Indians in, 7, 38, 77; John Galsworthy in, 69; Lawrence on, 96; Mabel Dodge Luhan in, 20–21, 52, 69, 70, 81; Mardsen Hartley in, 77; Mary Austin in, 69; modernism in, 7, 15, 51, 66–67, 113n69; northern, 7, 53; poems located in, 55, 56; race, ethnicity, and gender in, 7, 14, 52, 104–5; tourism in, 96, 100; and United States, 7, 96; wealth in, 97; Witter Bynner in, 69; Yvor Winters in, 69. *See also* Lawrence, D. H., in New Mexico
"New Mexico" (Lawrence), 25, 48, 51, 70, 110
New Poems (Lawrence), 74, 120n111
New Poetry, The (Henderson and Monroe), 66
New Republic, 28, 36, 48, 98, 105, 116n41
New York, N.Y.: Alfred Stieglitz in, 15, 34, 47; Georgia O'Keeffe in, 21; Mabel Dodge Luhan in, 20, 21, 49; modernists in, 15; plans to exhibit Lawrence's paintings in, 117n7; publication of Lawrence's works in, 83, 114n20
New York Call, 44
New York Evening Post Literary Review, 2, 31
New York Herald Tribune Books, 33, 115n26
New York Sun, 34
New York Times, 98
New York Times Book Review, 31
New York Times Magazine, 38
Nin, Anaïs, 27, 118n51
Nolan, James, 71–72, 74
North, Michael, 6
Norwood, Vera, 104, 105

O

Oaxaca, Mex., 25
Observations (Moore), 80
O'Keeffe, Georgia: and Alfred Stieglitz, 47–48; and Dorothy Brett, 25, 125n20; Lawrence on, 109; and Lawrence's New Mexico writings, 105, 108; and Mabel Dodge Luhan, 21, 117n4; in Manhattan, 21; as modernist, 113n69; in New Mexico, 21, 25, 107, 108, 125n21; paintings by, 107, 125n21; Paul Rosenfeld on, 107; photos of, 125n21; scholarship on, 59; and Tony Lujan, 39
Olson, Charles, 15, 27
Omoo (Melville), 28, 43
"On Coming Home" (Lawrence), 109–10
"On Creating a Usable Past" (Brooks), 45
Oppenheim, James, 49
"Orchard" (H.D.), 61–62
Organ Mountains, 97
Origins of Prohibition, The (Krout), 115n26
"Overtone, The" (Lawrence), 123n40

P

"Pact, A" (Pound), 72, 73
Padilla, Genaro, 97
Padstow, Cornwall, Eng., 123n41
Paleface (Lewis), 12
Palms, 120n96
"Pan in America" (Lawrence): analysis of, 85–86, 88, 123n40; description of pine tree in, 107–8; writing of, 25, 79, 85, 86, 122n24
Pansies (Lawrence), 23–24
Paterson (Williams), 51
Paterson Strike Pageant, 20
Patria Mia (Pound), 120n105
Pattee, Fred Lewis, 34, 35, 115n37, 115n39
Pease, Donald E., 3, 4, 13, 18, 83
Phillips, Bert, 113n69
Pickthall, Marmaduke, 115n26
Pine Tree with Stars at Brett's (O'Keeffe), 107
Pinkney, Tony, 57

Playboy, 120n111
Plumed Serpent, The (Lawrence): characters in, 44, 84, 96; publication of, 10; writing of, 24, 25, 42, 81
Poe, Edgar Allan, 27, 28, 31, 46, 50, 56, 122n18
Poems (Lawrence), 16
Poetry magazine: Alice Corbin Henderson and, 64, 67; Carl Sandburg and, 67; Ezra Pound and, 64, 71, 72, 76; Harriet Monroe and, 55, 64, 70–71, 120n96; H.D. (Hilda Doolittle) and, 61; and Imagism, 64, 76; Lawrence and, 55, 64, 120n96; purposes of, 70–71; scholarship on, 64; Whitman as inspiration for, 71
"Poetry of the Present" (Lawrence), 58, 73–74, 76, 120n111
Pollnitz, Christopher, 16
Pontesbury, Eng., 87
Poor Richard's Almanack (Franklin), 40
Porter, Carolyn, 8
"Portrait of Mabel Dodge at the Villa Curonia" (Stein), 20
Postmodern Geographies (Soja), 113n56
Pound, Ezra: and American democracy, 72; as émigré, 75; and H.D. (Hilda Doolittle), 58; and Imagism, 62, 63–64, 66, 119n59; and Lawrence, 63–64, 119n59; and modernism, 9, 54; and *Poetry* magazine, 64, 71, 72, 76; scholarship on, 9, 10; and *Smart Set*, 115n25; T. S. Eliot on, 72; and Whitman, 72, 73, 120n105; and William Carlos Williams, 50, 74, 121n121; works by, 62, 65, 66–67, 72, 76, 120n105, 121n120, 121n121
Pratt, Mary Louise, 8, 39
Preston, Peter, 114n24
"Priapus/Keeper-of-Orchards" (H.D.), 61
Primitive Culture (Tylor), 119n85
"Princess, The" (Lawrence): analysis of, 82, 94–97, 98–99; Dorothy Brett as model for Dollie in, 105; F. R. Leavis on, 95; Lawrence on, 122n13; New Mexico in, 96–97, 98; as New Mexico tale, 18, 82, 83; origins of, 94–95; publication of, 124n60; writing of, 25, 94, 95, 100

Princess and Other Stories, The (Lawrence), 122n1
Professor's House, The (Cather), 37, 92
"Protest of Artists and Writers Against the Bursum Bill," 38
Pryse, James M., 30, 114n13
Psychoanalysis and the Unconscious (Lawrence), 30, 32
Pueblo Indians, 10, 38, 86, 92, 103
Puritans and Puritanism, 33, 34, 49–50, 87, 100–101
"Purple Anemones" (Lawrence), 60, 61, 118n51

Q

Queer theory, 12
Quetzalcoatl (Lawrence), 24, 42, 81
Quintano, Pablo, 85

R

Race. *See under* New Mexico; *Studies in Classic American Literature* (Lawrence)
Rahv, Philip, 3
Rainbow, The (Lawrence), 11, 48, 57
Raine, Kathleen, 30
Ramazani, Jahan, 9, 15, 16, 53, 84
Rananim. *See under* Lawrence, D. H.
"Rappaccini's Daughter" (Hawthorne), 94
"Red Atlantis, The" (Collier), 38
Red Earth: Poems of New Mexico (Henderson), 66, 67
"Red Wolf, The" (Lawrence), 68–69, 78
Reed, John, 20
Reflections on the Death of a Porcupine (collection, Lawrence), 17, 25, 109
"Reflections on the Death of a Porcupine" (essay, Lawrence), 79, 97
Regeneration through Violence (Slotkin), 18
Reinterpretation of American Literature, The (Foerster), 115n39
Reising, Russell, 33
"Return, The" (Pound), 66–67

Return of the Vanishing American, The (Fiedler), 36, 112n37
Reworlding America (Muthyala), 1
Ripostes (Pound), 66–67, 121n121
"Rip Van Winkle" (Irving), 95
Roberts, Neil, 19, 37, 68, 100, 116n46, 118n43
Robin of Sherwood, 86
Rodriguez, Sylvia, 83
Romance genre, 83, 88, 92, 93, 94, 101
Romero, Margarito, 97
Rosenfeld, Paul, 48, 105, 107
Rowlandson, Mary, 100–101
Rudnick, Lois Palken, 103, 104, 113n64
Ruskin, John, 70
Russell, Bertrand, 8, 112n25

S

Sagar, Keith, 19, 23, 55, 91, 122n1
Saïd the Fisherman (Pickthall), 115n26
Sandburg, Carl, 38, 67, 69, 73
San Francisco, Calif., 116n63
Sangre de Cristo Mountains, 21, 97, 123n45
Santa Fe, New Mex.: Alice Corbin Henderson in, 21, 64, 105; as cultural hub, 49, 105; D. H. and Frieda Lawrence and, 21, 24, 49, 64; Maurice Sterne in, 21, 82; in "St. Mawr," 124n74; Witter Bynner in, 24, 64
Santa Fe Railway, 100
Santa Monica, Calif., 24
Santayana, George, 35
Santo Domingo, N. Mex., 77
Saturday Evening Post, 98, 124n60
Saturday Review of Literature, 109
Scarlet Letter, The (Hawthorne), 10, 42–43
Scrutiny, 46
Sea and Sardinia (Lawrence), 21, 81
Sea Garden (H.D.), 59, 61
"Sea Iris" (H.D.), 59
Secker, Martin, 122n13
Segal, Charles, 60
Self and Sequence (Laird), 15
Seligmann, Herbert J., 34, 48
Seltzer, Thomas, 28, 32, 34, 90, 113n77

Seven Arts magazine, 8, 11, 49, 50, 71, 111n24, 120n99
Sexual Politics (Millett), 99
Sherman, Stuart Pratt: and American Moderns, 33; on Benjamin Franklin, 40; and *Cambridge History of American Literature*, 115n39; as critic, 4; death of, 115n26; as editor of *New York Herald Tribune Books*, 33; and H. L. Mencken, 31, 32, 33; influences on, 33, 46; and Lawrence, 49, 115n26; on "St. Mawr," 89, 93; on *Studies in Classic American Literature*, 2–3, 4, 6, 31, 32–33, 34; works by, 32; and World War I, 49
"Ship of Death, The" (Lawrence), 62–63
Shropshire, Eng., 87, 88
Shumway, David R., 115n39
Sicily, It., 1, 36
Siegel, Carol, 60, 91–92, 99, 124n69
Sleeping Beauty, 95
Slotkin, Richard, 18, 87
Smart Set, 33, 115n25
Smith, Henry Nash, 3, 13
"Snake" (Lawrence), 80
"Snap-Dragon" (Lawrence), 59
Snyder, Gary, 37, 51, 53, 67, 68
Soja, Edward, 113n56
Some Imagist Poets, 1915 (Lowell), 59
Some Imagist Poets 1917 (Lowell), 57
Song of the Lark, The (Cather), 92
Son of Woman: The Story of D. H. Lawrence (Murry), 103
Sons and Lovers (Lawrence), 25, 62, 95, 114n20
Sontag, Susan, 13–14
Spingarn, J. E., 31–32, 115n29
"Spirit of Place, The" (Lawrence), 70
Spivak, Gayatri Chakravorty, 68–69
Spring and All (Williams), 15, 53, 74–75
Spud Johnson and Laughing Horse (Udall), 124n74
Steffens, Lincoln, 20
Stein, Gertrude, 20, 21
Stein, Leo, 21
Sterne, Maurice, 82

Stevens, Wallace, 15, 50, 53, 74
Stieglitz, Alfred: as avant-garde/modernist leader, 8, 15, 20, 34, 47–48, 49, 76; dedication of Seligmann's study of Lawrence to, 34, 48; and Dorothy Brett, 106, 125n20; galleries of, 47, 48, 49, 76, 107; and Georgia O'Keeffe, 47–48; and Lawrence, 34, 48, 109; Paul Giles on, 50; and *Studies in Classic American Literature*, 47, 50; Walter Benn Michaels on, 50; and William Carlos Williams, 48, 76; and World War I, 48
Still Life with Apples (Cézanne), 121n131
St. John de Crèvecoeur, Hector, 28, 40–41, 55, 56, 62, 109
"St. Mawr" (Lawrence): analysis of, 18, 87–89, 90, 91–92, 93, 94, 99; Carol Siegel on, 124n69; characters in, 61; Dorothy Brett and, 105; F. R. Leavis on, 95; Georgia O'Keeffe and, 108, 125n21; James C. Cowan on, 88; Lawrence on, 122n13; as New Mexico tale, 82, 83, 91, 100; Richard Aldington on, 25; Santa Fe in, 124n74; Stuart Pratt Sherman on, 89; "wild America" in, 124n74; writing of, 25, 99, 105, 122n24
"Story of a Panic" (Forster), 122n18
Strand, Paul, 47, 48
Studies in Classic American Literature (Lawrence): Alfred Stieglitz on, 34, 47, 50; on America, 29, 50, 55; and American pastoral, 92; audience for, 11; and believing communities, 23, 50–51; and Benjamin Franklin, 27, 30, 40, 41; and Book of Revelation, 30; and Brook Farm, 22; characteristics of, 31, 35; and Crèvecoeur, 29, 40–41, 55, 56; as criticism, 14, 26, 27, 34–35, 45, 83; *Current Opinion* review of, 28, 114n7; David Cavitch on, 31; and democracy, 27; and Edgar Allan Poe, 46; and Europe, 29; foreword of, 26; Fred Lewis Pattee on, 33; and Freud, 30; and gender, 14, 39, 43, 104; and Hawthorne, 37, 42–43, 46, 86; Henry Irving Brock on, 31; and Herman Melville, 43–44, 46; and homoerotism in, 116n60; and homosocial aspect of American fiction, 92; and homosocial bonding, 42, 44, 92; Indians in, 35–36, 37, 38, 39, 40, 41, 42, 43, 68; influences on, 30; and James Fenimore Cooper, 39, 41, 42, 90; John Macy on, 31; Kurt L. Daniels on, 114n4; Lawrence on, 11, 14, 26; and locality, 80; market for, 30; and modernists, 27; Neil Roberts on, 37; and new science, 29–30; origins of, 10, 28; Paul Giles on, 101; pieces omitted from, 13, 36; price of, 28; publication of, 10, 12, 18, 26, 28–29, 47; and Puritans and Puritanism, 29, 33–34, 35–36, 39, 40, 87; and race and ethnicity, 14, 39, 42, 43; and reanimation of American literature, 16; and Richard Henry Dana, 43, 46; Richard Slotkin on, 18; scholarship on, 4, 12, 38, 39; and spirit of place, 4, 29, 33–34, 87; Stuart Pratt Sherman on, 2–3, 4, 6, 31, 32–33, 34; Susan Sontag on, 13–14; and transcendentalists, 27; and Whitman, 5, 27, 28, 44, 45, 46, 56, 72, 73, 74, 115n26; William Carlos Williams and, 50, 76; works and authors influenced by, 8, 12–13, 27; writing of, 5, 6, 10–11, 14, 22, 24, 28, 29, 30–31, 32, 36, 38–39, 40, 49, 81, 83, 109
"Supermarket in California, A" (Ginsberg), 73
"Surgery for the Novel--or a Bomb" (Lawrence), 114n7
Survey Graphic magazine, 48, 117n4
Sussex, Eng., 113n76

T

Talisman magazine, 109
Tanner, Tony, 88
Taos, N. Mex.: artists' colony in, 21, 113n69; as cultural hub, 105; D. H. and Frieda Lawrence in, 6, 21, 22, 24, 38, 49, 65, 81, 85; Dorothy Brett in, 24, 85; Fiesta of San Geronimo at, 52, 77; Georgia O'Keeffe in, 21; Kai Götzsche in, 22; Knud Merrild in, 22; Mabel Dodge Luhan in, 19, 21, 24, 38, 65, 70, 81, 100; Mary Austin in, 65

"Taos" (Lawrence), 25, 51, 52, 77
Taos Indians, 68, 82–83, 119n85, 125n18
Taos Moderns, 113n69
Taos Pueblo, 23, 51, 67, 85
Taos Society of Artists, 113n69
Tapscott, Stephen, 74
Templeton, Wayne, 116n46
Tendencies in Modern American Poetry (Lowell), 64, 74
"Terra Nuova" (Lawrence), 57–58
Tewa Indians, 66
"Thimble, The" (Lawrence), 49
"This Is Just To Say" (Williams), 77
Thompson, Jon, 4, 39
Thorp, N. Howard, 69
Through Other Continents: American Literature across Deep Time (Dimock), 9–10
Tindall, William York, 24, 77
Toomer, Jean, 21, 53
Toomer, Margery, 103
Totemism and Exogamy (Frazer), 119n85
Trachtenberg, Alan, 13, 71
"Tradition and the Individual Talent" (Eliot), 45
Transcendentalists, 9
"Trans-National America" (Bourne), 8
Transnationalism, 14, 112n29
Transnational literary scholarship, 2, 7–8
Transnational Poetics, A (Ramazani), 53
"Transnational Turn, The" (Gross), 14
"Traveling Genres" (Cohen), 54
Treaty of Guadalupe Hidalgo, 96
Treaty of Versailles, 5
Trent, William Peterfield, 115n39
"Tribal Esthetics" (Hartley), 77
Tribute to Freud (H.D.), 58
Tuan, Yi-Fu, 51
"Turkey-Cock" (Lawrence), 55
Turner, Frederick Jackson, 89
Turner, Victor, 23
Turquoise Trail, The (Henderson), 17, 69
Tuscany, It., 52
Twain, Mark, 91
Twice-Told Tales (Hawthorne), 86

Tylor, E. B., 119n85
Typee (Melville), 28, 43

U

United States, 3, 13
Upper Rio Grande, N. Mex., 7

V

Van Doren, Carl, 115n39
Van Doren, Irita, 115n26
Vanishing American, The (Grey), 37
Vanity Fair, 107
"Violets" (Lawrence), 115n25
Virgin Land (Smith), 13
Vision, A (Yeats), 30
Vita Nuova (Dante), 57
Voice of Africa, The (Frobenius), 118n51

W

Wanamaker, John, 40
"War and the Intellectuals, The" (Bourne), 49
Waste Land, The (Eliot), 75, 95
Weaver, Raymond, 28
Western genre, 93
"What I feel about Walt Whitman" (Pound), 120n105
"What's Become of the Punchers?" (Thorp), 69
White, Eric, 117n17
"White Stocking, The" (Lawrence), 115n25
Whitman, Walt: and American democracy, 72; and *Birds, Beasts and Flowers*, 16, 56, 73; Ezra Pound and, 120n105; as influence on Lawrence, 10, 16–17, 28, 45, 54, 56, 57, 58, 61, 72, 74, 120n111; later poets and, 16, 71–72, 73, 74, 76; in "Poetry of the Present," 73–74, 76; and relationship with public, 71; *Seven Arts* magazine and, 120n99; space and place in works of, 6, 9; and *Studies in Classic American Literature*, 5, 27, 44, 45, 46, 56, 73, 74, 115n26

"Whitman" (Lawrence), 44, 45
"Wilful Woman, The" (Lawrence), 81, 82–83, 122n1
Williams, Ellen, 64
Williams, Raymond, 5
Williams, William Carlos: on 1913 Armory Show, 20; on Alfred Stieglitz, 48; on America as place, 53; and American democracy, 72; and American expatriates, 15; and audience, 76; as cofounder of *Contact* magazine, 74; and Ezra Pound, 50, 74, 121n121; and Lawrence, 15, 48; and modernism, 54; on origin of ideas, 77; Paul Giles on, 50–51; role of, in American literature, 15, 16; and *Studies in Classic American Literature*, 50, 74, 76; on Thomas Morton, 123n41; on T. S. Eliot, 46, 75; Wallace Stevens on, 50; Walter Benn Michaels on, 50; and Whitman, 16, 71, 74, 76. See also *In the American Grain* (Williams); *Kora in Hell* (Williams)
Winter in Taos (Luhan), 103
Winters, Yvor, 69
"Woman Who Rode Away, The" (Lawrence): analysis of, 18, 99–100, 101; Dorothy Brett and, 105; Lawrence on, 122n13; location of, 100; Mabel Dodge Luhan and, 103, 125n21; as New Mexico tale, 82, 83, 100; origins of, 95; Siegel on, 124n69; writing of, 25, 99, 105
Woman Who Rode Away and Other Stories, The (Lawrence), 84, 105–6, 124n72
Women in Love (Lawrence), 10, 57
"Women Who Rode Away" (Chabot), 125n21
Wordsworth, William, 86
"Work of Iron in Nature, Art, and Policy" (Ruskin), 70
World War I: Alfred Stieglitz and, 48; and art, 47; D. H. Lawrence and, 5, 11, 48–49, 51, 63, 70, 83; Frieda Lawrence and, 48; and literary criticism, 27, 45; Mabel Dodge Luhan and, 21, 70; U.S. entry into, 48
Worthen, John, 52
Wright, T. R., 41, 75

Y

Yale Review, 28
Yeats, W. B., 29
Yépez, Heriberto, 9
Young Intellectuals, 31, 33

Lee Margaret Jenkins is professor of English at University College Cork. Her publications include *Wallace Stevens: Rage for Order* and *The Language of Caribbean Poetry*. She is the editor, with Alex Davis, of *Locations of Literary Modernism*, *The Cambridge Companion to Modernist Poetry*, and *A History of Modernist Poetry*.

www.ingramcontent.com/pod-product-compliance
Lightning Source LLC
Chambersburg PA
CBHW032100230426
43662CB00035B/864